New Buildings
on
Old Foundations

Studies in

THE WORLD MISSION OF CHRISTIANITY

NEW BUILDINGS ON OLD FOUNDATIONS

A Handbook on
Stabilizing the Younger Churches in Their Environment

BY

J. MERLE DAVIS

Director of the Department of Social and
Economic Research and Counsel

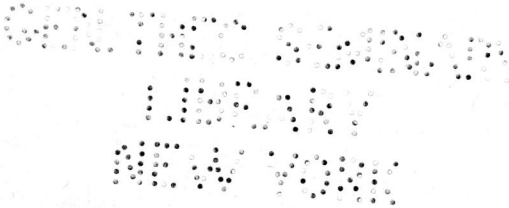

INTERNATIONAL MISSIONARY COUNCIL

New York and London

1945

PRINTED IN THE UNITED STATES OF AMERICA

SOWERS PRINTING COMPANY, LEBANON, PENNSYLVANIA

INTRODUCTION

THE author of this work, J. Merle Davis, possesses unique qualifications for his great achievement.

He was born in a missionary family, his father being Dr. J. D. Davis of Kyoto, one of the principal missionaries of Japan. After his thorough preparation at Oberlin College and Hartford Theological Seminary, and postgraduate study at Göttingen and Leipsic Universities, he served as a missionary in Japan for fifteen years with the International Committee of Young Men's Christian Associations.

After jointly directing with the late Robert E. Park the Survey of Race Relations upon the Pacific Coast and Canada between 1922 and 1924, Mr. Davis served for five years as the first General Secretary of the Institute of Pacific Relations during the foundation-laying and precedent-setting period of the life of this significant agency.

Shortly following the meeting of the World Missionary Conference in Jerusalem in 1928, he was appointed to serve as chief executive of the Department of Social and Economic Research and Counsel of the International Missionary Council in Geneva, Switzerland, and he has occupied this important post ever since.

Thus from boyhood and since his period of college life, he has been intimately related to the missionary enterprise in both national and world-wide aspects.

Mr. Davis's work has involved a life of extensive travel. Since his period of service in Japan, he has for twenty-three years been occupied with thorough tours of service which have taken him to southern and central Africa, to many parts of eastern Asia, and many sections of India, to most of the more important parts of the Pacific island world, and in recent years to the principal Latin American republics and the West Indian islands.

His traveling record has been quite unique, not only in extent but also in point of intimacy of contacts with governments as well as with missionary and other cultural movements and agencies. I do not recall another author or research worker who has had wider or more influential contacts.

At representative conferences of most experienced and best informed leaders of different phases of the missionary enterprise, and of various Christian communions, as well as in the archives of national and international Christian councils, he has prosecuted various research projects and familiarized himself with necessary source materials.

In the present volume, the author presents us with a fresh, comprehensive, and thought-provoking characterization of the culture changes throughout the world. These were never so much in evidence as in the present period of convulsion, near and far.

He focuses attention most effectively on the unique and powerful impact of Christian missions upon non-Christian peoples.

Notwithstanding the greatness of this contribution, this work, more than any other since the notable volumes of Dr. James S. Dennis on *Christian Missions and Social Progress,* constitutes a convincing summons to rethink, to revise, to restate and above all, greatly to enlarge the missionary program of both Older and Younger Churches.

The basic question of a far more adequate support of the world mission is wisely lifted into a place of central importance. Here we are presented with a remarkable conspectus of most fruitful experience in different parts of the world.

As in the case of all his published studies, Mr. Davis sounds out the prophetic note and opens up vistas of triumphant hope.

JOHN R. MOTT.

FOREWORD

THE World Missionary Conference at Madras stressed a new dimension:—The environment of the Church in the foreign mission enterprise.

Side by side with the more familiar themes of evangelism, education, and medical work, the economic and social mediums in which the Church is planted were studied and discussed in relation to its growth.

The Department of Social and Economic Research and Counsel of the International Missionary Council, for many years, has been studying the environmental problems of the Younger Churches and gathering economic and social data that bear upon their progress and stability.

Within this frame of reference, such matters as industrialization, the land, labor, livelihood, living standards, growth of population, problems of youth, the home and family, the liquor and narcotics traffics and vocational education have been examined.

More recently the Department has studied the economic basis of the Younger Churches with the problem of their attaining financial independence. The principal findings of these studies are here brought to bear upon the question of stabilizing and rooting the Younger Churches in their environment.

Foreign missions provide a unique example of planned culture change. However, they are a part of a yet wider movement of world-wide culture diffusion and are examined in this universal context. The rôle of missions as carriers of culture, the characteristics and limitations they share with secular culture carriers, their sources of strength and unique responsibility among the many influences that are changing the life of peoples are examined. The anthropological approach, the significance of environment for the Church, the problem of attaining self-support, with the obstacles encountered and the resources and methods available, together with the experience of outstanding independent churches, are all reviewed.

Finally, there is a characterization of the factors of the environment of the Church in the post-war age and suggestions for training the missionary and national pastor to deal with them.

The book does not attempt to make a case for the principle of self-support among the Younger Churches. This would be like trying to prove that, to endure, a tree must be able to draw nourishment through its own roots and leaves. Rather, it aims to make clear the interrelation of the Church and its environment. While self-help is a basic condition of health and survival for the Church, it is not an end in itself. It is a means for releasing the spiritual power that is latent within its members, power through which the redemptive purpose of God for humanity may be furthered.

The book is an answer to requests received from many mission fields and missionary societies for practical help in planting the indigenous Christian movement, and for definite plans and methods which may serve in achieving this central task of the Church.

While there are essential contrasts between the economic and social orders of the peoples of mission lands, the problems of the Younger Churches in their adjustment to environment and in attaining self-support fall into certain common patterns.

It is probable that there is no church anywhere today struggling with problems and obstacles which, in the past, have not in a measure been faced and overcome by some other church in some other part of the mission world.

I have drawn freely upon the previous studies, surveys, and notes made in preparation for the Madras Conference and wish to acknowledge the valuable collaboration of my many associates in India and China who shared in preparing the resource material for that meeting. I am further indebted to the National Christian Councils and to a very large number of national pastors, missionaries, public officials and laymen whose help in supplying information and counsel made possible the field surveys of the Department in African, Asiatic, Latin American and West Indian countries, both preceding and following the Madras meeting.

Special acknowledgment is made to the Missionary Research Library of New York and to its Director, Mr. Charles H. Fahs,

for his counsel and for placing the rich resources of the library at
my disposal. Our thanks are due to Mr. John Ritchie of Lima, Peru,
and to Fleming H. Revell Company of New York for permission
to place in the Appendix a digest of a chapter of Mr. Ritchie's forthcoming book. We also make acknowledgment to the John Day
Company, D. Appleton-Century Company, Columbia University
Press, Yale University Press and Harper and Brothers by whom
permission has been granted to quote from copyright material.

The book has been written with a belief in the power of facts
as applied to the problems of the Church, the principle of cooperation in securing data, and the value of the interchange of ideas
and experience between churches and between fields. It is presented with the conviction that the post-war era offers an incom-
parable opportunity for using these principles in the world-wide
program of missions.

J. Merle Davis.

New York, N. Y.
September 1945.

CONTENTS

PART FOUR

STRENGTHENING THE STRUCTURE

PART FIVE

BUILDING IN THE POST-WAR AGE

———

PART ONE

CULTURE CHANGE IN THE
MODERN WORLD

CHAPTER I

COMMON FACTORS IN CULTURE CHANGE

THE last one hundred years have witnessed the widest and most rapid diffusion of cultures among the races of the world that human history has experienced. Science, education, industry, commerce, imperialism, wars, foreign missions, the spread of literacy and literature, steam navigation and railways, the automobile and airplane, the radio and the motion picture—each has furthered the kaleidoscopic changes that have been taking place in the thinking and the ways of life of the various races of the world.

The amazing era of geographic discovery of the Renaissance carried Dutch, English, French, Portuguese and Spanish arms, religion, and trade to the seven seas. For centuries the movement was largely a one-way movement and the backwash of the wave of Westward expansion and cultural diffusion was negligible until the early decades of the Nineteenth Century. The culture diffusion which is taking place in the modern age even yet is only to a minor degree a reciprocal process. It has been most evident from the expanding, aggressive peoples to the more static, passive, and self-contained races but it is taking place everywhere.

With the passing of the first shock of Western contact, a counter-current of culture diffusion began to appear among the civilizations of the East. This arose partly from the conviction of their peoples of the inevitability of participating in world life, and partly from the emergence of nationalism among the culture-receiving nations.

This cultural Renaissance of Eastern peoples has been stimulated by the disillusionment that has accompanied two world wars and the new perspective of the worth of their own cultures and sources of power which has been gained from a growing familiarity with the ways of Western peoples. Modern education and literature are further powerful influences that have set in motion the currents of culture exchange from the East. The systematic diffusion of Western

3

science, ideals of human rights, and self-determination among these peoples has carried many of the keenest young minds of Asia and Africa to North American, English, and European universities where they have familiarized themselves with the store of principles, tools, and practices of Western culture. Through this opening of their educational facilities to retarded peoples, the Western nations have planted widely the seeds of their own political and social theories and institutions in nation after nation, and now the harvest in the form of demands for larger liberty and opportunity is being reaped.

The political and economic rivalries of the Powers which have extended their struggles for mastery to the ends of the earth laid the foundation of the colonial system of the Twentieth Century. The immense economic power of Europe and America, the masses of idle capital clamoring for investment, and the technical skill and leadership available have exerted a further irresistible pressure from the West.

Finally, the urge of the Christian Church to extend its faith to all the peoples of the earth has been a most powerful factor in culture change and diffusion.

The terrific impact of Western energy, its material power, institutions and prestige upon non-Christian peoples has created a sense of bitterness in some, of inferiority in many, and of weakness in all. Japan alone accepted the challenge of the West by sending commissions to Europe and America to learn the sources of their strength and, upon them, to reorganize her national life.

DEFINITION AND FUNCTIONS OF A CULTURE

What is meant by a "culture"? What are its rôle and functions and how does it serve a people?

Hallowell defines culture as the tested and traditionally established means that a people employ in solving the fundamental problems of human living. In other words, culture is the unique instrument of human adaptation.[1]

There are four services that a culture performs. First, it accommodates the life of the group to its physical environment. House

---

[1] A. Irving Hallowell, "Sociopsychological Aspects of Acculturation." Reprinted from Linton, *The Science of Man in the World Crisis,* by permission of Columbia University Press.

types suited to climate, implements suited to the local terrain, food crops adapted to altitude, rainfall and soils, handcrafts and arts related to the elements of earth, forest, plant and animal life.

Physical geography and climate are basic arbiters of culture. Arctic cold and torrid heat, the oceans, plains, rivers and mountains have each produced different ways of living, different physical types, different degrees of energy and different outlooks upon the world: in short, different cultures.

A second rôle of the culture of a people is to rationalize their thinking and concepts regarding their origin and destiny and to explain and putatively to influence the physical elements and the life cycle—birth, disease, disaster and death. Thus it attempts to make intelligible the whole scheme of things of which man is a part.

A third useful service of a culture is to create values, criteria of good and evil, standards of conduct, rules of behavior and patterns of relationships, obligations, rewards and penalties.

Finally, culture attempts to satisfy the social, aesthetic, and spiritual needs of a people and to provide for their expression.

Culture gives direction to a people's aims and motivations, serves to allay their doubts and fears, mitigates their ills, guides their ambitions, and provides a frame in which the individual and the group may find their place and function. To disturb this complicated structure by the introduction of a new culture is to accept a responsibility of the utmost magnitude. It may start a train of developments that disintegrates a people as a political, economic, and social unit, but on the other hand, the introduction of a new culture may serve to reintegrate and strengthen them and insure their stability.

Linton points out that "the comparatively rapid growth of human culture as a whole has been due to the ability of all societies to borrow elements from other cultures and to incorporate them into their own." Through this diffusion or transfer of culture elements from one society to another mankind has been able to pool its inventive ability, enrich the content of its culture and go forward.[2]

CULTURE CHANGE

Culture change is the process by which the existing order of a society, that is, its social, spiritual, and material civilization, is trans-

[2] Ralph Linton, *The Study of Man*, p. 324. D. Appleton-Century Company, New York, 1936.

formed from one type to another. It covers the processes of modification in the political constitution of a society, in its domestic institutions, in its beliefs and systems of knowledge, in its education and law, as well as in its material tools and their use, and the consumption of goods on which its social economy is based.

Culture change is a permanent factor of human civilization; it goes on everywhere and at all times. It may be induced by factors and forces spontaneously arising within the community, or it may take place through the contact of different cultures by the process of diffusion.

In discussing the conditions under which successful culture changes take place, Malinowski observes that

Whenever effective cooperation occurs a new form of social organization is engendered: A native Christian congregation under the guidance of a white staff, a bush school where African children are taught by European teachers, an organized system of native administration under European control. Thus what results from the impact are new institutions organized on a definite charter, run by a mixed personnel, related to European plans, ideas, and needs and at times satisfying African interests.[3]

Here is the interaction of two institutions and the resulting creation of a third composite one.

Another universal feature of culture change and the successful transmission of any form of culture to an indigenous culture is the principle that we have two cultures to deal with, namely, the impinging culture and the one which receives, instead of only one. There are the modifications wrought on the recipients by the aggressors, and also vice versa.

The study of culture change must take into account three orders of reality: the impact of the higher culture, the substance of native life on which it is directed, and the phenomena of autonomous change resulting from the reaction between the two cultures.[4]

The foreign influences impinging upon Asiatic and African peoples are both positive and negative, both constructive and disintegrating in their effects. Influences of a positive character such as schools, improved agriculture, public health measures, nutrition, sanitation and the multitude of amenities introduced by science

[3] B. Malinowski, *The Dynamics of Culture Change*, pp. 65, 66. Yale University Press, New Haven, Conn., 1945.

[4] *Ibid.,* p. 26.

are so obvious as to call for little comment. However, such influences together with the teachings of liberty, justice, and religion are not susceptible of so simple an analysis. New ideas and ideologies and those instruments of Western civilization which expand the physical, mental, and spiritual horizons of peoples provide a basis for the integration of the old ways of life with the new, but they are also potential destroyers of ancient cultures.

Western civilization in its impact upon primitive or backward peoples is handicapped for forming a synthesis with the old culture and for exerting a constructive influence. This is due to a series of antitheses which exist between the East and the West, and between modern orders of society and the older civilizations.

MATERIALISM AND WESTERN CULTURE

The first and most obvious impact of Western culture is materialistic while the core of the culture of these other peoples is religious. Western culture, except for the message of the Christian Church, does not deal with spiritual values, relationships, duties and disciplines which make up a very large part of the scheme of life of non-Christian peoples. Western science and education, with their mechanistic formulas and sanctions, tend to shatter the foundations of the beliefs and values of these peoples and they do not provide the society whose culture is displaced with a compensating faith or a discipline by which life may be given meaning and guidance in the modern age. In this connection Malinowski says,

Just now, however, culture change has assumed in both its variants a rapidity and magnitude unprecedented in human history. The technical inventions, the developments of industrial enterprise and of financial and mercantile organization have speeded up evolution in the Western world, giving it a far-reaching mastery of the material environment. Mechanical progress, however, has not been paralleled by a corresponding control of social conditions and spiritual culture.[5]

ECONOMIC DETERMINISM

Another limitation of Western culture as it impinges upon other races is the principle of economic determinism which it uses in all its contacts. The rapid expenditure of $70,000,000 between 1911 and 1930 by British, American, and Belgian mining syndicates in the

[5] *Ibid.*, p. 1.

development of the huge mines of the Copper Belt of the Belgian Congo and Northern Rhodesia has brought far-reaching consequences to African tribal discipline and social and family solidarity from the Union of South Africa to the Sudan and from the Atlantic to the Indian oceans.[6]

In another continent, the use of millions of American dollars by the Office of the Coordinator of Inter-American Affairs[7] in the effort to implement the "Good Neighbor" policy confuses Latin American peoples. It also arouses jealousies, suspicion, and scorn at such prodigal use of gold as a medium for winning understanding and friendship. The North American has become so accustomed to measure progress in terms of finances that he has difficulty even in his cultural and religious approaches to other nations in avoiding the pitfalls of economic determinism.

The economic disparities which exist between the monetary systems, purchasing power, wage and living standards of East and West disturb still further the normal interplay of culture change.[8] These disparities are, in some cases, so enormous as to cause the Westerner to lose his perspective and sense of proportion and to put the whole economic picture out of focus. For example, a mill worker's wage in the United States amounts to as much as twenty times that paid to the cotton mill worker in Peru or in India.[9] From this inaccurate evaluation of the people's inner life and from these striking disparities, an unwarranted assumption of the economic and social helplessness of the group is readily made.

To the older economic order, the Western government, bank, commercial firm, college and mission represent imposing power and affluence. The Western institution is frequently the most conspicuous and costly architectural unit in an Oriental city. Employment within its organization is sought because it insures economic

---

[6] J. M. Davis, *Modern Industry and the African,* Chapter XVI, Part 5, p. 279. Macmillan and Co., Ltd., London, 1933.

[7] Formerly Coordinator of Commercial and Cultural Relations between the American Republics.

[8] Madras Series, Vol. V, pp. 36, 37.

[9] a) Gerard Swope, "The High Cost of Living in South America," *Atlantic Monthly,* June, 1940, pp. 777-779.

b) C. W. Ranson, *A City in Transition,* p. 68. The Christian Literature Society for India, Madras, 1938.

c) M. C. Matheson, *Indian Industry,* pp. 39, 56. Oxford University Press, London, 1930.

security, not only for the individual, but for the circle of relatives for whom he is responsible. It is difficult completely to divorce the new culture from this economic alliance and to allow it to make its own case for what it is worth in other than monetary terms. On the other hand, the judgment of the Westerner as to realities and values of the new culture is impaired by the economic disparities between the unfamiliar society which surrounds him and that in which he was reared.

INDIVIDUALISM VERSUS COLLECTIVISM

The genius of Western culture is individualism while that of Asiatic and African society is collectivism. These two philosophies of life are as far apart as the poles and this dualism complicates every cultural approach between East and West. The individual in a collectivist society is valued to the degree in which he can contribute to the solidarity and welfare of his group and he has no significance apart from it. Western society, on the other hand, is valued for the success with which it is able to develop efficient, healthy, happy individuals. The person is an end in himself. Thus Western culture tends to separate the individual from the old social order with its public opinion as the stabilizing influence of family and village while on the other hand, it can make real to him, but slowly, the sanctions of the foreign social order to which he is introduced.

Within recent decades as a result of Western culture contact, the small independent Chinese family has appeared in contrast to the patriarchal or extended family. T. C. Chao stated in 1938 that the family system of China was rapidly passing, and that the social order of the nation would be permanently altered due to the appearance of the small independent family impelled by economic and individualistic influences, and by the break-up of population caused by the war.[10]

For one hundred years the missionary in the Far East has been demonstrating the practice of monogamy and the small family unit. This has been supported by education in hundreds of mission schools and by the example of thousands of Christian Chinese families scattered throughout the land. The homes of Western business

[10] T. C. Chao, "The Future of the Church in Social and Economic Thought and Action," 1938.

men and diplomats, the outlook of students returning from study abroad, together with the growth of modern urban Chinese life with its new economic pressures, have all furthered this trend toward the independent family. In the family a major strand in the web of China's social life is disintegrating, but the process has been supported by so many converging cultural influences as to allow in a measure for the splicing of the new strand with the old. What is actually resulting is a new type of social unit, a family that is neither wholly Chinese nor Western, but one which shares the attributes of both cultures.

THE SPEED AND DRIVE OF MODERN LIFE

The speed and drive of Western civilization also complicate the process of culture change. An ox-cart or mule-back way of life has little in common with a culture whose energy is typified by the internal combustion engine. The West finds it difficult to accommodate its abrupt cultural approaches and high-speed projects to the slower tempo and unperturbed poise of the older civilization.

The factor of speed is present in all its contacts with other peoples. The Anglo-Saxon, and particularly the North American, is geared to a different tempo from the rest of the world. Programs must move and keep up to schedule, for to him time is money, while to many other races time is a medium for enjoyment. The easy-going Latin American is irritated by the efforts of the North American to exchange cultural amenities and to create mutual understanding and appreciation on the basis of intensive and high-pressure programs.

The importance of the time factor in the sphere of culture change is seen in the contrasted results of the policies of the United States Government in Puerto Rico and in the Philippines. In the Caribbean Island the intensive rehabilitation program of the Puerto Rico Reconstruction Administration backed by the expenditure of millions of dollars over a period of six or seven years has been aimed at improving the efficiency and the way of life of the rural masses. However, the Puerto Rico program calls for the withdrawal of financial aid to its rehabilitation projects after a ten year period. It has largely been directed at rural farm improvement although practical vocational training also has been provided for a limited number of children. The program has touched but a very restricted group and has not yet materially affected the way of life of the masses.[11]

In contrast to this short-term project stand the results of the forty-four years of popular education in the Philippines. In this period there has been sufficient time to bring about far-reaching transformations in the national culture. A new generation of Filipinos, imbued with democratic ideals and prepared for self-government, has come forward through the schools of the nation.

RURAL VERSUS URBAN-CENTERED CULTURE

The contrast between the rural way of life of the non-Christian races and the urban-centered, mechanized civilization of the Anglo-Saxon peoples works against the normal operation of culture change. The West has not fully grasped the meaning of the fact that the genius and culture of nearly all of the non-Christian peoples of the world are rural in character. The land is the cradle of all civilizations and is the source of the livelihood, values, and motivations of three-quarters to nine-tenths of the populations. Neither Western governments, commerce, industry, education or missions have as yet adequately understood the profound implications of the fact that outside of western Europe and North America the peoples of the earth still, to a very large extent, are thinking and functioning in the rural moulds in which they were shaped.[12]

British administration in India has been marked by monumental efforts to undergird the economic life of the peasant, such as the vast irrigation schemes of the Punjab,[13] and the increased national facilities for transportation,[14] but it has awakened belatedly to the necessity of shaping its economic and social policies to meet the basic needs and conditions of India's three hundred million farmers. Modern education in many Asiatic and African lands has been so far modelled after the urban school of the West, with its orientation

---

[11] a) Annual Reports, Government Soil Conservation Service, U. S. Department of Agriculture, Washington, D. C.

   b) Annual Reports, Puerto Rico Reconstruction Program, San Juan, Puerto Rico.

   c) J. M. Davis, *The Church in Puerto Rico's Dilemma,* Chapter V, International Missionary Council, New York, 1942.

[12] Kenyon Butterfield in the Report of the Jerusalem Meeting, International Missionary Council, 1929.

[13] Report of Royal Commission on Agriculture in India, 1928, Chapter VIII, "Irrigation," pp. 324-366.

[14] Report of Royal Commission on Agriculture in India, 1928, Chapter IX, "Communications and Marketing," pp. 267, 280.

upon city-centered activities, that the natural future leaders of the rural communities have been drawn away to the urban world and, consequently, rural society has remained in a static condition.

DISINTEGRATING EFFECTS OF WESTERN CULTURE CONTACT

The culture of a people may be likened to a spider's web—a frail and highly complicated creation built up by scores of connected strands. Touched from without at any point, the whole fabric trembles, while if only one of the main supporting cables is broken, the entire structure may be ruined. Like the strands of the spider's web, the importance of each element of a people's culture and the rôle which it plays should be understood before it is supplanted. The representative of the new culture should be able to integrate its values with the old in a way to cause the least possible destruction. The experience of British governments in Africa with the policy of "Indirect Rule" illustrates the difficulty of reestablishing the customary tribal rule of the native chiefs after a period of supplanting their authority.[15]

The Gold Rand of the Transvaal and the Copper Belt of central Africa illustrate the shattering impact of modern industry upon tribal Bantu life and its institutions.

The modern mine, like a magnet with steel filings, draws out hundreds of thousands of native workers from the old society. The disintegration of the social order occasioned by the absence of this army of men from their home communities[16] is only partly compensated by the worker's learning a few mechanical operations which have little relation to native life, and by the discipline of regular work and a standardization of diet and health. The significance of mining in the life of the world, the constructive use of unaccustomed liberties, the beneficial use of wages and any other than the physical adjustment of the worker to the strange surroundings are not a concern of the management. In the mining industry the African meets Western culture in one of its crudest forms. He is in contact with white foremen, mechanics, and superintendents

[15] a) Lord Lugard, *The Dual Mandate in British Tropical Africa,* Chapters X, XI, XXI, William Blackwood and Sons, Edinburgh and London, 1923;
   b) Chapter XIV, "Indirect Rule," by Leo Marquard in *Modern Industry and the African.* Macmillan and Company, Ltd., London, 1933.
[16] Lord Hailey, *An African Survey—A Study of Problems Arising in Africa South of the Sahara.* Chapter XI, "The Problems of Labour," Oxford University Press, 1938.

who are neither interested in nor able to interpret to him clearly the meaning of the other elements of the Western cultural stream of which their mine is a part. The techniques, amenities, manners, disciplines, morals and values of the Western mining world alone are communicated to the African. Whatever else he learns of Western culture is accidental and not intrinsic in the mining process. Thus the Bantu miner returns to his home having acquired new patterns of behavior, values, and motivations which are related only to one of the most mechanistic of the great variety of elements which form the composite of Western culture.

It is doubtful whether the New York or London stockholder in the Rhodesian and Transvaal mines has any conception of the disintegration of African society caused by the mining enterprise. It would be illuminating for these stockholders to have attached to their certificates of annual earnings the debit account which their investments have piled up for native society. These are some of the items on that account:[17]

1. A weakening of tribal bonds, authority of chiefs, tribal discipline, laws and taboos.
2. The withdrawal for long periods of the able-bodied men from the villages with the breaking up of homes and families.
3. A loss of respect for and interest in the old culture and institutions.
4. Dependence for livelihood upon foreign capital and foreign markets.
5. Decline in native agriculture and food supply.
6. Decline in native arts, skills, and crafts.
7. The spread of venereal disease among the villages.
8. A loss of faith in native religion and its controls.
9. The creation of urban slums into which natives detached from their tribal centers drift—slums that are breeding crime, disease, lawlessness and degeneration.[18]

INCREASED TRAVEL AND MOBILITY

First the sailing ship and then the steamship, railway, and motorbus have exerted a profound effect upon culture diffusion. From the years of the early slave trade in which millions of Africans were transported to the New World[19] to the modern migrations of Euro-

[17] J. M. Davis, *Modern Industry and the African*, Chapters VI, XI, XVI.
[18] Ray E. Phillips, *The Bantu in the City*, Chapter V, "Crime and Delinquency," Lovedale Press, South Africa, 1939.
[19] Raymond Leslie Buell, in *Problems of the New Cuba*, states that it is estimated that altogether, until the abolition of the slave trade, more than a million Africans were carried to Cuba alone. (Foreign Policy Association, Inc., New York, 1935)

peans, Chinese, British Indians and Japanese, the peoples of the earth have been distributed to distant centers of life with a resulting change both of their own culture and that of the peoples among whom they have settled.

The railways and bus lines of India have been actively breaking down the taboos of the caste system. Although the railways provide separate communal restaurants and water taps at stations and class compartments in the passenger trains, the democracy and congestion of modern travel undermine the barriers between the castes. A Brahmin who hurries to catch a train cannot avoid letting the shadow of an outcaste fall on him, and only with great difficulty can he escape the contamination of riding with passengers of other religious faiths. The business life also of Indian cities is moving at such a quickened pace and with such an intermingling of caste groups as to weaken the distinctions of the old social order.

The periodic leaving of their homes for distant industrial centers is, as has already been stated, a practical education for the hundreds of thousands of African miners of the Gold Rand of South Africa and the Copper Belt of Northern Rhodesia and the Belgian Congo. Of the 341,207 Africans employed in 1936 by the mines of the Union of South Africa, 157,356 came from other parts of the continent. It is estimated that an average of fifty per cent of the adult males of Basutoland are constantly away at the mines, while in the Herschel district of the Transkei, in 1930, seventy-five per cent of all adult males were absent six months every year.[20]

The speed of culture transmission has been profoundly conditioned by the mobility of the culture carriers. The substitution one-hundred years ago of steamship and steam railway for sailing ship and horse-drawn vehicles enormously accelerated the mingling of diverse peoples. The development of the automobile and even more that of the airplane has carried forward that acceleration to a point where peoples living on opposite sides of the globe are but a few hours removed from one another. The next one hundred years will undoubtedly see the vehicles of culture transmission still further developed beyond the powers of today's imagination. This will put an extraordinary strain upon the capacity of the human race to absorb and appropriate diverse cultures and not to be demoralized or destroyed by them.

[20] Lord Hailey, *op. cit.*, p. 700.

WAR AND CULTURE DIFFUSION

From the beginning of history wars and invasions have served as active carriers of cultures. The effect of the Norman Invasion upon the life of England, of the Moorish Conquest upon the peoples of Spain and Portugal, and of the Crusades upon western Europe are classic examples. In modern times, we have seen the cultural influences of the Japanese conquest of Korea, the American occupation of the Philippines and Puerto Rico, and the spread of British, French, Spanish, Portuguese and Dutch culture in the great areas which have come under the control of these Powers.

Contrary to popular opinion, there are many constructive by-products of modern war. The Russian and Polish *intelligentsia* who as refugees found asylum in Japan during the First World War taught European art and languages to the upper-class citizens of Tokyo. In a few years Japanese galleries were flooded with oil and water color paintings, and European art motifs crowded upon Japanese color prints and *genre* works while street bookstalls displayed European books in many new languages.

Pianos were installed in better-class Japanese homes. Stringed orchestras, operatic singers, and choral societies were trained, and concerts were given in Tokyo's public halls. From this backwash of international conflict a generation of Japanese has appeared with an appreciation of the works of Chopin and Tschaikowsky, the writings of Tolstoy and Dostoyevsky, and a knowledge of Western art.

The 150,000 Chinese of the Allied labor battalions of Flanders and France carried back to China from the first world war a thirst for reading. Welfare officers and Young Men's Christian Association secretaries organized classes for the illiterate coolies and a simplified system of Chinese ideographs was devised through which the men were trained to use their own written language. This became the source of the nationwide literacy movement of China led by Dr. Y. C. James Yen which has taught millions of Chinese to read and write.[21]

The cultural effects of the present global war are literally worldwide. Over against its colossal destruction, disillusionment, and confusion, there are definite constructive results. The war has been

---

[21] a) Y. C. James Yen, "The Thousand Character System," in *The Talking Leaf*, Foreign Missions Conference of North America, 156 Fifth Avenue, New York, 1944.
b) Pearl Buck, *Tell the People*, The John Day Co., New York, 1945.

changing the outlook, widening the horizons, and stimulating the interests of hundreds of thousands of Asiatics and Africans who have been serving in the Allied armies and labor battalions upon many different fronts. An intensive process of culture change has been at work among these young men. Not only have they learned a wide variety of new skills and disciplines, but in many cases they have gained a desire for higher standards of diet, sanitation, and orderliness which will make them dissatisfied with the confusion, squalor, and depressed conditions of their native communities.[22]

British colonial governments and the leaders of New India already are planning to capitalize on this great fund of war experience through using the discharged service men in far-reaching rehabilitation programs among the rural masses.

Millions of American and British service men will carry back to their homes a lively interest in and a respect for the unfamiliar peoples with whom the war has thrown them into contact.

The European war refugees, including scientists, writers, master craftsmen and professional men who have come to North, South, and Central America have been enriching the culture of the countries they enter. New factories, industries, commercial enterprises and crafts with new technical and professional leadership are emerging.

THE GREAT SOCIETY

The ever-accelerating pace of culture diffusion in the modern world has created what the late sociologist, Robert E. Park, has called "The Great Society,"—a pool of racial and national standards which, for better or for worse, is spreading over the entire earth.

Within the framework of the existing world economy which European commerce and industry have imposed upon the rest of the world, there is growing up a body of custom and social practices which are now more or less understood and accepted by all the diverse peoples that have come within the sphere of their influence. These constitute a culture or a civilization that is no longer local but world-wide and destined, it seems, to inherit the cultural traditions of all earlier and simpler peoples, so that there is now probably no racial minority and no local culture that has not made its contribution to the cultural resources of this Great Society.

22 From *Oversea Education*, Vol. XV, No. 4, July, 1944.

Every member of the Great Society, whether he be politician, laborer, trader or craftsman, is affected by this ever extending and ever tightening nexus. A sudden decision by some financier whose name he has never heard may, at any moment, close the office, mine or factory in which he is employed and he may either be left without a livelihood or be forced to move with his family to a new center.

What seems to have held the ancient empires together . . . was . . . the possession by the diverse nations and peoples involved of a body of common customs and fundamental beliefs in accordance with which they sought to direct their individual and collective lives—that is to say, a common culture and a common religion.[23]

No people is so isolated or so encased in protective armor as to escape the diffusion of the culture of this Great Society. Until recent decades and except in rare cases, the carriers of this universal culture have been impelled by the self-interest of the culture carriers, viz., the investment of capital in areas of low economic standards and unused resources, the opening of mines, plantations and mills, the extension of trade routes, railways and steamship lines, banking facilities and the political domination of weaker peoples. The West has siphoned off into its own pockets the great bulk of the material advantages which are derived from normal human intercourse with the more passive and static peoples. Because of their superior experience in technology and trade, their knowledge of science, their economic power and ability in transportation and war, the Western nations have established an enormous superiority over the East.

It is important to consider that the criteria of the superiority of their culture claimed by Western peoples and demonstrated with such overwhelming evidence of mechanical power by these founders of the Great Society have been so largely in the realm of the material and, furthermore, that the peoples of the West are profoundly convinced of the complete superiority of their culture over that of all other societies.

This claim is challenged by thoughtful Asiatics and Africans. As a Japanese delegate to the biennial conference of the Institute of Pacific Relations at Honolulu, in 1927, expressed it:

We Orientals do not concede our culture to be of a lower order than yours because you use metal bathtubs, central heating, automobiles and elevators. We believe that all these mechanized devices may even exist

[23] Robert E. Park, "Missions and the Modern World," *The American Journal of Sociology,* Vol. L, No. 3, November, 1944.

in a low order of culture and that it is possible for a superior culture to function without them.

Ako Adjei, a highly educated West African, in his address upon "Imperialism and Spiritual Freedom: An African View," at Fisk University in April 1944 commented:

The term "European" has come to be identified with an advanced stage of civilization and a higher order of life. Consequently, any culture or civilization whose basic ideas are not rooted in the European tradition is generally looked upon by Westerners as being backward and retarded. . . . The Asiatic cultures and civilizations are older than the European, and they are even the fountain source of many of the values which the Western mind has come to accept as noble and sublime. . . . The popular mind in Europe and America has not yet developed to the point where it would accept alien cultures as being equal to the Western.[24]

PLANNED CONTROL OF CULTURE DIFFUSION

With the greatly accelerated speed of culture diffusion and particularly in view of the terrific material impact and destruction of the world war upon human societies, the builders of the Great Society are under the necessity of demonstrating to the peoples upon whom the new order is being superimposed its superiority in terms of economic, social, and spiritual values and its capacity for providing a better and more satisfying way of living than that which has been superseded. This means that the major Powers must create a measure of planned control of culture diffusion. If this is not done, the uncontrolled investment of capital among backward peoples will continue to disintegrate their societies with no comparable values substituted for such an irreparable loss. The result is apparent in many parts of the world which have been colonies or protectorates of the Western Powers. The system has created the so-called "Slums of Empire," the peonage, serfdom, and helplessness which accompany the loss of the land, forced labor, and the development at best of a second or third-rate class of citizens.

These conditions cannot be changed without the acceptance of a new responsibility by the dominant Powers and dominant stockholders of the world for the people of their dependencies who are producing so much of their wealth. The post-war world must apply

[24] *The American Journal of Sociology*, Vol. L, No. 3, November, 1944.

to itself the dictum of Abraham Lincoln, "No nation can endure half slave and half free."

A beginning has been made by governments and by private corporations in the planning of a better balance of culture diffusion for the masses under their control.

The housing, gardens, schools, hospitals and mother and baby care of the Union Minière in the Belgian Congo,[25] the amenities for recreation and high standards of health maintained for the miners on the Rhodesian Copper Belt[26] and on the Gold Rand of the Transvaal, the sanitary living quarters, farm plots, milk-cattle, home and agricultural advisers and schools provided for the workers on the extensive sugar plantations of the United Fruit Company at Preston, Cuba,[27] are all evidence of the acceptance of a new measure of responsibility for their workers which is growing among powerful industrial corporations. However, a beginning only has been made in returning to the workers a fair share of the financial earnings which their labor has helped to create.

The British Government has recently taken notable forward steps toward rehabilitating the people of its dependencies. The British Colonial Development and Welfare Act of 1940 is based upon the contention that "the primary aim of colonial policy is to protect and advance the interests of the inhabitants of the colonies."[28] Under this Act, since 1941, The Imperial Commission for Development and Social Welfare in the West Indies has been setting up far-reaching instruments of social and economic betterment among the depressed peoples of Jamaica, Trinidad, Barbados and other islands. Vocational training, land settlement projects, improved farming, schools, traveling libraries, motherhood and child welfare, four-H Clubs and social-worker training centers are being organized. One million pounds annually for ten years have been allocated by the Imperial Government in this effort to lift its West Indian subjects to a greater participation in the cultural benefits of the British Empire.

[25] J. M. Davis, *Modern Industry and the African*, pp. 176, 308, 310.
[26] *Ibid.*, pp. 305, 309, 310.
[27] a) Raymond Leslie Buell, *Problems of the New Cuba*, pp. 99, 479. Report of the Commission on Cuban Affairs, Foreign Policy Association, New York, 1935.
   b) J. M. Davis, *The Cuban Church in a Sugar Economy*, pp. 121, 124.
[28] *Statement of Policy on Colonial Development and Welfare*, United Kingdom Colonial Office, Cmd. 6176, 1940.

The Mass Education Plan for the British African dependencies,[29] and the so-called "Sargent Plan" for India[30] call for the rehabilitation of the peoples of those lands upon a scale that dwarfs any measures yet projected for their uplift.

The governments of the Dutch East Indies, France, Belgium, the Union of South Africa and the United States, under difficult war conditions, have been initiating or are making definite plans to initiate fundamental economic and social reforms among the peoples for whom they are responsible. A similar acceptance of responsibility must be manifested in the post-war age by every government which controls masses of backward and dependent peoples.

It has been only within recent decades that serious efforts have been made to promote a reciprocal interchange of cultural understanding between East and West. The Institute of Pacific Relations, formed in 1925 at Honolulu, is probably unique in this field. Through its ten national councils and offices, its biennial conferences, its continuous program of research, its imposing list of published studies and its periodic journal and bulletins, the Institute has exercised a considerable influence in creating an informed public opinion in the nations bordering the Pacific Ocean with respect to many aspects of the life of their neighbors.[31]

The International Institute of African Languages and Cultures offers an excellent example of an intercultural society aimed at throwing light upon the different types of life of a great continent. A notable series of field studies in the languages, lore, and social and political structure of African races from the Cape to the Mediterranean has been carried out and a first-class journal, *Africa,* has been published.[32] This organization is typical of the best of a group of international scientific and economic societies which have arisen through Western initiative for the purpose of securing, organizing, and spreading knowledge of the culture of relatively unknown parts of the world.

The Institute of International Education, a subsidiary of the

[29] "Mass Education in African Society," Colonial Office, Advisory Committee on Education in the Colonies, Colonial No. 186, London, 1941; also British Information Services, 30 Rockefeller Plaza, New York.

[30] Report by the Central Advisory Board of Education on Post-War Educational Development in India.

[31] Office of Central Secretariat, One East 54th Street, New York.

[32] Central Office, Seymour House, 17, Waterloo Place, London S.W.1.

Carnegie Endowment for International Peace, has a most successful record in promoting effective cultural exchange. For two decades it has brought about the exchange of graduate and undergraduate students and teachers of many lands for international travel and study. The Institute has developed a most efficient reciprocal technique and organization for culture exchange which has introduced thousands of educational leaders to the culture of widely diverse peoples.[33]

The work of the League of Nations and its International Labour Office, the Pan-American Union, and more recently, the Office of the Coordinator of Inter-American Affairs, all take high rank in the field of the interchange of cultures. The first three offices possess international secretariats, and all four have maintained national representatives in their participating member countries, have held periodic conferences, and have attempted the gathering and disseminating of data upon an international scale.

At the twenty-sixth session of the International Labour Conference, held at Philadelphia in 1944, a comprehensive memorandum on "Minimum Standards of Social Policy in Dependent Territories" was discussed as the fifth item upon the agenda and its provisions were recommended to all member governments of the International Labour Office.[34]

At the San Francisco Conference, plans were studied for creating an International Authority and for Regional Commissions which would devise and encourage the application of minimum standards of economic and social welfare for the peoples of dependent territories. The willingness and the ability of the ruling Power to accept and implement these standards would be a test of its fitness to control the destiny of a subject people.

The participation of a backward society in world life is dependent upon the introduction of the people to many aspects of the new culture as presented by different types of carriers. The trader, missionary or government official is definitely limited as a culture carrier by the scope and representative nature of his interests.[35] A balanced understanding of the new world order cannot be transmitted by secular agents alone. Such an understanding calls for the presenta-

[33] Central Office, Two West 45th Street, New York.
[34] International Labour Office, Montreal, 1944.
[35] Linton, *op. cit.*, p. 336.

tion of the aesthetic and spiritual aspects of the new culture and this must be integrated in its values and practices with the elements of permanent worth in the old culture. This presentation and integration is the task of religion: in short, the task of the Christian mission.

CHAPTER II

MISSIONS AND CULTURE CHANGE

ONLY in recent decades has it been widely recognized how vital to the missionary task is culture change. Governments are concerned with the inner life of peoples to the extent of adjusting their culture to the laws which they have enforced and to the provisions for health, education, industry and trade which they have established. As we have seen, the secular culture carrier—planter, trader, or industrialist—is intent upon promoting his own interests and is indifferent to the inner life of the people about him and to the effects upon it of the particular facet of culture that he represents.

Among culture carriers the missionary alone aims at the spiritual transformation of native society and brings to it an organized philosophy of life, a social structure, a scheme of conduct and a moral discipline of a new faith—in short, a Christian culture.

"The Great Society" which is spreading to every race is, as has been already stated, creating a body of common custom, social practice, concepts of morality, justice and interdependence. Without such a basis for world life chaos lies ahead of humanity. Modern missions for one hundred years have been preparing peoples for membership in this Great Society. Governments can build their framework and establish their laws, but they cannot create the inner disciplines of such a world culture: secular education stops short of providing the moral dynamic required. The disciplines, sanctions, and dynamic needed for effective participation in The Great Society must come from the hearts of individual men. This is a supernatural phenomenon and is the task of religion.

Conversely the only medium in which religion can take root and have a certainty of permanence is a culture medium. Christian character and the Christian Church cannot exist apart from a society, nor apart from its culture, for culture is the air that a society breathes. Therefore, the strategy of foreign missions is to create a social and cultural medium that is favorable to the reception and the rooting of its message.

The path of the missionary movement is strewn with the wreckage of churches and mission projects which have ignored this principle. One of the earliest examples is that of the extension of Nestorian Christianity to China. After two long periods of activity in many parts of China between the eighth and fourteenth centuries, this early Christian movement completely disappeared. Latourette states that in the spread of Christianity eastward, it was represented by merchant communities and monasteries which tended to be closed enclaves guarding their own peculiar culture, but not consciously reaching out to alter the culture about them. They were established *in* the country but were not *of* it. This tendency marked the spread of Christianity to the East in contrast to its penetration of western Europe. Except for Mesopotamia and southern India, Eastern Christianity did not become deeply rooted nor an integral part of the culture of any one people.[1]

In modern times, among widely contrasted social orders and racial types such as Japan and Ecuador, we find examples of the failure of Christianity to integrate with the culture that surrounds it. Churches that were established by earnest missionary effort which were unrelated to their environment and which neglected to create a new or modified culture as a soil for Christian growth have disappeared in the course of a generation. Many mission fields have experienced this phenomenon.

It is clear that the Kingdom of Heaven of which Jesus so often spoke cannot be identified with The Great Society of the Twentieth Century sociologist. However, the philosophy of life, the relationships of man to man, and of man to God which Jesus taught, envisage a scheme of things and a way of life capable, if followed by the nations, of making a reality of The Great Society and of preparing the way for the Kingdom of Heaven.

Among the influences which are affecting the change in cultures in the modern world, the foreign missionary movement holds a very high position. It also holds a unique position. The sources of the uniqueness of the cultural influence of Christian missions upon the non-Christian peoples are not hard to find:

[1] Kenneth Scott Latourette, *A History of the Expansion of Christianity*, Vol. II, pp. 280-285, Harper and Brothers, New York, 1938.

1. The missionary movement has exerted a *continuity of contact* with non-Christian peoples which has been equalled by no other Western influence. Missions entered many of the non-Christian lands in advance of the representatives of Western governments or commerce. The Roman Catholic fathers in North and South America, Xavier in China and Japan, Livingstone in central Africa, Cary in India, Morrison in China, Judson in Burma, Nommensen in Sumatra, and Chalmers in the South Seas were not only founders of the Church but were forerunners of Western culture and of organized political contacts. In most cases, the footholds secured for the Church by the early missionaries have been resolutely followed up and built upon by the societies which commissioned them through an unbroken stream of successors that has been maintained to the present. No other form of Western cultural penetration can match the persistence and continuity of the Church in its occupation and in the backing of its representatives in non-Christian countries.

2. The position of modern missions in the lands to which they have gone is unique because of their *singleness of purpose*. Whatever broadening of its scope and program it has experienced, the central and impelling force of the Christian mission to make known the saving power of God and to win disciples for Christ, has remained unaltered through the succeeding generations. The steady reiteration of this message has given to it an accumulated momentum and a strength of impact through the years.

3. Missions are unique in their contacts because of the *unselfish character* of their aims and programs. Their representatives have spent their lives in foreign lands without the drive of personal gain or advantage. They have gone in the conviction that they carried God's greatest gift to humanity, that their message, if accepted, would bear the fruit of the same privileges which the West has found in its Christian faith. This conviction backed by a continuous stream of workers eager to give all they had to world evangelism has been irresistible in its cumulative effect.

4. As a medium of culture change, missions have had the outstanding advantage of an extraordinary *diffusion of their representatives* in the inner recesses and throughout the length and breadth of the lands to which they have gone. While political and commercial agents are established in the capitals and great cities of

non-Christian lands, the missionary is found in hundreds of the inland cities, towns, and rural localities. The China Directory of Protestant Missions for 1936 lists 784 cities and towns where missionaries resided and for Japan the figure for the same year was 116.[2] The missionary distribution in India is equally wide and each mission station is a center of culture diffusion. Beyond the mission stations, the 55,000 Protestant mission churches of the world also are effective diffusers of Christian culture (J. I. Parker, *Statistical Survey,* 1938, p. 18). In 1936, it was estimated that Christian churches were located in 1,726 of the 2,423 rural townships of Korea.[3]

5. The Christian missionary, by reason of the *stable nature of his work, his knowledge of the language,* and *his intimate contacts with the common people,* is in a position to secure an understanding of their character and their way of life which is a basis for appreciation and friendship rarely equalled by secular agents. The criticism, prejudice, cynicism and ignorance with regard to natives, together with avoidance of social contacts with them which are frequently displayed by Western business men in the great port cities of the East, are seldom, if ever, found in the missionary.

Scholarly missionaries have enriched scientific knowledge of the peoples of many countries. Until the appearance of the modern school of anthropologists, the most acute interpretations of Asiatic and African life and the cultures of the South Seas were made by the missionary. Edwin W. Smith, one-time president of the Royal Anthropological Institute, has stated that "Because of the missionary's contribution to anthropology, as well as because of the utility of this science for the missionary in his daily activity, Social Anthropology might almost be considered a missionary science."[4]

Professor E. A. Hooton of Harvard University states, "As an anthropologist, I have completely reversed my opinion of missionaries. These men and women have contributed more to our knowledge of the peoples of the world than have the entire ruck of professional travellers and explorers. They may have done more than the anthropologists themselves."[5]

[2] Japan Christian Year Book, 1936.
[3] Ralph A. Felton, *The Rural Church in the Far East,* p. 107.
[4] E. W. Smith, Presidential Address, *Journal of the Royal Anthropological Institute,* Vol. LXIV, 1934.
[5] *Christian World Facts,* p. 96. Foreign Missions Conference of North America, New York, Autumn, 1941.

M. Searle Bates observes that in linguistics, history, ethnology, archaeology and the social sciences, Far Eastern missionaries have made studies of lasting value not only to cultural understanding but in the fields of exact science.[6] This insight into and appreciation of the nature and value of non-Christian societies have exerted a unique influence upon the West in its understanding of these peoples.

6. Throughout the history of modern missions, the intimate *contacts established between the "sending" and the "Younger Churches,"* have provided a unique medium of appreciation of one another's cultures between East and West. Many missionaries return to their homelands saturated with the culture of the people among whom they have been living; much of the period of furlough is spent in visiting the home churches and in explaining to the congregations the meaning of the ways of life and the nature of the foreign culture. For one hundred years this process has been at work in thousands of communities throughout North America, Britain, and Protestant Europe, and has been one of the chief sources of knowledge of Western peoples about the non-Christian world.

Our most general information of China came through the great missionary movement. . . . The breadth and influence of that movement have not always been adequately appreciated by historians. Throughout those years, in almost every fair-sized American community . . . there had been situated one or more churches each of which was in whole or in part supporting one or more foreign missionaries. . . . The news of the work of these missionaries coming through their reports and letters reached a large number of our people living in almost every quarter of the land. To many of them the progress of this work was one of their keenest interests.[7]

7. *Christian education* is one of the most powerful of all the agencies which has been changing the cultures of the people of the non-Christian world. "In recent years the Protestant secondary schools and colleges (of China) have provided for nine to ten per cent and fifteen to twenty per cent respectively of the nation's youth in those two grades of training."[8] The thirteen Christian

[6] M. Searle Bates, "Missions in Far Eastern Cultural Relations." Paper prepared for the American Council of the Institute of Pacific Relations for the Eighth Conference held in December, 1942, at Mont Tremblant, Canada.

[7] Henry A. Stimson, *The Far Eastern Crisis*, (pp. 153-194) quoted by M. Searle Bates in "Missions in Far Eastern Cultural Relations," p. 6.

[8] M. Searle Bates, *op. cit.*, p. 4.

colleges and universities, the 255 middle schools, and the many hundreds of primary schools which were maintained by missions up to the outbreak of the war with Japan have had an incalculable influence upon the ideology and culture of the Chinese nation. The same may be said of the thirty-five Christian colleges of India and the many higher mission educational institutions of Japan, Korea, and other Asiatic countries. Until recently the bulk of the modern education of the people of a very large part of Africa, of the Near East, and of the islands of the Pacific has been in the hands of Protestant missions. Before the war it was estimated that there were in the city of Shanghai alone 10,000 former students of Christian schools and colleges. These men and women are all active diffusers of Western culture. The head of one of the departments of the Government of China in 1936 stated that one-half of his official associates had been educated in Christian schools and were either Christians or were imbued with Christian principles. He further stated that the same would apply to several of the other government departments. Not a few of the graduates of the Christian women's colleges of Japan, because of their knowledge of Western culture, have been sought as wives by official and commercial leaders.

8. The Christian mission has exerted the most active influence upon the *social and moral rehabilitation* of the non-Christian peoples. In his three-volume work, *Christian Missions and Social Progress,* Dr. James S. Dennis observes, "Christianity, however, does much more than provide a redemption from sin. It brings the soul under the sway of loftier incentives."[9] The moral dynamic to which Christianity introduces the community, the incentives to a disciplined life and to the regeneration of the underprivileged are apparent on every mission field. This is evident in the gradual emergence of a new middle class among many humble Christian constituencies. The Church appears among the depressed classes as a new social group and brotherhood and provides a unique corporate life and fellowship. The people are helped to new standards of self-control, conduct, discipline, progress and goals. These, together with the spiritual dynamic of the Gospel, the inspiration of trained leadership, and the moral support of a new brotherhood, furnish a foundation to the individual for progress. The trend is nowhere more manifest than in Brazil where the members of many

[9] Vol. I, Chapter IV, Fleming H. Revell Co., New York, 1897.

Evangelical churches who were recruited from the humble ranks of society are advancing into the middle class.[10]

A similar influence is operating among the depressed classes of India where whole communities and groups of villages have broken their caste relationships to form a new type of cultural group.[11]

9. Finally, the Church of Christ is unique among all culture contacts with non-Christian peoples in that it alone provides *an adequate interpretation of life* to take the place of the native religious philosophies and beliefs which are being destroyed so rapidly by the secular carriers of Western culture.

The responsibility of Western peoples for contributing to the non-Christian world their spiritual and religious philosophy and moral dynamic, along with the materialistic and irreligious aspects of their culture, is inescapable. The attributes which have produced the scientific spirit and the principles of freedom of Western democracies have their roots in the concepts of intellectual honesty, of personal worth, of liberty, of justice, of personal integrity, of social responsibility and of the dignity of womanhood. These foundations of Western culture are direct outgrowths of the Christian religion and must be offered to non-Christian peoples if the West is true to itself and to the values which give meaning and worth to its own culture.

The non-Christian cultures are essentially religious. Impersonal and materialistic forces such as economic determinism, power politics, and selfishness are sweeping away the moral and religious foundations of non-Christian societies. Rationalism, secularism, and the materialistic implications of science strike at the roots of the religious interpretation of life which is embodied in the great ethnic faiths and the animistic beliefs of half the population of the globe. The leaders of these peoples are losing faith in the gods of their fathers. The masses, on the other hand, are confused, disillusioned, and resentful at finding themselves pawns upon the chessboards of war and of economic exploitation by the Western Powers and by their own privileged classes.[12] Christianity alone in this

[10] J. M. Davis, *How the Church Grows in Brazil*, pp. 83, 123, 124.

[11] J. Waskom Pickett, *Christian Mass Movements in India*, pp. 178, 195, 203, 204, 206, The Abingdon Press, New York, 1933.

[12] R. E. Phillips, *The Bantu Are Coming*, Chapter III; F. M. Keesing, *The South Seas in the Modern World*, pp. 227, 228; W. C. Willoughby, *Race Problems in the New Africa*, p. 255.

disintegration, disillusionment, and helplessness has a clear word of hope for humanity. That word centers in the Christian rationalization of the universe and man's place and destiny in it. And this, in turn, is based upon the Father-love of God who cares for the individual man because of his sonship, and who has provided for him a means of victory through the way of the Cross.

THE LIMITATIONS OF FOREIGN MISSIONS IN FURTHERING A CHRISTIAN CULTURE

It is of utmost importance to understand that foreign missions are subject to many of the same limitations and encounter many of the same pitfalls as are experienced by the secular mediums of culture diffusion among non-Christian peoples. Indeed, because of the supreme values it offers and its avowed purpose of uplift, the prestige of its authority and its supernatural origin, the missionary enterprise is peculiarly open to the dangers that beset all cultural approaches from the West to the East.

Unless these limitations are recognized and measures taken to counteract them, the Church of Christ may inadvertently contribute to the disintegration and weakening of societies which, as we have seen, attend culture change between the younger and older civilizations. Among these limitations are:

1. *The Revolutionary and Arbitrary Aspects of Missions.* Malinowski stresses the important part of missions in the process that is everywhere bringing about culture change. He calls the work of the Western Church no less than revolutionary in the life of the African and of the peoples of the South Seas. He points out the one-sided nature of the early stages of all culture contact. European agents constitute everywhere the main drive in change and they themselves are in most of their actions determined by instructions, ideas, and forces which have a foreign origin.

Take the missionary: He is the initiator and center of the religious revolution now taking place in Africa. He would not be true to his vocation if he ever agreed to act on the principle that Christianity is as "any other form of cult."

As a matter of fact, his brief is to regard all the other forms of religion as misguided and to regard Christianity as entirely different, the only true religion to be implanted.

Much the same process goes on under the administrator who is representing a foreign order which is superseding the tribal order. It may be a paternal form of Government exercised from motives of concern for the welfare of those governed, but it nevertheless supersedes and replaces the old authority and code of laws with a foreign authority and a foreign code.

Likewise with the contact of the Western industrialist, commercial firm, banker, and settler, the process of culture change is predicated upon a pattern brought in from without and imposed upon native life.

However, culture change is as dependent upon the reaction of indigenous cultures as upon the impact of Western civilization. We must treat the plans, intentions, and interests of white contact agents as something which can only be realized through cooperation with the African. Such cooperation is as essential to the missionary enterprise as to the Government administration, the mining enterprise, the commercial firm or the settler. With each of these contact agents their enterprise may fail in case there is a real conflict of interests, faulty planning, misunderstanding and a lack of a common ground for effective joint work.[13]

2. *Economic Determinism.* A baffling factor in its work which the foreign mission encounters in common with other carriers of Western culture is that of *economic determinism.* The controlling power of money in Western civilization prevents the healthy integration of Eastern and Western culture and tends to defeat or postpone the realization of the central purpose of the Christian mission, i.e., the development of an indigenous church.[14]

The Protestant Church in Anglo-Saxon lands is a middle-class institution and is based upon the assumption of the existence of a prosperous middle class, with middle-class interests, leisure, incomes and a marginal economy. However, in a majority of the lands of the Younger Churches, the middle class is extremely small or nonexistent. In many of the great rural areas of the mission fields there are only two classes—the landed aristocracy, and the peasant farmer or land serf who lives on scarcely more than a subsistence level. The support of a Christian church and its pastor requires money and among the rural masses money is a rarity. Consequently the mission assumes the responsibility, supports the pastor, and pays

[13] B. Malinowski, *The Dynamics of Culture Change,* Yale University Press, New Haven, Conn., 1945.
[14] Madras Series Vol. V, pp. 36, 37, 38.

for the purchase or rental of a suitable building for use as a church. The church members may contribute a portion to the upkeep of their church life, but the project is essentially a mission project. Wiser's study of rural congregations in the United Provinces of India records that ninety-one per cent of the congregations in Aligarh District felt no sense of ownership in their churches.

Such churches are found in nearly every foreign missionary field and they are related to practically all church denominations.

An even greater handicap suffered by missions from the economic aspects of their programs is with respect to the spiritual values which they carry to the non-Christian peoples. The spacious buildings of the mission represent princely sums to an Oriental community. An inconsistency appears between expensive programs and equipment and the way of life and teachings of the Son of Man who had not where to lay his head.

Sitting in his mud and wattle-built office, the secretary of the Committee on Education of the All-India Congress Party at Seva-gram, India, stated that three of Mahatma Gandhi's lieutenants, including himself, had left the employ of the Christian movement because they felt that the simplicity and poverty surrounding the Mahatma were closer to the Spirit of Jesus than the way of life represented by costly mission-built institutions. "If Jesus should come to India, I think he would feel more at home here than in the imposing halls of a Christian university."

Furthermore, the dilemma of the disparity of economic resources and standards of living, as between the missionary and the people he is endeavoring to win to the Christian way of life, is one that cannot but affect his spiritual relationships with the indigenous church.

No satisfactory solution of this problem has yet been discovered although notable examples of self-sacrifice and simplicity of living are to be found among missionaries in many fields. At this point the celibacy of the Roman Catholic priesthood allows a degree of identification with the way of life of their people that is practically impossible for the missionary family.

Frank Rawlinson, former editor of the *Chinese Recorder,* resolutely grappled with this dilemma in his "Western Money and the Chinese Church." He says,

Unless the modern missionary is willing to step down from his level of economic superiority and live like his economically weak Chinese brethren, he cannot disassociate himself entirely from economic power and significance. . . . Missionaries in China do not demonstrate the economic equality that Christ taught and practised. . . . Since in China to most of their fellow Christians they live like rich people they are liable to be understood as holding on the one hand that for themselves a fairly high economic level is essential to spiritual vitality or physical efficiency but that, on the other hand, the Chinese can attain both on a much lower level. . . . For a rich man to tell a poor man that he can and should be as good and happy though poor, is really to expect the poor man to make a bigger effort than himself.[15]

3. *The Factor of Time.* The Christian mission also has to reckon with the time factor in its work of culture change. Central among the motives which have carried the missionary to his field is the conviction of the urgency and immediacy of his task. The mission-sending churches are eager to hear of progress in terms of churches founded and converts baptized and it is difficult to wait for the slow processes of preparing the ground, sowing the seed, and cultivating it. It is irksome for the missionary under this pressure to use methods which seem to postpone harvests. The annual progress report which is expected of him and the immediate tasks put on him by the mission or the National Church seem to preclude the possibility of using more deliberate methods.

The element of speed not infrequently is a pitfall for the modern missionary in the rural field. Although time-saving devices have greatly enlarged the scope and intensity of activity in supervising his field, as a means of deepening his spiritual influence in a backward society, the use of an automobile may prove to be a handicap.

The head of one of the largest Church bodies in Jamaica described the dilemma in relation to his rural churches in which the use of his motor had placed him: "The car enables me to visit four times as many of my scattered parishes as I formerly managed on my horse, but the speed with which I travel and the inaccessibility of the remote hill communities preclude the possibility of unhurried visits in the homes of the people which the old horseback days permitted."

Upon the mission field it is difficult to get the perspective of the Creator of the universe who measures time by the life cycles of the stars and to whom a thousand years are as a watch in the night.

---

[15] Frank Rawlinson, *The Chinese Recorder,* Vol. LX No. 2, p. 97.

The Church of today must be aware of its responsibility not only for redeeming individuals but of its further responsibility for helping to create social and economic conditions in which these individuals and also future generations will find it possible to live as Christians. This is an inescapable obligation upon missions for culture change.

In various fields, time has not sufficed for the building up of strong indigenous churches and a trained national leadership to minister to them and the pressure to "snatch brands from the burning" has been too great to permit an attempt to put out the fire. In the great rural hinterland behind the port city of Kobe, Japan, some thirty years ago several churches were formed among the farmers through missionary evangelism. Eventually the missionaries withdrew and the congregations were left without leadership. Ten years ago when the Northern Presbyterians entered this rural field not a single congregation, and only two or three scattered believers from the earlier era, could be found.

In the highlands of Ecuador, the Quechua Indians present to external influences one of the most impenetrable cultures existing in the modern world. None of the missions which are trying to evangelize these people has taken the time adequately to study their culture, to ascertain their values or motivations or to understand why, after a missionary occupation of over forty years, in an Indian population of more than one and one-half million, there are so few baptized Protestant Quechuas and no organized churches among them.[16]

4. *Social Disintegration.* A baffling dilemma of the Christian mission in its contact with a non-Christian community which it shares with secular culture carriers is its tendency to disintegrate the established fabric of society. Religious conversion in Anglo-Saxon communities is essentially an individual experience. In the closely knit family and tribal organization of a collectivist society, the conduct of each member is a matter of concern to all the other members and decisions are reached by the group rather than by the person.[17]

Under such a social and economic order, conversion tends to isolate a person from his social unit, destroy his sources of support, render him a ward of the mission and deprive him of those normal

---

[16] Report of the Commission to the Indians of the High Andes, Committee on Cooperation in Latin America, New York, 1945.

[17] See Pickett, *op. cit.,* pp. 26, 27.

human relationships and obligations through the exercise of which his own Christian experience may best be strengthened. It also deprives the group to which the new convert belonged of the daily witness of his Christian faith.

The dilemma of leaving a few converted people who are subjected to the pressure of an intensely hostile environment is familiar to missions in many fields. The experience of an isolated Indian peasant who was attempting to live a Christian life in a caste village in the United Provinces is revealed in his remark: "We Christians are like people sailing down a river in two canoes, who stand with one foot in each canoe and alternately shift from one craft to the other. When the evangelist visits us, we step into one canoe and when he has gone, we step back to the other."[18]

5. *Adapting the Church to Rural Needs.* A serious handicap of modern missions among non-Christian peoples is the difficulty of adapting the Christian message, education, church program and worker training to the realities and culture of rural communities. Christianity as carried to the great rural populations of the world has been developed in an urbanized civilization. The typical mission church is a city church, its pastor a city-trained man, and its schools are based on the model of city schools.

A majority of missionaries are unacquainted with rural life and do not readily adapt the Christian enterprise to its genius. The mission working under such handicaps may even contribute to the weakening of the rural community. In the Rhodesian colonies of Africa the commission which studied the impact of modern industry upon African tribal life repeatedly questioned Bantu men who were employed along the railway zone and Copper Belt as to where they lived and why they were working at such great distances from their families. A frequent reply was that the cost of keeping one or more children in the mission school obliged them to leave home to earn more money. In this respect, Christian missions were having the same disruptive influence upon native society as the copper mines. In both cases, Bantu fathers found it necessary to be absent for long periods with the ensuing moral, social, and economic deterioration of their home communities.[19]

[18] N. Timothy, St. John's College, Agra. Memorandum on "Economic Implications of Conversion in the Rural Church."

[19] J. M. Davis, *Modern Industry and the African,* p. 344. Macmillan and Company, Ltd., London, 1933.

One of the serious aspects of Western culture contact in non-Christian lands centers in the fact that much of the education, whether conducted by government or missions, tends to disintegrate and even to retard the progress of rural society. The orientation and instruction of the schools have been such as to prepare the pupils for city careers and to magnify urban rather than rural interests. In this way the most promising future leaders have been drawn out of their villages, diverted to urban activities, and permanently separated from their own rural world. The backwardness of hundreds of rural communities and the weakness of their churches are due in part to this cause.

The isolation of the graduates of African mission schools from their home communities in "the bush" is marked. The world for which they are being prepared and to which they aspire is a totally different world and the interests and skills which they have acquired have little relation to the needs and activities of the African kraal. Moreover, a well-educated Bantu young man or woman would not be able to earn a living in a tribal village.[20]

The officials of the Department of Education of Peru stated that Government efforts at educating the Quechua Indian children in the rural primary schools are neutralized by the indifference of the parents and by the deeply grooved patterns of family life and tradition which cancel the influence of the school. If basic progress is to be made, the process of culture change of the classroom must be related to and paralleled by culture change in the home and village. It is futile to expect school children to keep up such newly acquired habits as face washing, teeth brushing and the use of sanitary latrines that are provided by the school when their homes are places of filth with no facilities for washing but the stream or pond and where the public road or courtyard serves as a toilet. The educated Indian of the Andes, no less than the Sioux or Apache of North America, does not return to live among his people but is absorbed into the modern activities for which he has been prepared.[21]

On the other hand, we cannot expect primitive farm households to appreciate a schooling which does not help their children to be more skillful cattle herdsmen and farmers or to increase the comfort

[20] L. A. Notcutt and G. C. Latham, *The African and the Cinema*, p. 9. Edinburgh House Press, London, 1937.

[21] Report of the Commission to the Indians of the High Andes, Committee on Cooperation in Latin America, New York, 1945.

and prosperity of the family in its village environment. This conflict between the outlook of the village world and modern education gives point to the new emphasis of missions and governments upon rural vocational training, the woman visitor for home and family counselling, and more recently the mass education of the villagers.

6. *The Conflict in Culture Diffusion.* A familiar limitation of the effectiveness of the missionary as a culture carrier, and one that he shares with secular carriers, is the presence in his field of other agents of Western culture which neutralizes or blocks his work. A similar conflict exists between government efforts at native betterment and the exploitation of native labor by private interests.[22]

Malinowski in describing this conflict in culture diffusion says, "Culture contact" does not mean that the cultures influence each other as wholes. The contact is only partial. We do not bring Western civilization as a whole to the natives and the fragments which we do bring are distorted or remoulded in the process: Employment of labor . . . is accompanied by Pass Laws and the prohibition of trade unions; Christianity becomes almost unrecognizable in the presence of the Color Bar; "Education" is given to the natives without facilities for the attainment in adult life of the social and economic status for which it is a preparation.[23]

An illustration of this conflict between Western culture carriers is provided by the commercialized cinema. It may be questioned whether the power of the motion picture as an interpreter of Western culture to the masses of Asia, Africa, and Latin America is generally understood. The cinema at its best is a mighty force for furthering international relations, but at its worst it is devastating to such understanding. The low order of commercialized films is probably more responsible than any other single agency for giving to the people of many countries a distorted conception of American life.

In 1934, in commenting upon the influence of the cinema, Dame Rachel Crowdy, director of the Social Section of the League of Nations, said,

I once travelled from San Francisco to Shanghai upon an American

---

[22] R. E. Phillips, *The Bantu in the City,* Lovedale Press, South Africa, 1939.
[23] B. Malinowski, *Methods of Study of Culture Contact in Africa,* as quoted by John M. Graham and Ralph Piddington in "Anthropology and the Future of Missions," p. 8, The University Press, Aberdeen, 1940.

ship. Each evening on the main after-deck, melodramatic motion pictures depicting gun-play, murder, and bedroom episodes of the lowest order were displayed to an absorbed Chinese steerage audience. There were fifteen Christian missionaries on the ship bound for China. One could not but wonder which influence being carried to the non-Christian East by the same ship was more powerful: that represented by the sensational films, or that represented by the missionaries.[24]

7. *An Understanding of Racial Cultures.* An inadequate knowledge of the content and significance of the culture of the people to whom he is sent is a serious limitation which the missionary shares with other carriers of Western culture. An acute and sympathetic observer of missionary work among primitive peoples states that

. . . missionaries assume a tremendous responsibility when they decide to destroy the laws, customs, beliefs and rites by which a people has been adapting itself to the needs of life in relation to its own environment and in accord with its own historical development. For in so doing, they will, if successful, uproot the people from its own past and so mould it that it will no longer be able to meet life in its native setting. This type of missionary policy must therefore include such an alteration in the social and economic environment that the people concerned will be at home in it. Now here is a great opportunity for missions. . . . This, however, demands an understanding by the missionary of the social function of religion.

It is amongst peoples whose social and economic life is in process of change that the greatest opportunity for effective missionary service is presented. Their ultimate moral and social sanctions have been religious, spiritual, magical and superstitious. But as a result of culture contact . . . respect for these sanctions gradually weakens, with consequent loss of respect for the authority of head men, chief, or elders. Disunity and disruption must follow unless a new principle of unity is established based on new sanctions or a modification of the old.

If they do not plan to destroy the past and substitute from without their own beliefs and particular form of social life, then the policy of missions must include a thorough understanding of native thought, social life and religion, a knowledge of the principles of social cohesion, development and change and a grip of the problems of culture contact. As a result they should be able to guide their people through the difficult transition stages, and to do so in such a way that eventually *this people will be still themselves,* though transformed and Christianized. . . . With these fateful alternatives in mind, missionary organizations must

[24] Statement made to the author at Geneva in 1933.

decide what their policies really are and what methods are to be employed in putting them into operation.[25]

8. *The Assumption of Cultural Superiority.* A state of mind common to all carriers of Western culture, and one from which the missionary is not entirely free, is the ready assumption that their own civilization is superior to that of the people to whom they go. It requires clear thinking and trained insight on the part of the missionary to discriminate between the universal validity of the Gospel he preaches and that of the civilization he represents.

As expressed by Dr. Westerman, "For the missionary of today the Gospel is supernatural and supercultural, suitable for any type of culture and capable of establishing its own forms to meet the peculiarity of each people."[26]

The difficulty is a subtle one and requires in the missionary a clear appreciation of the elements of permanent worth in the way of life of the people to whom he is presenting Christianity. A. T. Fishman in his studies of "Madigas under Christian Guidance in South India," lists fifteen characteristics of Indian culture that with great advantage may be used by the Christian Church. He also names a longer list of customs that contain nothing essentially hostile to Christian teachings or the Christian way of life which should be considered in any serious attempt to develop an indigenous church.[27]

Somewhat extreme examples of perverted missionary conceptions of the rôle of the Church in relation to native usages are found in various mission fields. The European mission to a matrilinear tribe in Northern Rhodesia for many years had attempted to transform its church community to a patrilinear society. This was in the conviction that the Biblical pattern of a family in which the father is the head was basic for the Christian way of life.

An even greater confusion of social and spiritual values was the policy of a small mission in the Belgian Congo among a tribe which had the tradition that the washing of clothes was the work of the men. The missionaries were distressed at this unaccustomed re-

[25] A. P. Elkin, "Missionary Policy for Primitive Peoples," Reprint from *The Morpeth Review*, No. 27. University of Sydney.

[26] *The African Today and Tomorrow*, p. 223. Oxford University Press, London, 1939.

[27] "Culture Change and the Underprivileged," The Christian Literature Society for India, Madras, 1941.

versal of the duties of husband and wife and earnestly taught and demonstrated to their people that laundering in a Christian household should be done by the women.

THE CHURCH AS A NEW SOCIAL AND TRIBAL UNIT

The Christian Church is not only a unique religious phenomenon but a unique social phenomenon. There is nothing like it in any of the non-Christian societies. In providing the family, which has broken with the old order, with a new corporate life and fellowship, and a new code of conduct and a public opinion, the Church takes the place of many former group and clan relationships.

Numerous non-Christian peoples are in the grip of world forces which they cannot rationalize. Family and clan ties have become loosened; old sanctions, disciplines, and authority are disappearing; faith in their gods, in themselves, and in their destiny is gone. Their security and, with it, their interest in life are shattered. On the other hand, they have not gained an appreciation of the values of the strange culture into which they have been projected.

Robert E. Park asserts that missions create a solidarity that helps the races to survive the convulsions through which they are passing.

Modern civilization has changed the functioning not only of economic institutions but of every other type of social institution. Everywhere the diffusion of European culture has been accompanied by an increasing relaxation of the familial and tribal bonds which formerly in some fashion held society together. . . . European culture has tended to plow under the local and traditional religious beliefs and to substitute a secular for a religious social order. The religious sects which have sprung up on the frontiers of European civilization and in the United States have, in some sense, performed in the modern world the function of the tribal unit in more primitive societies.[28]

The Christian mission alone, of all the approaches of Western civilization, comes with a new scheme of life, a faith, a social orientation, and a program that is capable of refilling the empty vessels of the native's world. But the message of his personal salvation cannot be separated from the message of redemption of the evil estate to which maladjustment to modern life and contact with the secular forces of European culture have brought him.

Educated Christians and non-Christians alike from the Union of

[28] Robert E. Park, "Missions and the Modern World," *The American Journal of Sociology*, Vol. L, No. 3, Nov., 1944.

South Africa to the Gold Coast are pointing to the weakness of the Church in failing to deal resolutely with basic injustices and discrimination against Africans. The teachings of the Church with respect to the spiritual claims of Christianity increasingly are losing their power with thoughtful Africans because of the Church's silence upon such questions as the alienation of the land, the color bar, restrictions upon employment and freedom of movement, inadequate wage schedules and the withholding of political rights from qualified natives.

As is the case with many non-Christian peoples, life to the African is essentially a unity, but this concept is violated and confidence in the Church is undermined by its silence upon conditions which destroy his self-respect and handicap his progress in every direction.

Ako Adjei of the Gold Coast states,

Without minimizing the importance of education and also medical attention, political and economic issues are the main problems confronting Africans today. But since the members of the Church are the same members of the community who are affected by the ravages of European imperialism, Christian Africans feel disappointed by the indifferent attitude of the Church toward the other aspects of community life that are not directly within the province of religion—according to the excuses of the foreign missionaries—but which really are inseparable from religious theory and practice.[29]

A somewhat similar criticism of missions is evident in India and China where increasingly people look to the Church for a clear voice and leadership with respect to the political, economic, and social disabilities which fill the whole horizon of their lives.

Paul's injunction, "Bear ye one another's burdens and so fulfil the law of Christ,"[30] is reflected in the *Biradari* or brotherhood sanctions of the low caste British Indian, in the *minga* or mutual aid teams of the Indians of the high Andes, and in the reciprocal obligations recognized by many other non-Christian communities. The brotherhood responsibilities and mutual aid obligations of the Western Christian Church, however, are not conspicuous. The traditions of an individualistic society with its public care of unfortunates have relieved the Church in America and Europe of many social responsi-

[29] "Imperialism and Spiritual Freedom, An African View," *The American Journal of Sociology,* Vol. L, No. 3, November, 1944.

[30] Gal. 6:2.

bilities for its members. In this respect the transfer of the Western type of Church to collectivist civilization has serious limitations. A natural pattern of church function among many old social orders probably would be nearer that which is described in the Acts of the Apostles and the Epistles of Paul as a brotherhood of believers which provided a central ministry for relieving distress.

Thus the Christian Church has the superhuman and majestic task of rationalizing, purifying, and reconstructing the disintegrating native world. The Church provides a new social grouping to satisfy the craving for tribal solidarity and support. It creates a new fellowship and obligations based upon common beliefs and aspirations to take the place of the old brotherhood; it substitutes a new type of relationships, sanctions, and disciplines for the old; it creates a new center of authority, a new public opinion, a new self-respect, new interests and a new leadership for the old system which has been discredited; it sets up a new tribunal of moral conduct and ethical judgments and finally and most vital of all, it introduces man to a new Source of Power which energizes him and provides the strength which will enable him to meet the demands of the strange economic, social, and spiritual order that he has entered. No less than this is the opportunity of the Church in the midst of culture change.

In conclusion, it is important for the missionary and native pastor rightly to assess the unique resources and power for culture change of the Christian way of life which they represent:

First, Christianity possesses in the Bible a new source of authority. In the face of the controversies over its literal interpretation and the relative value of its utterances, the Bible stands as the authoritative and complete expression of the will and love of the Creator.

A *second* and basic asset of the Christian culture is its rationalization of the universe including the stage upon which man finds himself together with a solution of the riddle of the life he is sharing with all animate creatures.

A *third* attribute of Christian culture is the revelation of a new relationship between God and man. Supplementing the concept of a God of power and of punishment is that of a God of love, of compassion, to whom even the fall of a sparrow is not unnoticed. From the Father-God relationship arises man's sonship and illimitable destiny, and the way of victory provided for him through Christ.

Fourth, and unique in the history of religious cultures, is the new valuation placed upon man and his responsibility for society. Christianity answers Cain's tragic question, "Am I my brother's keeper?"[31] and thus lays the foundations of a Christian social order.

Fifth, Christian culture provides an incentive to progress, new criteria of values, new standards of conduct, goals, motivations and aspirations. The horizons of life have been lifted and widened by Christian missions and men are given a vision of the high estate that God has provided for them.

Sixth and finally, the crowning attribute of Christianity, which lifts it above all other religions and makes possible the implementation of its culture, is the moral dynamic which it provides.

The old Batak chief of Sumatra told the missionary, Nommensen, after a two-year period of explaining the Christian religion that the *Adat* or common law of the Batak nation was very similar to the teachings of the Mosaic Ten Commandments and the Sermon on the Mount.

"We are in full agreement with what you have told us." Nommensen realized that he had failed to make clear the uniqueness of the Gospel. Later the old chief again came to the missionary and said, "Our Adat tells us not to steal, lie, commit adultery and bear false witness and to treat our neighbors justly, but we do not obey it. We are bad Bataks for we break our own laws. You have for the first time told us of a way by which we can find strength to obey our Adat. If Jesus can give us the power to be good Bataks, we want Him as our Master."

After eighty years, more than 400,000 Bataks or one-third of the nation, are enrolled in the Christian Church because they discovered in Jesus the power to fulfil their own culture.[32]

[31] Gen. 4:9.
[32] J. M. Davis, "The Batak Church," pp. 17-19.

PART TWO

USING THE OLD FOUNDATIONS

CHAPTER III

THE ANTHROPOLOGICAL APPROACH

ANTHROPOLOGY is commonly defined as the study of man and his works.[1] This includes the study of human origins, the classification of human varieties and the investigation of the life of peoples.

For the purpose of this discussion, the third only of these classifications, including the social and cultural emphases of the science, will be considered.

Since man is the subject of foreign missions and since the social order he creates is the field in which they operate and in which they seek to plant the Christian Church, there is every reason for the missionary to secure an intimate understanding of Social Anthropology—its insights, its methods, and its findings.

Social Anthropology deals with the techniques of observation, with the analysis, and the description of man as a gregarious, reasoning, and developing being. It is concerned with his social, cultural, and psychological inheritance, his habits and folkways. It introduces the student to the family and tribal structure, relationships, and obligations, to the manner of living, means of livelihood, and the ways in which man has adapted himself to his environment. It reveals the values, motivations, religious beliefs, superstitions and ideology of a people. It also traces the relation of conduct patterns to the physical surroundings, social structure, and the body of common knowledge and beliefs. In short, anthropology provides answers to the question: Why does a man think, feel, and act as he does? Such a science is indispensable to those who would understand or influence an unfamiliar society and to no one is it more vital than to the missionary for, without such help, he is handicapped from the very beginning of his work.

The Swiss missionary, H. P. Junod, in commenting upon the

[1] Ralph Linton, *The Study of Man*, p. 4. D. Appleton-Century Co., New York, 1936.

47

necessity of a knowledge of anthropology for the Christian approach to the Bantu says,

I believe that anthropology can help us greatly. It can widen our views, it can open our eyes, it can teach us to understand, it can improve our educational policy and point out to us the dangers of the way. . . . A missionary who does not study the African soul, its intuitions, fears, and longings, as well as African institutions and customs, a missionary who purposely or through negligence ignores this seems to me to betray our Master. If we have lacked foresight and insight, it is there: We have not sufficiently and patiently searched for the image of God in the soul of the Umuntu himself.[2]

D. Westerman observes,

How could I be a witness in an African village to what God has done for me if I am not familiar with the language, the mode of thinking and arguing, the religious views, fears and hopes of the people to whom I am talking? How am I justified in presenting myself as guide if I have not been willing or able to learn from them? What right have I to ask from them the renunciation of their religion, their traditions, their tribal ideals if I do not even know what they are and am not in the position to judge whether their content is good or bad? How are they to respect my message if I show disrespect and crass ignorance in things that are dearest and holy to them?[3]

This principle applies to our dealing with people regardless of their type or stage of culture. The strategy of an inquiring approach to the religious beliefs of a non-Christian community was that used by Watts O. Pye of the American Board mission in north China. On entering a village, his practice was first to seek out the elders who were best versed in Confucian philosophy and patiently listen to their description of the religious beliefs of their people. Not until this was done did he point out to them the nature of the Christian faith, its similarities and differences, and its power to fulfil the precepts of Confucius and to vitalize the conventional Chinese ethics by personally relating the individual to God.

The Gospel record reveals Jesus as a practical social Anthropologist. Jesus gained His introduction to anthropology by living for thirty years as a participant in the daily drama and tragedy of His people. He knew their history, background, inheritance, common law and

---

[2] "Anthropology and Missionary Education," *International Review of Missions,* Vol. XXIV, No. 94, April, 1935, pp. 226, 228.

[3] "The Place and Function of the Vernacular in African Education," *International Review of Missions,* Vol. XIV, No. 53, January, 1925, p. 27.

motivations. He was familiar with the land and the people's struggle for livelihood, their social structure, family life and responsibilities. He knew the obligations and limitations of the political environment and the demands upon His people of the tax collector and the Roman soldier. He was acquainted with the Mosaic Law and the organization and ritual of the Temple.

Jesus' conversation abounds in references to intimate daily life. He knew the Jews—their thoughts, hopes, aspirations and hatreds, their religious faith, patriotism and pride in ancestry, the ways by which they gained a living. His parables are alive with references to homely matters: The sheep caught in a pit, the leaven hidden in the meal, the traveler robbed and left on the road, the barren fig tree, the tax money paid to the publican, the wise and foolish virgins, the pearl of great price, the fowls of the air, the hard, stony, thorny and good soils, the talent hidden in the napkin, the householder and his steward.

A secret of Jesus' power in presenting new ideas to the people of His time and in moving them to action lay in the fact that "He knew all men," and "He knew what was in man,"[4] and how to relate His message to that knowledge, and He used this as a key to unlock men's hearts.

The task of the modern missionary in presenting new ideas and in influencing men's wills is similar to that of Jesus. Jesus bade His disciples to follow Him and proclaim the Gospel to all peoples. The record of His life and teachings gives us a clear picture both of the content of His Gospel and the methods and techniques which He used in presenting it.

However, the work of the foreign missionary in interpreting Christ's message to the people to whom he goes is even more difficult than that of Jesus. Jesus was at home in Palestine. He was a product of His environment. He shared the cultural, racial, and religious heritage of His countrymen. He based His teaching upon the Old Testament Law and ethics which He honored in common with them.[5] The modern missionary is handicapped at all these points. He seeks to attach the loyalty of his hearer to a new source of ethics and of authority. He has to acquire a new language and an understanding of a new environment while the language and

---

[4] John 2:24, 25.
[5] Matt. 23:2, 3; Matt. 12:3, 4, 5; Mark 10:19; Luke 3:4; Luke 4:16-21.

surroundings of Palestine were as familiar to Jesus as the air He breathed.

If the modern missionary is called to preach the Gospel of Jesus in an unfamiliar environment and cultural order in a way which will win disciples to an acceptance of His Lordship, he must set himself to the task of knowing "what is in man." Without that knowledge, Jesus could not have accomplished His work. Surely His missionary disciple cannot expect to do his Master's work without using every possible means to equip himself, so far as is humanly possible, with the insights into humanity which Jesus possessed.

While not the place for a discussion of the science of Social Anthropology, this chapter will aim to relate its significance, principles, and techniques to the understanding and practice of the missionary.

Anthropology stresses the richness and variety of the elements which compose a racial culture and the inadequacy of any one carrier to represent more than a fraction of the cultural stream from which he comes. The process of diffusion and integration depends upon the scope and quality of the culture content carried by the individual or group. Linton asserts that culture is something which lies entirely outside the range of physical phenomena. It cannot be exported or imported or bought or sold, but it can be transmitted, acquired, and appropriated by well-defined processes. The form, content, and even the existence of a culture can only be deduced from the human behavior to which it gives rise.[6]

Since behavior is the medium through which culture is transmitted, demonstrated, and understood, the commanding part that the individual plays in culture change becomes clear. Whether as trader, soldier, miner, diplomat, teacher or missionary the individual is the indispensable medium of diffusion. This is a challenge to each culture carrier and the culture group that he represents. It follows that the individual missionary depending upon the quality of his personality, the depth of his insights, and the range of his gifts becomes a unique medium for the transformation of non-Christian society.

There are basic elements of a people's culture with which the missionary must deal in presenting the Christian message. The

[6] Ralph Linton, op. cit., pp. 288, 289.

means which they have evolved for solving their problems of living and the customs which they hold as satisfying their physical, social, and spiritual aspirations will not be set aside until more effective means and conclusive beliefs and practices have been demonstrated to their own and not the missionary's satisfaction.[7]

With this in mind, the first principle of introducing the new culture and the new faith is *utility*—not utility from the missionary's point of view, but from that of the people to whom he goes. The new faith must be shown to be practical and applicable to every sphere of their life. As Dale states,

Before the Indian can accept the Gospel, he must see that it aids him to meet the present world with confidence and the next with assurance. Not only must he be given a well-defined group of ideas, values, and motives which are Christian, but these must be presented to him directly and objectively in concrete patterns of behavior. Otherwise, the Indian in times of crisis will revert to the old patterns. The Gospel must be concerned with the whole of the Indian's life—his person, mind, soul, his home, work, pleasures, attitudes and his values.[8]

In a society which for a thousand years has placed confidence in and depended upon a particular philosophy and practice for meeting its problems and crises, for the missionary without discrimination to assert the falsehood of these foundations and to substitute a new source of supernatural power, there is always the risk that the superstitious native will regard it as a new and stronger type of magic.

Keesing tells of a Samoan chief (quoted by John Williams) as haranguing his people as follows:

It is my wish that the Christian religion should become universal amongst us. I look at the wisdom of these worshippers of Jehovah, and see how superior they are in every respect. Their ships can traverse the tempest-driven ocean for months with perfect safety. Their axes are so hard and sharp. Now I conclude that the God who has given to His white worshippers these valuable things must be wiser than our gods, for they have not given the like to us. We want all these articles; and my proposition is, that the God who gave them should be our God.[9]

For a people to whom the services of the witchdoctor are their mainstay against disease, evil, and the unknown, the teaching of

[7] A. P. Elkin, "A Missionary Policy for Primitive Peoples," Reprint from *The Morpeth Review*, No. 27. University of Sydney.

[8] Rev. J. T. Dale, joint author of *Indians of the High Andes*, Section III, Committee on Cooperation in Latin America, New York, 1945.

[9] Felix M. Keesing, *The South Seas in the Modern World*, p. 230. The John Day Company, New York, 1941.

preventive medicine, sanitary measures, and simple remedies for common diseases must supplement and parallel condemnation of the witchdoctor and of belief in evil spirits.[10]

Witchcraft serves useful functions in primitive society. It supports tribal morality, it reinforces tribal authority, it serves to explain and putatively to control the incalculable forces of destiny. For these reasons, it is deeply rooted in primitive culture. Yet witchcraft is inconsistent alike with Christianity, with scientific knowledge and with our conceptions of legal and moral responsibility. What is to be done? The first step is to emphasize the things which witchcraft endeavors to explain and control—disease, death, disaster and the frustration of human hopes. Our own scientific knowledge gives us a large measure of control over these, and until we have made this fully available to the native we have no right to condemn the superstitious beliefs by which he tries to defend himself and his fellows from despair or disaster. More than this, our attempts completely to eradicate witchcraft are not only unjustified, they are doomed to failure.[11]

No problem of the Church in relation to the life of primitive societies is more difficult than the necessity of ruling in the practice of plural wives. The problem is not only to maintain Christian standards but also to do justice to the intricate system of responsibilities and obligations that have developed in a polygamous society.

A frontal attack alone upon polygamy increasingly is seen to be insufficient. The African delegates to the Madras Conference in 1938, appointed from ten different areas of the continent, unanimously requested the International Missionary Council to carry out objective studies of marriage customs and witchcraft in relation to Church discipline and practice. The delegates pointed to the confusion resulting among African Christians from the lack of uniform Church rulings on these matters and also the unfairness of basing modern Church discipline upon the inadequate understanding by early missionaries of the inner social structure of African tribal life.[12]

If Christianity is to change the traditional, polygamous structure

---

[10] *Africa*, Vol. VIII, No. 4, October, 1935. Articles on Witchcraft by E. E. Evans-Pritchard, G. St. J. Orde Browne, Frank Melland and Audrey I. Richards.

[11] J. M. Graham and R. Piddington, "Anthropology and the Future of Missions," p. 9. The University Press, Aberdeen, 1940.

[12] *The World Mission of the Church*, pp. 157-159. Findings and Recommendations of the Meeting of the International Missionary Council, Tamberam, Madras, December, 1938.

of African society, preaching against the custom of multiple wives must be accompanied by training in midwifery, proper diet, care of infants, and cleanliness in the home, together with other practical measures to reduce the high infant mortality which is a basic cause of polygamy among many African tribes.

Dr. John Hubbard asserts that it is useless to try to change African morals without reference to the place that reproduction occupies in the African's world. The average African woman bears ten living children of whom an average of not more than two reach maturity. On this basis monogamy would not guarantee the continuance of the race. The concepts of a woman as a child-bearing machine and an income producer are underlying urges to polygamy and must be thoroughly understood by anyone who attempts to change the practices of the African. Since practically the whole of the great reproductive activity amongst Africans is an effort to make good the loss due to excessive mortality of infants and children, missionary societies would be well advised to take the most active measures possible for reducing it. The causes—abortions, faulty midwifery, still-births due to venereal disease, female circumcision, improper feeding of children, entire lack of parental child control—are, to a very large extent, preventable. The task of the mission, then, is to plan a preventative and curative program which may be summed up as maternity and child welfare work and the training of native midwives. This approach to the problem of African morals is attacking the problem at its very source and there is little hope of making headway on any other basis.[13]

Ancestor worship can be modified and Christianized so that its strength for family solidarity may be conserved to the lasting benefit of social orders which are rapidly losing their respect and honor for parents and with it their social cohesion.

The experience of a missionary in Japan who modified the Oriental practice of ancestor worship is illuminating. On the anniversary of his father's death, a simple family service was held in his honor. Upon the mantel in the living-room, flowers were placed at either side of the father's photograph. After singing together his favorite hymns, passages were read from the Bible he had used. Stories were then related to the children of their grandfather's boy-

---

[13] "The Cause and the Cure of African 'Immorality,'" *The International Review of Missions,* Vol. XXI, No. 78, April, 1931.

hood and later life which revealed his courage, struggles, defeats and victories. The sources of his strength and beauty of character were made vivid to the children. The little service closed with a prayer of gratitude for such an inheritance and for strength that each member of the family might prove himself worthy of it.

Anthropology reveals the values which a culture treasures. The missionary who understands and honors these values, and so far as possible incorporates them into the Christian way of life, will make progress in reaching the heart of the people.

Such basic values as the initiation school training, the celebration of events in the life cycle—birth, marriage, anniversaries and death, and the ceremonies of planting, harvesting, and house-building— have for unnumbered generations characterized the education and the social life of the people and can in very many cases be modified, carried over, and used in the Christian way of life.

The long and hard discipline of the initiation school is the cornerstone of the social, moral, and tribal education of African youth from the Cape to the Sudan as it is of other primitive peoples. Through this rigorous training the lore, discipline, obligations and skills of manhood and womanhood are passed on to the rising generation.

Because of certain sexual rites and practices offensive to Christian standards, the Church has commonly proscribed the whole institution and in doing so has furthered the disintegration of native society. No substitution of an education modelled upon the European type can take the place of this foundation stone of African life. Too often such substitution detribalizes the individual and renders him ignorant of the basic virtues and *mores* of his group. As a result he becomes a hybrid who is neither African nor European and is accepted by neither society.

In discussing the subject of the sublimation of Bantu life and thought, Edwin W. Smith says;[14]

Surely there is something admirable and well-suited to the needs of the Bantu in that severe preparation by discipline for the duties of adulthood. . . . Our education in the mission field aims too exclusively at the acquisition of facts and the fitting of boys to earn money; though they may have perverted it, the natives themselves have in their initiation

[14] E. W. Smith, "The Sublimation of Bantu Life and Thought," *International Review of Missions,* Vol. XI, No. 41, January, 1922, p. 89.

schools the right principle—the making of men and women.[15]

The craving for self-expression and prestige that exists in every society is a value which is easily overlooked by the missionary in planning for the development of the Christian community. The Church should reckon with this instinct and, through the placing of responsibility upon its members in a varied program of activities, provide for its expression.

A fertile source of the extraordinary growth of the Fijian Church has been the early giving of responsible tasks to large numbers of the Christians so that nearly every family was related through one of its members to some definite responsibility for the Church.[16]

The reciprocal obligations and community teamwork of many non-Christian societies are other values that often remain unused by the missionary. The individualistic Westerner easily overlooks this basic characteristic of communal life and fails to build it into the Christian structure.

Robertson Smith in his book, *The Religion of the Semites,* discusses the importance of establishing a point of contact with people in presenting the Gospel. He says,

No positive religion that has moved men has been able to start with a 'tabula rasa' and express itself as if religion were beginning for the first time. A new scheme of faith can find a hearing only by appealing to religious instincts and susceptibilities that already exist in its audience and it cannot reach these without taking account of the traditional forms in which all religious feeling is embodied and without speaking a language which men accustomed to these old forms can understand.[17]

Social Anthropology and studies in comparative religions are keys which will unlock these existing instincts and susceptibilities. Both Jesus and the Apostle Paul, and after them the great evangelists and missionaries of modern times, established their points of contact with their hearers as a first step in presenting their messages.[18]

The land, the struggle for livelihood, the family, disease and death, fear of the unknown and of disaster, security in this life and the life to come, the craving for contact with Divinity and the sense of failure are among the virtually universal points of contact

---

[15] A remarkable experiment in the sublimation of the central principle of the initiation school and its adaptation to the Christian training of Bantu youth has been attempted by the Universities Mission at Masasi, Tanganyika.

[16] J. W. Burton, The Madras Series, Vol. II, page 80.

[17] Robertson Smith, *The Religion of the Semites,* p. 2.

[18] Luke 4:16-21; Acts 13:14-41; Acts 17:22-31.

with non-Christian peoples. However, to be effectively utilized these factors must be approached from the point of view and understanding of the hearer.

The anthropological approach is a deliberate approach. It demands patience, self-discipline, faith, the ability to use the imagination and to be content with the investment of time in laying foundations of understanding.

The anthropological method as a preparation for missionary work has useful analogies in secular activities. The North American mining engineer in Peru or the Belgian Congo is confronted with different geologic and ore conditions than those of his homeland. The composition of copper is the same but frequently the processes of separating it from the ore are different. Metal ingredients mixed with copper ore in Peru resist the formulas used in the Lake Superior region or in Arizona. For several years the Cerro de Pasco Mining Company of Peru, one of the largest producers in South America, mined a mountain of low grade ore from which they could extract only a small percentage of copper. The metal was present in enormous quantities but it was so mixed with other metals that it defied the usual processes of separation and flotation. It was decided to let these huge stocks stand while some of the best ore analysts of North America worked on the problem. For ten years they studied and experimented. In the eleventh year the secret was discovered, the copper was separated in highly paying proportions and the basis for the great output of the Cerro de Pasco Company was laid.[19]

The problem of foreign missions in the post-war age will be similar to that of the Cerro de Pasco Company. The precious metal will be present but it will be found in combination with new elements which may baffle accepted methods. Moreover, old factors in modified or heightened forms will be present with the new. Communism, nationalism, antagonism to the entrance of missionaries, the discounting of Western culture and leadership, newly found abilities and self-reliance, a disorganized national economy, a disrupted social and moral order, famine, disease, malnutrition and desperate poverty—all these will have been intensified by the World War, and will combine to create situations of unprecedented difficulty for the Christian movement. The mis-

[19] The Cerro de Pasco Mining Corporation, Lima, Oroya, and Cerro de Pasco, Peru.

sionary should go to his work equipped with skills and with insights into the underlying social, economic, and political conditions of the mission land that will aid him to meet these situations and to secure results which the use of the old methods and equipment alone could not bring about.

The anthropological approach as a step preliminary to the opening of a new mission was used in 1943 by the Commission to the Andean Indians.[20] The purpose of the Commission was to secure a comprehensive picture of the Quechua and Aymara Indians who live in the highlands of Ecuador, Peru, and Bolivia against the background of their culture which would serve as a guide in planning a united mission. Each member of the Commission had had experience on mission fields either as evangelist, anthropologist, physician, agronomist, educator or economist. The problems of livelihood, farming, stock raising, health, diet, education, schools, social structure, festivities, recreation, superstitions and religion were all studied.

While the Quechua and Aymara Indians constitute two-thirds or more of the populations of the Andean republics, they are almost completely isolated from the main stream of national life. They have been crowded off their lands and have either submitted to peonage on white-owned *haciendas* or have retreated to the lofty recesses of the Andes where they live at heights difficult of access for their oppressors. The Indian culture is little changed from the days of the Incas. They live on a subsistence economy basis. Toward the whites, they hold a deep suspicion and hatred. Protestant missions, after fifty years, have made little progress with the Andean Indians.

If the Church that the missionary seeks to establish is to endure, the foundations of a new culture must be laid which is either integrated with or substituted for the old. The Indian has to be convinced that the Christian way of life is superior to his own and, to accomplish this, the missionary must introduce the Christian culture to him in terms which are familiar.

The new mission will be based upon the land which is the dominant interest of the Andean Indian. The first step will be the pur-

[20] The Commission was appointed under the auspices of the Committee on Cooperation in Latin America in 1943.

chase of an *hacienda* with its attached peon population. This will serve as a foothold and experimental ground for further work. On the *hacienda,* Indian life is found at its lowest level and here a beginning of rehabilitation and redemption must be attempted.

Such an approach calls for long preparation of the Indian peon family for land ownership as a basis for freedom and for a Christian and a better way of living. The missionary personnel will include in addition to an evangelist, an agronomist, a medical expert, and a worker versed in the problems of home and family rehabilitation. The use of the Indian language and an introduction to Social Anthropology will be essential for each worker. Each member of the staff must consider his aim the spiritual regeneration of the Indian and through his part in the program, contribute to that aim and to the establishment of the Church of Christ.

With this purpose in view, Indians will be trained for church leadership and for the extension work to the free Indian communities which ultimately will be attempted.[21]

A plan for an experimental mission, organized upon the anthropological approach, was proposed some years ago to several members of the Conference of Missionary Societies in Great Britain and Ireland.[22] An English missionary of an interdenominational society working among the primitive Indians of Venezuela, became convinced of the inadequacy of the methods used by his mission. Though only one per cent of the Indians spoke Spanish, this language with interpretation was the medium through which the Gospel was preached. The mission personnel had not studied the culture of the communities they were attempting to convert to Christianity. Many years of using such methods had produced but meagre results. The missionary resigned and returned to England determined upon equipping himself thoroughly for the task of reaching primitive peoples.

After three years of training in Social Anthropology at the London School of Economics, he devised a plan for an experimental mission, based upon the anthropological approach, to be set up in an untouched area of Africa by the joint action of several missionary societies. Its personnel was to include an anthropologist, a

[21] The United Andean Indian Mission is a joint project with five cooperating societies.

[22] Cecil W. Gibbons, "Project for An Experimental Mission Centre in Africa," London, 1933.

doctor, an agriculturalist, an educator and an evangelist. Each staff member would have had missionary experience in Africa, and would be allocated to the project by his own missionary society which would be responsible for his support and for a pro rata share of the operating expenses of the mission for an initial term of five years. The anthropological member would serve as an adviser to the mission and the others would be guided in starting special lines of work by the results of language and culture study. During the first three years, progress reports would not be required, but at the end of this period an "umpire"—an experienced board secretary— would visit the mission, remain for several months, and assess the results of the project. The "umpire" would then return to London and report his observations and recommendations. At the end of a second period, during which the team might modify its methods, another "umpire" would visit the project. After these experimental years, the mission personnel and the cooperating societies would be in a better position to determine whether or not to continue the project and to consider the type of program to be employed. This experimental mission plan was somewhat in advance of the times and was, therefore, not realized, but it merits the careful study of all who are concerned with the task of evangelizing primitive peoples.

The last two decades have seen in parts of British and French Africa an increasing number of anthropological studies carried out under government and private auspices. Following the first World War, The International Institute of African Languages and Cultures[23] initiated a plan by which a succession of anthropologists have been sent to make field studies in French Equatorial Africa, the Union of South Africa, and British East and West Africa. These studies have dealt with the language, proverbs, and place names of tribes, their arts, crafts, hut construction, diet, kinship obligations and relationships, marriage customs, sex relations, dances, initiation rites, crop cultivation, hunting, the social life and occupations of the women, the training of children, the taboos and rituals, superstitions, magic, witchcraft and other aspects of African life.[24]

[23] Central Office, Seymour House, 17 Waterloo Place, London S. W. 1.

[24] The monographs produced by this school of cultural anthropologists have appeared for a number of years in *Africa*, the Journal of the International Institute of African Languages and Cultures. Outstanding names among this group are G. Gordon Brown, M. Fortes, Monica Hunter, L. P. Mair, S. Nadel, K. Oberg, M. Read, A. I. Richards, I. Schapera and Godfrey Wilson—all of whom were trained in the London School of Economics under the late Dr. Bronislaw Malinowski.

Dr. Audrey I. Richards, a disciple of Malinowski, has made an invaluable contribution in recent years through her intimate studies of Bantu life.[25] The modern missionary could, with profit, ponder her patient methods in studying the home and the daily life of Bantu women. Dr. Richards spent several months in intimate companionship with the women of a Babemba village in Northern Rhodesia in order to learn the nature of their problems, their interests, and the trend of their thinking and conversation. Sitting on the ground in the circle of village women, she joined them in pounding the mealies, in preparing food, and in the care of babies and little children. Day by day she listened to the banter, palaver, and gossip, observed the conduct and techniques of the group and noted the subjects of conversation. The reward for this painstaking process is a book unrivalled in its revelation of the inner life, thought, daily activities and motivations of the African woman.

A group of able anthropologists led by such scholars as Professor Agnes Winifred Hoernlé of the University of the Witwatersrand, Professor Ernst G. Malherbe of Pretoria, and Professor I. Schapera of Capetown[26] has been at work for many years in the Union of South Africa. A pioneer among modern African anthropologists and for many years a missionary of the Swiss Romande Mission among the Thonga tribe of southeast Africa was the late Dr. Henri A. Junod. His two-volume work, *The Life of a South African Tribe*,[27] stands as a classic and is characterized by Paul Schebesta as the finest description of an African people. Schebesta[28] mentions the work of two other missionaries as being in the forefront of studies of African life, i.e., *The Ila-speaking Peoples of Northern Rhodesia* by E. W. Smith and *The Baganda* by Roscoe.

There are great areas today peopled by primitive races or by populations so isolated and deeply set in their peculiar culture as to

---

[25] *Hunger and Work in a Savage Tribe*, George Routledge and Sons, Ltd., London, 1932 and "The Village Census in the Study of Culture Contact," *Africa*, Vol. VIII, No. 1, January, 1935.

[26] Among the many anthropologists who have produced first-rate monographs and articles on culture contact in the South Seas and contiguous areas are Beaglehold, Brown, Buck, Dollard, Elkin, Firth, Groves, Hogbin, Keesing, Mead, Powdermaker, Reed and F. E. Williams. The writings of Brown, Elkin, and Keesing are peculiarly rewarding for the missionary student.

[27] Second Edition, 1927, Macmillan and Co., London.

[28] Paul Schebesta, "Recent Literature on Bantu Tribes"—Some Ethnological and Linguistic Publications, *Africa*, Vol. I, No. 1, January, 1928, pp. 116-124.

be all but inaccessible to the frontal approach of Christianity. Under this category would be included many African tribes from the Sudan to the Cape of Good Hope and from the Atlantic to the Indian oceans and a large majority of the seventeen million Indians living from Mexico to Cape Horn. The border tribes on the confines of China, Indo-China and Burma, the Bhils and Ghonds of India, the Thibetans and many of the nomadic races of central Asia and the head hunters of New Guinea and Borneo all are groups that are peculiarly open to the anthropological approach.

The anthropological approach need not be limited to primitive, isolated or backward societies alone.[29] The science may be used for gaining insights into the culture of the most advanced peoples— not excluding European or Anglo-Saxon societies. Very much remains to be done to secure an accurate understanding of many of the small and the great nations which have begun to modernize their life, but whose culture and springs of conduct are rooted in a medieval or prehistoric past. The peoples of India, China, Japan, Korea and Burma and the widely scattered Malayan race are still moulded by the impress of cultures which antedate the Christian era and from which there linger mental processes, values, and attitudes which baffle the Westerner.

[29] B. Malinowski, *The Dynamics of Culture Change*, p. 2.

CHAPTER IV

THE SIGNIFICANCE OF ENVIRONMENT

THE environment of the Church, for the first time in the history of modern missions, was discussed at the world missionary gathering at Madras in 1938, along with evangelism, education and medical work as a major factor or "fourth dimension" of the Church.

What is meant by the environment, or this "fourth dimension," and what part does it play in building the Christian movement?

The fourth dimension connotes the soil in which a man—or a society—is rooted, from which he takes his nourishment and through which his stability is insured. It is the air that a man breathes of whose presence and support he is scarcely aware until it is withdrawn. The fourth dimension is the medium in which a man makes his struggle for livelihood. It includes the social structure, the relationships and influences of family and community with their responsibilities and mutual obligations. It is the inherited body of tradition and folkways. It is the source of a man's values, his motivations and the things which impel him to action. It also embraces a man's fears and superstitions, his hopes and beliefs. In short, the field of the fourth dimension is the medium in which a culture is rooted and in which it is shaped. In the fourth dimension are many obstacles which prevent a man—or a society—from accepting the Lordship of Christ, but, on the other hand, it also holds the key which may open the door to His entrance.

The environment of the Church and the attitude of the Church to it may be a matter of life and death to a missionary enterprise.

Science tells us that the dinosaur and other mammals of the Miocene Age disappeared because of changing environmental conditions to which they could not satisfactorily adjust. The Christian Church possesses supernatural sources of power but it is also a natural organism and is subject to the laws of survival of other living organisms. The Church, no less than the dinosaur, is bound by the same condition of survival.

Church leaders may with profit ponder the history of two missionary ventures of the early Church. The Nestorian missions to China in the eighth and fourteenth centuries have already been mentioned as examples of the failure of an alien church to make a satisfactory integration with its environment. The reasons why the Nestorian movement in China so completely vanished are shrouded in mystery. The two chief sources of the eastward spread of Nestorian Christianity during the T'ang Dynasty, 635-850, viz., the travel and residence of Syrian merchants and the planting of monasteries, were open to the same weakness. The merchant communities became closed enclaves apart from the Chinese people and were intent upon guarding their own forms of worship. The priests and monks in their monastic foundations were almost entirely foreigners. There was apparently no integration of their activities with their surroundings and little missionary outreach to the Chinese. When, under these circumstances, the Christian movement was involved in the edict of Emperor Wu Tsung in 845 A.D., which dissolved the powerful Buddhist foundations, after two hundred years of life it entirely disappeared.[1]

In contrast to this experience, an offshoot of the same Nestorian faith—the so-called Syrian Church—gained a foothold in south India in the fifth century and after fifteen hundred years, with its various branches, numbers two million members—the largest non-Roman Christian Church in India and in the missionary world. The Nestorians of Travancore and Cochin made an adjustment to Indian environmental conditions by intermarriage, by accepting a modified form of caste, and by successfully entering the economic activities of their surroundings, which made it possible for them to survive in an unfamiliar cultural order. This Church also guarded the central citadel of Christianity: belief in one God, the Saviorhood of Christ, the Scriptures as a basis of Christian teaching and the sanctity of the marriage bond. Today the Nestorian Christian communities of Travancore and Cochin, although possessing a different tradition from that of the modern mission churches around them and having integrated in many ways with Hindu society, nevertheless,

[1] a) Kenneth Scott Latourette, *A History of the Expansion of Christianity,* Vol. II, Chapter V. Harper & Brothers, New York, 1938.
   b) A. C. Moule, "The Primitive Failure of Christianity in China," *International Review of Missions,* July, 1931.

after fifteen centuries, have kept a reality of faith and an integrity of life.[2]

THE ECONOMIC ENVIRONMENT

The economic environment is of profound concern to the Church since it conditions the struggle for a livelihood of all of its members and this, in turn, governs the possibility of creating a deeply rooted and a self-sustaining church. There are, however, broader grounds for the Church's concern over economic trends than their bearing upon the interests of its own members. The economic developments in the fields of modern missions, such as heavy industry in mines and plantations, the massing of workers in city factories and in modern transportation and commerce, the huge international investments and public works, with their myriad subsidiary enterprises, have been changing the face of non-Christian society and conditioning the development of a Christian order.

The pressure of expanding populations on the land, the increased growth of tenancy with loss of land ownership, the inadequacy of wage and income schedules in face of the rising costs of living, the resulting undernourishment and squalor of the masses, are all of vital concern to the Church for they not only limit the possibility of its own stability and expansion but also of the existence of a stable society.[3]

The monastic orders of the early middle ages in their missionary expansion to the pagan tribes of western Europe recognized in the environment the medium in which a Christian church and community were to be built and they accepted the task of creating a new economic and social environment. The Benedictine and Cistercian monks took large numbers of lay Brothers with them into Germany, Switzerland, and the Low Countries. These missionaries could not think of a Church as existing in a wilderness nor of a Christian community of barbarians. To them the two concepts were contradictions in terms. The Way of Christ called for better and nobler living and so the monks made of their monastic establishments little

[2] a) Kenneth Scott Latourette, *op. cit.*

b) P. C. Joseph, "The Economic and Social Environment of the Church in North Travancore and Cochin."

[3] a) R. Ishii, *Population Pressure and Economic Life in Japan*, p. 155.

b) Edmund deS. Brunner, *Rural Korea—A Preliminary Survey of Economic, Social, and Religious Conditions*, p. 104.

islands of Christian culture, activity, and worship where such a way of life could be demonstrated. The monks cleared the land, tilled the soil, introduced new varieties of grain, vegetables and fruit trees. They brought cattle, sheep, hogs, and poultry. They introduced fish and bee culture. They built looms for textiles, tanned hides, made brick and blew glass. They puddled, poured, and moulded iron. They planted vineyards for wine and made cheese, butter, candles and soap. Along with the farming, stockraising, and artisan trades went the practice of medicine and training in silver and goldsmith work, weaving, embroidery, painting, illuminating and music. These industries and arts were needed for the furnishing and maintenance of the church and monastery but their practice passed on to the community which clustered around them an appreciation of better and gentler ways of living together with the skills required for following them. It is important to note that the monks did not bring a program of economic and social uplift into the wilderness for its own sake, but that the culture-building activities emanated from and were organized around a Christian church. Wherever they settled, the monks also established schools, not only to train the novitiates for the Church, but to educate the children of the countryside. Some of these schools such as Fulda and St. Gall were noted throughout Europe and were the forerunners of the universities. Through this wide program of activities, the monasteries laid the foundations of civilization in western Europe. After several hundred years of leadership in the arts of Christian living, these cultural functions of the Church were largely taken over from the monasteries through the rise of the free cities of Europe with their universities and their artisan and commercial guilds under the patronage of the princes.[4]

The environment not only is the medium in which a people's culture has been shaped and culture change takes place: it is the medium in which the Christian Church, if it is to endure, is rooted. From the outset of its life the soil of a Christian culture is needed

[4] a) Pertz, *Monumenta Germania Historica,* Vita St. Sturmi, p. 371.
  b) *Acta Sanctorum,* Edition Mabillon, Vita Wilfridi, April 24, p. 293, Feb. 27, p. 712.
  c) James Thayer Addison, *The Medieval Missionary,* International Missionary Council, New York, 1936.
  d) Montalambert, *Monks of the West,* Vol. II, Book 6, Chapter 5.
  e) Von Stein, *Kloster und Kultur,* pp. 51, 52.

for the roots of the young church to find their nourishment. If this is neglected and the environmental factor is ignored, the effort to establish an indigenous church may be completely thwarted.

The environment offers to the Church both stubborn obstacles and mighty aids in its work of creating a Christian culture.

A notable example of constructive dealing with the environment and the use of the land as the foundation for a spiritual enterprise is the work of the Canadian Baptist Mission to the Aymara Indians at Guatajata on the shores of Lake Titicaca, Bolivia. Twenty-five years ago, with a farm of 1,000 acres, the mission took over fifty peon families which, in the Latin American tradition, were bound to the soil as serfs. These Indians had only squatter's rights to small fragments of land and worked without wages for their *patron*. They possessed a serf mentality and were lazy, degraded, suspicious, diseased and resentful. They were sodden with liquor and drugged from chewing the coca leaf. They listened to the Gospel message with indifference and were uncooperative in sending their children to school. Under these conditions the mission made but little progress.

Ten years ago a new director became convinced that Christianity and serfdom could not exist side by side and, unless the inner motivations of the people could be stirred, preaching alone was useless. He saw in the land the key to the mental and spiritual awakening of the Aymara Indian, and he determined to free his peons and make them land owners. But to create free, self-respecting farmers from this human material was a Herculean task. The missionary set in motion the slow processes of surveying, land courts, and registration and began to prepare his people for the responsibilities of land ownership and the management of home and farm. After eight years both goals were reached. Each family owned title to from three to ten acres of land; they had been trained in efficient methods of cultivation, they had learned to build houses with windows, floors, fireplaces and chimneys. Gardens were protected by picket fences and these, together with the cottages, were white-washed. Rugs of the Indian's own weaving were on the floors and curtains were at the windows. The children were in school, the mission clinic was serving a wide countryside, and coca cola had replaced hard liquor as the popular drink. One hundred and thirty adult Indians were baptized members of the Church and ten schools—

each also a preaching center—were scattered through the district.[5]

The Guatajata farm experiment is unique in the experience of Bolivia,[6] as well as in the experience of Christian missions in Latin America. It is an unusual example of how the land may be used for releasing the spiritual powers of a backward community.

There is a tendency to deplore the entrance of economic forces with the consequent break-up of social orders into fields in which the Younger Church is planted. However, such forces belong to God's world and are subject to His will in that they may be used to serve constructive as well as destructive ends. When left to selfish interests, economic determinism may be a menace to mankind, but the possibilities of using the same factor to extend God's Kingdom are seen in different mission fields. The investments that have drawn thousands of tribesmen from their villages to the great mines of Africa have also given the Church an opportunity to make contacts with hitherto inaccessible peoples. The Bantu miners frequently have spread the "good news" on returning to their distant villages. More than one hundred "bush" churches and schools have sprung up in Portuguese East Africa through the return to their homes of Bantu miners who first heard of Christianity in the mission chapels along the great gold reef adjacent to Johannesburg.[7]

The Chinese colony which, because of economic pressure, migrated forty years ago from south China to Sarawak, Borneo, through the witness of a few Christian emigrants, became a Christian community that numbers several thousand members and has influenced the native people of Sarawak.

In somewhat similar fashion economic pressure among the Filipinos of Luzon and the Toba Bataks of Sumatra has extended the Church to Mindanao and to Moslem communities in Sumatra.[8]

The Western commercialized cinema, by its distorted presentation of life in so-called Christian lands, often is a source of demoralization to the youth of Asia and Africa. On the other hand, the motion picture may be a powerful aid to education and for interpreting new ethical, social, and religious principles. Economic forces may serve the noblest purposes but we must be alive to the perils,

[5] Report of Commission to the Indians of the High Andes, 1945.

[6] Statement of Senator Jose Salmon, La Paz, Bolivia, September 7, 1943.

[7] Statements of Dr. James Dexter Taylor and Mrs. Frederick B. Bridgman, American Board mission, Johannesburg, Transvaal.

[8] The Madras Series, Vol. V., p. 422.

as well as the opportunities, latent in the world of economics which this swiftly-moving age lays at our doors. The long rollers of the Pacific that break upon the beaches of Hawaii may batter the life from the body of the tyro who opposes them, but to the surf-rider who has measured their strength and timed their speed, the same waves become the steed which bears him to the shore.

THE SOCIAL ENVIRONMENT

The social environment of the Younger Churches is a product of the cultural inheritance of the people. With the spiritual inheritance it is the most important of all the factors with which Christianity must deal in an approach to the non-Christian world. Into this fabric, the most characteristic and precious possessions are woven: the *mores,* the traditional way of life, the body of common law, the moral and religious sanctions and the code of social relationships. Here we are standing at the threshold of the genius of the race. Here are found the source of a man's aesthetic values, his forms of speech, and his mental and spiritual processes. It is these things that have made one man a Japanese, another an Indian, and a third an Englishman.[9]

If the Church of Christ is to be established as an indigenous institution in non-Christian lands, it must deal fearlessly, patiently, and intelligently with the fourth dimension. The mission comes as a foreign institution to a deeply entrenched order of society and brings to it a foreign faith and a foreign culture presented in strange terms and concepts. In introducing a non-Christian society to the Christian way of life, it is necessary, in addition to preaching the Gospel, to take the slower step of discovering the needs, values, and aspirations of the people which their culture endeavors to satisfy. The missionary who understands these things is in a strong position to present the claims of Christianity. In order to lead a man to new evaluations of God, of himself, and of his fellow man, one needs to understand the nature of his old evaluations. Equipped with such knowledge the missionary will know how to present Christianity to a people in terms which they can recognize as a superior way of life and a fulfilment of their own culture.[10]

---

[9] *Ibid,* p. 109.

[10] a) John T. Dale, Report of Commission to the Indians of the High Andes, 1945.

    b) D. Westerman, "The Place and Function of the Vernacular in African Education," *International Review of Missions,* Vol. XIV, No. 53, January, 1925, p. 27.

Early missions considered as heathen not only non-Christian religions but the social and cultural systems with which they were allied: it was a simple and convenient classification. Social Anthropology, the comparative study of religions, archaeology and art had not as yet come forward to assist the West to understand Asiatic and African peoples. The political and economic exploitation of Western imperialism was in its early stages; the inconsistencies and sins of the civilizations of the mission-sending countries were not yet known. All these factors have greatly complicated but also enriched the work of modern missions. The Twentieth Century missionary needs to approach his task with an open mind first, with respect to the social and religious endowment of the non-Christian peoples and, second, with regard to the alleged superiority of the social and economic order of the West.

The social and cultural environment of the non-Christian lands may be looked upon not as obstacles to be overcome, but rather as storehouses of the experience that the races have gathered in their efforts toward self-fulfilment. God has been dealing with each of the non-Christian peoples throughout the millenniums of their history. In various ways and in varying degrees, He has revealed Himself to them. The acceptance of the revelation has been imperfect and mixed with error, but it is present in every race. God's hand is found in attitudes of worship, codes of conduct, moral sanctions, aesthetic appreciations, philosophy, and in types of human relationships, respects, and loyalties. The fact that some of these values differ from those of the Western cultural stream does not, of itself, render them inferior or hostile to it.

The Christian mission should face these life patterns reverently and try to discover the foundation stones and main beams in the *mores* of the people which have made them Asiatic or African rather than Anglo-Saxon or European and, wherever possible, build them into the structure whose cornerstone is Christ. This is a delicate and costly process—costly in time, study, experimentation and faith—but it must be attempted if we are to honor God's own workmanship and build with Him rather than inadvertently pull down what He has built.

One reason for the slow progress of the Church in many parts of the world has been the inability of Christ's messengers to distinguish granite from rubble in the culture about them, or to appreciate the suitability of using the old framework to carry the new structure.[11]

The thousand years' discipline of feudalism, active among the Japanese people until only seventy-five years ago, has deeply graven the character of the race. The instinct for following a lord to whom complete fealty can be given in which all personal considerations are lost, is still a powerful motivation. This finds expression in the rigid etiquette, the impassivity of face and demeanor, and the unquestioned obedience to authority. It appears in the architecture of the castle town and the private home; in the honorific usage of language and the indirect syntax—all are reflections of a political and social system in which the people were schooled to protect the interests of the lord of the clan. Christianity in its approach to the Japanese has not fully understood the power of this instinct nor its implications for Christ's claims of Lordship upon the race.

THE EFFECT OF THE ENVIRONMENT UPON CHRISTIANITY

The modern mission in its approach to non-Christian cultures can never forget the imprint of the non-Christian environment upon the Church of the first five centuries of the Christian era. Latourette stresses the environmental influence of its surroundings upon Christianity in each of the first four volumes of his *History of the Expansion of Christianity*. He observes,

However we must not attempt to disguise the plain fact that in the year 500 Christianity was not the same as at its inception. Thrust plastic into the medieval world it had been largely shaped by its environment. Some of the features then acquired persisted into succeeding ages and were accorded sanctity and were treated as norms. Indeed the vast majority of the Christians in the centuries since 500 A.D., have been in churches whose creeds, rituals, and organization are lineal descendants of the Christianity which took form in the period we have been describing.

Would Christianity have been different had the original impulse appeared in some other cultural area—India or China? Undoubtedly. How different we cannot know. In future generations or as its cultural environment changes or as it is introduced to non-occidental peoples, may it not acquire other forms? Very probably. The cultural environment of these initial centuries has left an indelible impress upon all that is later

[11] The Madras Series, Vol. V, pp. 110, 111.

called Christianity. For better or for worse the Christianity of subsequent ages has borne the marks of the world in which it was cradled.[12]

Over and beyond the deep impress of *Judaism,* with its sublime concepts of God as a Personal Being, Creator, Judge and Sovereign of the Universe, its strong ethical note, its organization, universalism, Old Testament Writings, extra-canonical literature, sacraments, liturgy, religious observances and festivals and cardinal concepts, stands the massive and permeating influence of *Hellenistic Judaism.* From this quarter came the impact of Greek philosophy, the Mystery Cults, Stoicism, Neoplatonism, miracles, festivals, including Christmas, architecture with the non-Christian basilica, literary forms, robes and vestments.

The Church in this era also took on the forms and organizations of its political environment from the imperial divisions of provinces and municipalities, its guilds and clubs and the concept of the official religion of the Empire.

Finally the powerful sects and offshoots of Christianity each left their mark upon the growing Church, such as the Jewish Christians, the Gnostics, Marcionites, Montanists, Donatists, Manichaeists, Arianists and the ascetic ideals of monasticism.

Against such a background of development of the Christian Church there is every reason to believe that the contribution to Christianity of the Asiatic and African peoples is being made today through the Younger Churches and that the central stream of Christianity is being and will continue to be enriched as the Younger Christians increasingly contribute to the World Church the God-given outlooks, insights, and values of their individual inheritances.

A half century ago, the high-spirited Japanese Christian leader, Uchimura Kanzo, after a period of study in the United States, recorded in his diary his belief in the Christian potentialities of his people:

I thanked God for having brought me out into this world as a "heathen" and not as a "Christian." For there are several advantages to be born a heathen. Heathenism I consider as an undeveloped stage of humanity, developable into a higher stage than that yet attained by any form of Christianity. There are perennial hopes in heathen nations still untouched by Christianity—hopes as of the youth venturing for life

---

[12] Latourette, *op. cit.,* Vol. I, p. 362, Harper and Brothers, New York, 1937.

grander than that of all his predecessors. And though my nation is more than two thousand years old in history, it is yet a child in Christ, and all the hopes and possibilities of the future lie shrouded in its rapidly developing days.[13]

[13] Uchimura Kanzo, *Diary of a Japanese Convert*, Chapter X, "Net Impressions of Christendom."

PART THREE

ADJUSTING THE LOAD
TO THE STRUCTURE

CHAPTER V

THE SELF-SUPPORTING CHURCH

AFTER one hundred and fifty years of modern foreign mission-ary effort, only a small minority of the Younger Churches have reached a position of financial independence of the Western churches that founded them. Of the 55,000 organized Protestant churches of mission lands, it is probable that not more than thirteen or fifteen per cent are self-supporting by the simplest definition of that term,— i.e., payment of the pastor's salary and the cost of operating the local church.

Should a higher test of self-support be applied, including the cost of local evangelism, Bible women and Church schools and a share in the upkeep of general church administration, the ratio would fall still lower.[1]

While it is true that large numbers of assisted churches are pay-ing a part of the cost of their upkeep, and some are nearly inde-pendent, the Younger Churches, to a very large extent, are subsidized churches.

Foreign missions here face a problem which is removed from the field of local tactics into that of the strategy of the World Mission of the Church. If the Church is to take seriously the injunction of its Founder, it will deal courageously and realistically with this situation and with the principles which underlie the extension of the world enterprise, and not allow the tactics of local campaigns nor the pressure to keep up the lines of supply to areas already evangelized to obscure the pattern of over-all strategy for the vast task that still lies before it. When it is considered that the net increase of the populations of non-Christian nations is, with rare exceptions, at a far higher ratio than the net growth of their Chris-tian minorities, the hopelessness of world evangelization with the

[1] The Madras Series, Vol. V, p. 265.

use of present policies and the necessity of devising a new missionary strategy become apparent.

Recent vital statistics for India alone reveal a crude annual population increase of between five and six million, a number greater than the combined membership of all Protestant Church bodies.[2] The forecast of some of the world's ablest experts on population indicates a steady rise in the ratio of increase of births over deaths during the next fifty years, not only for India but for various other non-Christian races.[3]

While through the centuries in the history of the extension of the Church unpredictable and immeasurable resources under the purposes of God have been unexpectedly released to upset human calculations and extend His Kingdom, the situation faced by His Church today calls for the discovery of new stores of spiritual power and the focusing of it upon the world mission. The subject of self-support is here presented as one of the indispensable principles of such a strategy.

It will help to clarify the discussion if at this point we consider just what is meant by a "self-supporting church." The replies to this question by representatives of thirty-one missionary societies in India in 1938 may be taken as typical of the understanding and practice of mission groups in many fields.[4] While the definition of the term "self-support" varied considerably as between denominational bodies and between groups of churches of different size and strength, the replies of the missions fall into three main categories:

1. Eight missions considered a church to be self-supporting which fully pays its pastor's salary and meets the expenses of its regular worship and local work.

2. A wider understanding of the term was indicated by six missions which added to the upkeep of pastor and internal church activities the responsibility of maintaining the evangelists, cate-

---

[2] A. V. Hill, "Health, Food and Population in India," *International Affairs*, Vol. XXI, No. 1, January, 1945, The Royal Institute of International Affairs, Chatham House, London S. W. 1.

[3] a) Kingsley Davis, "Demographic Fact and Policy in India," from *Demographic Studies of Selected Areas of Rapid Growth*, Proceedings of the Round Table on Population Problems, Twenty-Second Annual Conference of the Milbank Memorial Fund, New York, April 12-13, 1944.

b) A. V. Hill, *op. cit.*, p. 41.

c) Frank Lorimer, "Population Trends in the Orient," from *Foreign Affairs*, Vol. XXIII, No. 4, July, 1945, Council on Foreign Relations, Inc., New York.

[4] The Madras Series, Vol. V, pp. 264, 290.

chists, and Bible women attached to the district of the local church. Several missions also included the upkeep of local church schools as within the meaning of the definition.

3. Seventeen missions considered self-support to involve responsibility not only for a church's own pastor and program of activities and the upkeep of the local evangelistic and educational program, but also for contributing to the corporate activities of the Church, such as home and foreign missions, theological training, buildings, provident and superannuation funds and the cost of general administration. None of the missions included within the scope of the term "self-support" maintenance of the larger institutional work of the Church, such as higher educational and medical activities.

Bearing the above categories in mind, it is of interest to note that between forty and fifty per cent of the *urban* churches of the five countries included in the Madras preparatory studies were found in one or another of the three classifications. However, in Korea, over ninety per cent of the urban churches were entirely self-supporting.

The position of the *rural* churches offered a striking contrast to the urban churches of Asia. In 1938, not over fifteen per cent of the rural churches of China, ten per cent of India, and three per cent of Japan could be called self-supporting by even the lowest classification. However, to offset this rather sombre picture should be placed the sixty per cent ratio of self-supporting Korean rural churches, the ninety-five per cent ratio of the Karen Church of Burma, the similar record of the churches in Angola, and the one hundred per cent independent position of the great churches of Samoa, Fiji, and Tonga and the eight hundred Batak churches of Sumatra.

Against this background of light and shadow, it will be useful to discuss some of the reasons why the realization of self-help is basic for an expanding Christian Church.

1. When we speak of natural law, we speak of God's law. As already stated, in so far as the Church is a human institution, it is subject to the laws which God has created for developing all natural organisms. The Church can no more expect to escape the penalties of breaking a natural law than it can a spiritual law. Both realms of law are immutable and God cannot make exceptions in either realm without being untrue to Himself. If the long-

continued acceptance of financial help by a human being weakens him because he is relieved of the necessity of using to the fullest his own powers, it is difficult to see how the long-continued supply of funds to a congregation will not have a similar effect. Otherwise, we are forced to the conclusion that money which is dedicated to missionary work possesses a mysterious quality which exempts it from the influences attending the use of non-church money.

2. The mission subsidy not infrequently violates the elementary principles of psychology. Missionaries and board secretaries would not raise their own children on the principles which they apply to many of the congregations which are under their supervision. A church is a composite or corporate person and is subject to the same principles of growth, initiative, and discipline as an individual. A congregation which has been nursed not only in its infancy but through adolescence and youth is no more prepared for adult responsibilities than a person reared in the same way. Such a congregation acquires the dependent attitude of the child or adolescent.

S. J. W. Clark observes,

The chief difficulties with putting self-support into practice will be encountered not in starting new work but with work established from the first on a dependent basis. A church once accustomed to dependence is least attracted to independence. Dependence is natural to the child, but it is not to the Church, for the latter is often most virile in its infancy whilst the former is always feeblest then.[5]

3. A church which has long been dependent upon outside aid for its support cannot be considered a normal, healthy church. It has been deprived of the discipline and exercise through which it should develop the strength and initiative to walk by itself. Such a church is crippled. It can only walk by the use of crutches, but cannot know the real freedom and joy of walking until the crutches are thrown away.

A subsidized church can only with difficulty awaken full devotion, or the sense of ownership and responsibility in its members. A certain measure of loyalty and sacrifice is given in response to the aid of the mission, but this seldom represents more than a part of the resources of time, energy, and money that the congregation possesses. When another is responsible for financing one's project,

[5] S. J. W. Clark, "The Indigenous Church," Second Impression, World Dominion Press, London, 1928.

it tends to become a matter of his primary concern rather than one's own. After years of such help, it is natural to rationalize the practice and to find many reasons why it should be continued.

4. A subsidized church is handicapped in a non-Christian land because, to the community, it represents an alien project maintained by alien money and is open to the suspicion of being controlled by alien authority. This tends to shut the door to the upper classes of the nationalistic, non-Christian peoples. Foreign money is looked upon as a lure and the community leaders whose influence, abilities, and economic strength could be of greatest help to the young church are repelled. An American or a European should stop to consider what the reaction of his fellow countrymen would be to a powerful, foreign-supported cultural and religious center established in his own community, that promoted a way of life and taught a faith contrary to his own.

The shrewd insight of Dr. John Nevius into Chinese character deserves the attention of the missionary to any non-Christian people. In 1885, he wrote,

The use of money in starting a new church lowers the whole mission enterprise in the eyes of the Christians themselves and of all the non-Christian community. Not knowing spiritual things, they take it for granted that the average Christian is in it, as they would be, for financial advantage, actual or possible, and exhortations to them to believe are considered to be efforts to gather in members for the financial advantage of the exhorter. What the missionary is to get out of it they are not sure, but they are convinced that it is some material advantage as for the others.[6]

5. A serious effect of continued subsidy upon a congregation is to relieve its members of the discipline of Christian stewardship of themselves and their possessions. Self-sacrifice and the practice of generous giving can, with difficulty, be fully evoked from a congregation which knows that what they do not pay toward the pastor's salary or a new church building, the mission or a central fund will supply. Long-continued help from abroad tends to keep the standards of giving of church members at a comparatively low level and accustoms them to ratios of church contribution out of proportion to their financial capacity.

[6] C. A. Clark, *The Nevius Plan for Mission Work in Korea*, p. 16. Christian Literature Society, Seoul, Korea, 1937.

This statement is supported by studies of member-giving-ratios in the churches of many mission fields. Replies to the India questionnaire in 1938 revealed that the average Christian family gift to the rural churches of the United Provinces ranged between three and six annas a year.[7] This amount represented about one-three hundred and twentieth part of the average family income. The giving ratio of rural Christians in southern India was between six annas and one rupee annually.[8]

Frank Price concluded from his study in 1937 of seventy-three rural churches in thirteen provinces of China that the annual average per member contribution to the church was 1.38 yuan.[9] Mr. Price's survey further found that the non-Christian families of the same communities each year spent on an average of 6.88 yuan for religious practices. However, these non-Christians included a higher proportion of people of wealth than were found among the Christians.[10]

The replies to a questionnaire sent to pastors of two hundred and eighty-five churches of eight denominations, or nearly one-half of the organized Evangelicals of Mexico, revealed that only twenty-eight or 9.21 per cent of their churches were entirely self-supporting and that the annual average gift of the regularly contributing members was between one and two per cent of their incomes. Sixty per cent of the members gave nothing at all.[11]

Replies to a similar questionnaire returned by sixty-nine of the one hundred and forty-eight pastors of seven denominational church groups of Puerto Rico, indicated that forty per cent of the members were contributing to the church in amounts varying from one-three hundredths to one-tenth of the income. The average family gift was about two per cent of its earnings. Of the two hundred and eight churches covered by the pastors' replies only fifteen, or seven and one-tenth per cent were self-supporting. However, thirty-four per cent of the cost of operating these two hundred and eight church-

---

[7] One anna is about two cents U. S.

[8] J. M. Davis, "Mission Finance Policies and the Younger Churches," p. 12.

[9] One yuan is the equivalent of approximately thirty cents U. S. (1939).

[10] Frank W. Price, "The Rural Church in China," Nanking Theological Seminary, 1937.

[11] J. M. Davis, *The Economic Basis of the Evangelical Church in Mexico*, pp. 49, 50.

es was supplied by the members and the other sixty-six per cent by the missions concerned.[12]

A point on which the questionnaire replies from the pastors of Mexico, Puerto Rico, and also Cuba agreed was that, with less than ten per cent of their churches supporting themselves, no systematic effort was being made to stimulate the giving of the members. Not one of the theological seminaries of the groups studied in these countries provided training in Christian stewardship, in the business management of churches or in methods and techniques which would prepare pastors to build up the finances of their charges or to train their members in giving.

6. The subsidy not only relieves the church members from the exercise of the spiritual discipline of Christian stewardship but tends to deprive the pastor of one of the richest sources of developing spiritual vitality in his congregation. The Oriental is especially sensitive upon the subject of personal finances and needs to have the whole matter of giving to the Church lifted above the level of solicitation and placed upon the high plane of his relationship to the Lord of all life. This is a spiritual discipline, for pastor no less than for church member, which a dependence upon the mission rather than upon God tends to impair. In the transfer of their faith from God's missionary agents to God Himself, both pastor and congregation have access to a never-failing source of vitality.[13]

7. The use of mission subsidy in starting a new church is apt to deprive both pastor and members of the exercise of their own resourcefulness, taste, ingenuity and initiative in adapting the new enterprise to the conditions of the environment and thus postpones its indigenous development. The Church comes to non-Christian peoples as a prescribed pattern which has been moulded by nineteen hundred years of European and Anglo-Saxon culture. It is an alien pattern, highly organized, complicated and conventionalized. This type of church has sprung up in many parts of the mission field and its suitability for serving a totally different culture from that which gave it birth has rarely been questioned. It is not often questioned because it is the type of church in which the missionary

[12] J. M. Davis, *The Church in Puerto Rico's Dilemma*, pp. 36, 37.
[13] Frank Rawlinson vigorously defends the thesis that foreign money received by a Chinese Church does not inherently weaken the spiritual power or growth of its members. "Foreign Money and the Chinese Church," *The Chinese Recorder*, Shanghai, Vol. LIX, No. 11 to Vol. LX, No. 7,—November, 1928 to August, 1929.

was trained and he has the experience and means with which to build it. .

There are examples of congregations in various fields which without the help of foreign experience or funds have expressed their ideology in their church building. The farmer-fisher members of the Methodist church of Kozura, Japan, carried the timbers for their new building to the top of a hill which commanded an unbroken view of Mt. Fuji. They worked during the week on the plain, in the muddy rice fields, and with their nets along the seashore, but they wished to worship in full view of the towering, snow-capped summit. They built the church with the chancel end toward the mountain and in place of the usual chancel wall inserted a large window through which they could look up to Mt. Fuji and on up to God.[14]

8. Another pitfall to which the generous spending of money may lead a mission in the opening of a new church is the failure to use the high tide of enthusiasm, initiative, and willingness to sacrifice which accompanies the first experience of conversion. Upon this initial spiritual tide, power is generated of a quality that may never again be present. In every non-Christian society the Christian convert abandons many expensive personal vices and community obligations such as liquor, gambling, prostitution, temple fees, witchdoctor charges, upkeep of festivals, etc., which aggregate a large proportion of his earnings.[15] Here are potential reservoirs of church support which may be dried up by the generous use of mission funds. "How does the new Christian use the money which the giving up of expensive non-Christian habits enables him to save?" is a question that all who are concerned with the life of the Younger Churches realistically should face. A study of this problem would richly repay the missionary or National Church in making the attempt to start new groups of converts upon the basis of self-help.[16]

9. A subsidized church cannot adequately be a missionary church. For a congregation to receive outside aid need not of itself deprive its members from sharing in the missionary enterprise by their gifts and prayers or by personal service, but usually such participa-

---

[14] Ralph A. Felton, *The Rural Church in the Far East*, p. 234.
[15] Study of the Indian congregations of the Tamazunchale district, San Luis Potosi, as reported in *The Economic Basis of the Evangelical Church in Mexico*, by J. M. Davis.
[16] The Madras Series, Vol. V, pp. 50-65.

tion is limited to a few individuals. A member who is unwilling to give generously to support his own church will hardly sacrifice so that others may enjoy the same privilege.

The ultimate hope for the extension of the Church of Christ in non-Christian lands lies not alone in the missionary spirit and giving of the churches of the mission-sending countries, but equally in the awakening of the missionary vision and sacrifice of the members of the fifty-five thousand Younger Churches on behalf of their own and other unevangelized people.

10. A subsidized church has a precarious life expectancy. Unless the church is being led along the path of the regular decrease of outside aid and the systematic increase of self-help, it faces an uncertain future. One consequence of the long-continued foreign subsidy of a national Christian movement was the embargo placed by the Japanese Government in 1938 upon all foreign funds for Christian enterprises.

Similar restrictions upon the use of foreign gifts to other national churches may be expected with the reorganization of governments following the war, but it is a serious question whether such churches would at once be able to carry the whole financial burden of their work as the Japanese Christians have done.

The subsidy renders the life of a National Church dependent upon the economic power and the missionary zeal of the sending churches. It subjects it to the shock of international financial fluctuations and also to the rise and fall of the spiritual barometer among other peoples. The financial depression of 1929-1933 dealt a staggering blow to many fields of the Younger Churches. Sudden and drastic cuts of thirty, fifty, and sixty per cent in mission subsidies brought the Christian movement in some fields to a standstill. Where a policy of gradual reduction of foreign help was applied, there was a measure of adjustment among the Younger Churches, but where the cut was sudden and arbitrary and without a preparatory period, there resulted a shrinkage in churches, leadership, and members from which some fields have scarcely yet recovered.

The missionary movement of today is facing the prospect of a world financial crisis that economists predict may dwarf the depression that followed World War I, yet with a few notable exceptions, the great missionary societies have not put into operation policies and practices adequate for strengthening the economic base of the churches and institutions for which they are responsible that would prevent a repetition of the former disaster.

Furthermore, the non-Christian nations increasingly are challenging the right of religious and cultural groups to promote alien doctrines in their territories.

The Turkish Republic has held this position for many years. It remains to be seen what policy a free India will adopt with regard to foreign proselyting activities and there is uncertainty as to Thailand, Burma, Iran, Egypt and Iraq. The basic concern of the non-Christian nations is not so much with the presence of minorities which differ in faith with the prevailing religion, as it is with the challenge to their autonomy represented by groups of nationals which receive financial and cultural backing and the direction of their activities from abroad.

Drastic changes in the foreign missionary enterprise in the post-war world may be expected, i.e., the exclusion of the missionary from administrative or directive positions in the national Christian programs, an insistence upon his rôle as a specialist in ministering to some specific need of the community, and restricted financial aid of churches and institutions and possibly of evangelism as well. This calls for a mission strategy that centers upon the development of maximum spiritual power among the national Christians, power which is not dependent upon missionary leadership or financial aid and, quickly and by every possible means, helps them to rely upon themselves and upon their own spiritual resources.

11. A policy—financial or otherwise—which weakens or retards the steady expansion of the missionary outreach defeats or postpones the central purpose of foreign missions. The necessity of subsidizing large numbers of established churches deflects the funds and with them the attention of the missionary societies from the extension of the Church to new fields. This conclusion is supported by the records of many missionary societies.

The funds of those mission boards which have developed the widest degree of self-support among the churches they have founded, as a result are freed for the development of new congregations in unoccupied areas. On the other hand, a large proportion of the financial strength of missions whose established churches are being subsidized is absorbed in helping them, and the progress of the whole movement is slowed down. It would be pertinent for a missionary board to compare the aggregate annual cost of financing its established churches with the funds that it allocates to the evangelization of unreached areas. The secretary of a large North American mission board recently wrote,

If and when the Chinese Church has achieved the place where it is capable of directing the work of hundreds, possibly thousands, of missionaries and of administering a nation-wide program of educational and medical service, is it not questionable whether such a Church should any longer be regarded as a proper field for major foreign missionary assistance? Has not the time come when the missionary body should turn its eyes again to the vast untouched areas that wait to be developed, and let the indigenous church grow in her physical and spiritual proportions by the essential discipline of providing for and directing her own life?

With the certainty of portentous changes just ahead and with half the world that is still without the knowledge of Christ, we here face a question of Grand Strategy.

Before dismissing the question of self-support as not applicable to particular groups of churches, or as one that is fraught with dangers to their spiritual development, it will be well to note that:

1. Several of the great self-supporting Younger Churches have arisen among economically-depressed peoples: the Aboriginals of Chota Nagpur, the Karens of Burma, the Koreans, the Bataks of Sumatra and the Umbundu of Angola. These groups differ but little in the economic scale and in standards of living from the masses of India and China. While it is difficult accurately to compare the economic strength of peoples in lands with differing climate, soils, products, currencies and customs, the standards of living of the masses of the non-Christian races approach a common denominator of poverty that can be termed,—the bare subsistence level.

The struggle for existence is more acute on the semi-arid plains of India and in north China than in many parts of the tropics where nature provides more bountifully, while the caste system places an added burden upon the depressed classes of India.

2. The principle of self-help was very early accepted by each Church and has been consistently followed. This has been in striking contrast to the policy and practice of foreign missions in most of the other fields of the world.

3. These Churches without the help of foreign money are expand-

ing at a rate of growth which exceeds that of a majority of mission-assisted church groups.

4. It is an arresting fact that each of the five great groups mentioned, is notably a self-propagating, missionary Church. This is brought out in a later chapter on "Some Outstanding Self-Supporting Churches." Far from the result of centering their attention upon themselves, the experience of complete independence has kindled and released spiritual power in each church, power that has expressed itself in an acceptance of responsibility for evangelizing the non-Christian peoples about them.

5. These great Churches have demonstrated that the evangelization of the non-Christian world can be accomplished by the Younger Churches. This result has been brought about not by economic improvement and higher living standards alone, nor by the use of clever devices of earning and giving money to the Church; on the contrary, it may be traced to the release of spiritual power, vision, and belief in themselves as God's instruments for the redemption of the world. Doors to inner sources of strength somehow have been unlocked. The life of these Christians has not only been vitalized but from their churches it has overflowed into distant regions and, in turn, has there planted the Church. Here is a supernatural phenomenon, but it is also an example of the interaction of spiritual and natural law and of their dependence upon one another for the largest fulfilment of God's purposes for mankind.

Sydney Clark, in his essay on "The Indigenous Church" (See foot-note on Page 78), has put the whole missionary movement in his debt by his analysis of the relation of the growing, infant church to the sources of life. He says that it is as futile to plant a church without living resources in itself as to plant a dead stick. Life cannot be purchased: it is a gift. It can be handed from one to another but its price is not a money price. It came to the missionary himself as a gift and he must pass it on to the people he evangelizes, and these in turn must propagate what they have received.

Mr. Clark stresses four sources of life for the Church: *first,* direct communion with God, the Giver of all life. If, from the very beginning, the missionary emphasizes the Divine resources of the Christian his first thought will be toward God rather than toward men. If dependence upon the inexhaustible resources of God is made a reality, the chief step toward making a church independent of man has been taken. God answers prayer through human agencies, when He so desires, but it makes all the difference in the power of a church whether the members habitually turn first to Him, or to His agents.

The *second* basic source of power in the infant Church is the Word of God. If the Word is the Bread of Life, it is a matter of paramount importance that it should be accessible. Hence teaching each convert to read is a first duty. If a man is dependent upon a missionary or a teacher for his daily food, either the missionary or teacher needs always to be at hand or the man must go hungry.

The *third* resource of the Christian is in his fellow-Christians. The members of each little church have great resources in one another, in mutual teaching, encouragement, fellowship and growth. The missionary or the preacher cannot always be available, but one's fellow-Christians are at hand and can be turned to at any time. In proportion as this need is stressed in the early training of the Church, will its power from within grow and increase. Training in all that appertains to helpfulness in the welfare of its members will not only result in a growing interdependence, but what is equally important, a growing independence. This will increase the liberty of the missionary for wider work, not only without weakening, but actually to the strengthening of the Church.

The *fourth* resource of the new convert is Christian service. A church expands chiefly on the growing experience of its members. When a man ceases to grow, it will be found that his experience has become stabilized. A man does not grow merely on preaching or teaching: he grows on practicing what he hears or is taught. The emphasis today is laid too much on *services* rather than on *service*. One truth that a new Christian hears and practices will carry him further than many truths that are listened to but soon forgotten because left unpracticed. The man who is engaged in practicing is learning. He may listen to a thousand sermons and be the worse for them if he does not forthwith go out and do. The best way to bring dependent churches to an independent basis is to start new causes which will enlist the definite service of the members.

A church planted on the foregoing principles will be able to stand the shock of separation if for political or other reasons the missionary should suddenly have to leave. There is no more valuable test of the soundness of a policy than its bearing on the coming away of the missionary.[17]

THE DILEMMA OF SELF-SUPPORT

It is important to face the dilemma in which the foreign missionary movement is placed in this whole matter of self-support for it is real, stubborn, and baffling.

1. The Younger Churches have been developed upon the principle of the necessity of receiving foreign financial aid. It is neither fair nor profitable to take the position of Sydney Clark that the "young tree" has had faulty planting. There has been far too widespread and vigorous growth of the Christian movement to warrant such a sweeping criticism. But Mr. Clark's searching question, "Surely an indigenous church should have indigenous roots; with roots in Europe or America, how can a church be indigenous?" is one that cannot lightly be dismissed.

It is a serious step for a congregation, which through one or more generations has been receiving aid from abroad, to decide that it will forego that aid and will rely upon its own resources. Missionary, pastor, and church members have been trained to a different outlook and practice. Usually a period of time is needed for altering such a deep-seated trend.

On the other hand, missions have, as yet, an unwritten page before them in the history of the infant churches that will be born in the post-war age.

2. A decision by a church to forego long-continued help must be accompanied and sustained by very definite new factors that enter its life. The vacuum caused by withdrawal of the power represented by the monthly subsidy, must be replaced by new power and by the discovery of sources which will generate and sustain that power. The frequent failure of the policy of subsidy reduction to bring a church to a self-supporting basis lies here: no adequate steps have been taken to supply the equivalent of the vitality that has been withdrawn. This problem is dealt with in detail in the chapters on "Methods" and "Resources" for self-support.

3. Another horn of the dilemma roots in the tendency to consider self-support as an end in itself, instead of a means to a greater

[17] S. J. W. Clark, *op. cit.*

end. The phrase readily becomes a slogan. To reach an independent position a congregation may exhaust its energies and find itself in an ineffective and static condition. Not only have its energies been spent, but what is yet more serious, its vision has been dimmed and its interests have become self-centered. Such a course leads a church to a "blind alley," if not to a "dead end," rather than to a thorough-fare toward an expanding life.

4. A further difficulty in the way of a courageous application of the principle is the concern of church leaders lest the withdrawal from the Younger Churches of the gifts of Western Christians will impair the reality of world-wide Christian fellowship with the sense of solidarity and sharing in the common task of world evangelization.

If a complete withdrawal of financial aid were contemplated, there would be grounds for this concern. However, the billion or more of non-Christians in the world, the increasing ratio of their population growth, and the presence of many races among whom no missionary work is being carried on give assurance that the sharing of the Older Churches in the missionary task has an unlimited future. With the growth of the missionary outreach of the Younger Churches themselves this joint task will be an increasing bond.

CHAPTER VI

OBSTACLES TO SELF-SUPPORT

BEFORE discussing the methods and techniques used by Younger Churches for securing financial independence and before reviewing the resources available to the churches, it is important to consider some of the most common and stubborn obstacles that must be met in reaching this goal.

The relevance of the obstacles listed varies as between mission fields depending upon the pattern of the social order, the type of national culture, the degree of strength of the Younger Churches and the policies of the mission and church organization. But it would be difficult to name a field which has not experienced, in greater or lesser degree, a large proportion of the problems mentioned.

Bearing these handicaps in mind, we will be in a better position to evaluate the principles and methods by which they may be overcome or neutralized.

THE ECONOMIC WEAKNESS OF THE CHRISTIAN COMMUNITY

The first and the most obvious handicap to the establishment of a self-supporting Christian movement in non-Christian lands is the economic weakness of the Christian community. A very large majority of the church members in all Asiatic countries, except Japan, all African countries, all Latin American countries, except Argentina, and all the island races of the Pacific area, belong to the rural classes: people who are wresting their living from the soil. Even among the stronger city churches of mission lands, a large majority of members are in the lower economic and social brackets of society. It is seldom that families of wealth and high social position are found in the Church.

The problem of church self-support upon the mission field is complicated by the fact that the Western type of church which has been transplanted by the missionary societies is a middle-class institution and is dependent for its support upon a strong middle class. This middle-class institution has been planted in mission lands in an economic and social order in which a middle class, as known in the West, is extremely small or does not exist.

Here is the crux of the economic problem of the missionary church. How can a relatively expensive institution, the product of a high-grade economy and living standards, be financed and indigenized in countries of a lower economic order where the bulk of the church members are drawn from the depressed classes of society?

The middle-class Christians in mission-sending lands have answered this question by supplying, in large measure, the funds needed for the support of the missionary church.

The Christian Church is of a different genius and is organized and financed upon a different plan from anything to which these non-Christian populations are accustomed. The Church, its program of activities, and type of ministry does not fit into either the economic pattern or the social order of the community. Village people who are familiar with a priesthood that is supported by a landed hierarchy or by donations of handfuls of rice or by ecclesiastical levies for performing masses, baptisms, marriages and funerals are not prepared to make free-will gifts for the support of a minister. To a community of hard-working peasants barely extracting their subsistence from the soil, the additional support of the minister's family,—a family which is not a producer and whose standards of living and income are higher than their own,—appears as a calamity.

While in some fields, notably China, Burma, Korea, and parts of Africa and the South Seas, there are rural congregations which are successfully supporting a trained ministry, by and large, the missionary movement has as yet evolved neither a type of church nor an educated pastor which is adapted to the supporting power of the rural community.

EXTRAVAGANT SOCIAL AND COMMUNITY CUSTOMS

The costly social habits of the non-Christian society are a second obstacle to the development of the self-support of the Christian Church. Many of these customs are inherent in the civic and social obligations and relationships of the new convert, such as the caste brotherhood fees and fines of India, the obligation to participate in community feasts and celebrations and to maintain the expenses of village festivals.[1]

Another group of expenses is related to the old religious duties and charges such as contributing rice or wheat at the regular calls of the Mohammedan *Pir* or holy man in the Punjab of northwest India. Security in the Moslem community where the *Pir* is the most powerful member frequently outweighs the Christians' sense of loyalty to the support of their pastor. There are cases in the Sialcot district of the Punjab where Christians admit that they are giving more to the upkeep of the Moslem religious leader than to the support of the churches of which they are members.[2]

"In the villages with which I am familiar, the fakir, or religious mendicant, constitutes a real economic problem. In some villages four such mendicants visit the Christian quarters every morning taking their toll of wheat or wheat flour."[3] The Christians dare not refuse and much of the self-support strength of the Christian people is going to support this unwholesome class.

A further type of extravagance centers in the celebration of family events, such as marriages,[4] births, funerals and anniversaries. These family celebrations demand an expenditure out of all proportion to the income of the family. The "face" of the family in the community plays a very large part in the problem.

In a strong Christian group where a new morale and a changed social order have begun to develop, some of these traditional expenditures can be modified by mutual agreement. On the other hand, where the Christian element is weak and the family's position in the community depends upon conformity to custom, the pressure is very great.

TRADITIONAL SECURITY

The Asiatic or African who becomes a Christian is a product of his inheritance and environment. His outlook has been shaped by the impress of uncounted generations of a society whose experience, aspirations, and beliefs have been embodied in a particular way of

[1] J. Waskom Pickett, *Christian Mass Movements in India*, p. 218.
[2] E. D. Lucas and F. Thakur Das, *The Rural Church in the Punjab*, p. 65.
[3] *Ibid.*, p. 65.
[4] *Ibid.*, p. 23.

life. He is subjected to a maze of relationships and loyalties, some of which inhere in the family to which he belongs while others relate to the village, clan, or caste brotherhood. Still other obligations pertain to the temple and priesthood, to religious beliefs and practices, fears and superstitions and the methods by which the community has built up its security with respect to the spirit world.

Security is a key to human institutions and human behavior everywhere. But to be effective, security requires adherence to a fixed code of behavior from each member of society. The older the social order, the more rigid the code of behavior becomes and the more difficult the withdrawal of the loyalties which maintain the social balance. Such is the nature of the strain which is placed upon the member of a non-Christian family in these ancient social orders when he transfers his loyalties from the old to a new way of life.

THE PSYCHOLOGY OF DEPENDENCE

The individualistic Westerner who has been trained to an independence of outlook and to accept responsibility for his own affairs finds difficulty in sensing the psychology of interdependence of the family and clan organization of the collectivist social and economic order. Dr. Frank Rawlinson,[5] in his discussion of the unreasonableness of rigidly applying the principle of self-support to the Chinese Christian community, refers to the influence of this age-old habit of relying upon the larger group for economic stability. He states that this in a measure explains the common acquiescence of the Chinese Church with the system of foreign subsidy and that to some extent it offsets the weakening results of accepting aid which the West is inclined to associate with continued financial support by the mission.

G. E. Phillips, in *The Outcaste's Hope*, describes the helplessness of the Indian low caste people:

But it is not even poverty which is the greatest difficulty. It is the disposition to think of themselves as naturally dependent upon others as surely as the creeper on its supporting tree or the child upon its parents. This has been engrafted in them for 1,000 years and is now a part of their very nature. The sense of pleasure which self-respecting men have in standing on their own feet is at first totally incomprehensible to

[5] Frank Rawlinson, "Western Money and the Chinese Church," *The Chinese Recorder*, Shanghai, Vol. LIX, No. 11 to Vol. LX, No. 7, Nov., 1928 to August, 1929.

pariahs. God made them, they think, to lean on others; if it were not so, He would have created them in some other caste. Nothing annoys the missionary so much as the constant declaration by the village Christians that he is their "father and their mother"—a statement which is always the preface to some fresh appeal for help.[6]

In view of this inherited psychology of interdependence, it is not difficult to understand the readiness to accept the principle that the growth, leadership, and support of the church are a primary concern of the mission which founded it and that the mission is not only able and willing to provide workers but also should pay their salaries to do the work.

Such readiness to accept outside help among closely knit and interdependent social groups exists in not a few mission fields and lends itself to the assumption of native helplessness which has frequently characterized mission policy in the early organization of Christian communities. That this obstacle to the acceptance of the principle of Church self-support is not insurmountable the numerous Chinese, Indian, and other Younger Churches which are paying for the upkeep of their own local work, including the pastor's salary, are conclusive evidence.

INDEBTEDNESS

Indebtedness is a condition which attaches itself to the farmers of the non-Christian world more generally than to any other class of society. On the whole, the farmer carries his debt with less concern than the urban dweller. The farmer is subject to the vicissitudes of seasons and markets which leave him, in times of crisis, with no option but to seek help from the money-lender, but the immobility of his land and the assurance of future crops make him, in the long run, a good financial risk. Although the payment of compound interest keeps the farmer from economic progress and bound to the money-lender, there is a fatalistic acceptance of this condition from which it is difficult to arouse him.

A debt among the rural communities of Asia is considered a certificate of character, a proof that someone trusts the debtor sufficiently to risk money on him. Another factor is that the debtor needs protection and this the creditor provides, if only from mo-

---

[6] Quoted by J. C. Heinrich in *The Psychology of a Suppressed People*, p. 4. George Allen and Unwin, London, 1937.

tives of self-interest.[7] Pickett has shown that the *per capita* annual incomes of 3,744 families in ten different parts of India averaged Rs.33-9 and that 6.5 per cent of heads of 3,819 families of the same areas were in debt, with an average indebtedness of Rs.185 per family.[8] What makes the situation so serious is that much of the debt of the Indian peasant is incurred for unproductive purposes.

E. D. Lucas and F. Thakur Das in their study of 105 Christian families of field laborers in Pasrur, Punjab, found that the average debt per family was Rs.201-12 and 81.9 per cent were in debt. For 179 families in the same community, the average annual income in cash and kind was Rs.133 and 80.9 per cent were in debt.[9] In both groups, marriage costs were the principal occasion for heavy borrowing.

The Report of the Provincial Banking Inquiry Committee found that in the Punjab only five per cent of farm debts was incurred for productive purposes, such as land improvement or investment in stock, the balance being incurred largely in payment of compound interest and extravagant social expenditures. Darling estimates that from thirty-three to fifty per cent of the debt is due to compound interest alone. A large percentage of those in debt are inextricably involved and can never hope on their own resources to go free. After handing over to the money-lender most of what they produce, they live on the small balance that is left. The payment of prior debt is the largest single item of new indebtedness and this consists largely of compound interest and not a substantial reduction of the principal. Furthermore, an important part of the debt of the average individual is either inherited or is due to chicanery on the part of the money-lender.[10]

The Chinese farmer, too, is subject to the crushing load of inherited debt. In central Szechuan Province, in certain districts, the produce of farms has been mortgaged in advance for forty years.

That indebtedness is a formidable obstacle to the development of an economically sound church life is emphasized by the report of the Royal Commission on Labour in India under the heading, *Indebtedness and Efficiency:*

The evil done by indebtedness is not confined to the hardship involved

---

[7] E. D. Lucas and F. Thakur Das, *op. cit.,* page 17.
[8] J. Waskom Pickett, *op. cit.,* pp. 93, 98.
[9] Lucas and Thakur Das, *op. cit.,* pp. 14, 17.
[10] Laymen's Foreign Missions Inquiry, Fact Finders Reports, Vol. IV, pp. 79, 80.

in the loss of money. . . . Debt is one of the principal obstacles to efficiency, because it destroys the incentive to effort. The indebted worker who makes an extra effort has little hope of securing a proportionate reward; in many cases the only result may be to enrich the moneylender. . . . The most powerful incentive to good work with the great majority of mankind is the prospect of securing a better livelihood; for too many Indian workers there can be no such prospect.[11]

Bishop Pickett, in commenting upon the above statement, observes, "Indebtedness has done even more damage to the debtor than the Commission has indicated. Long subjection to the necessity of paying to creditors all earnings above a bare subsistence level of expenditure has left him without experience in the constructive spending of money."[12] When the debtor comes into the possession of funds, he begins an orgy of extravagant and harmful spending.

With such a background and under such circumstances the training of Christians in the support of their church life is a slow and difficult process.

POOR BUSINESS MANAGEMENT

A fertile source of economic weakness among the lower-class populations of some mission lands is the inefficient management of their own affairs, in saving, in buying, in marketing their crops and in the securing of loans. "To extricate the depressed-class villager from his debts is only a slight help unless accompanied by service that effects changes in him, so that he will use the funds released for constructive purposes and will not plunge in as deeply again."[13]

The improvidence of the palm tapper of south India is described by Professor J. S. Ponniah of the American College at Madura:

The people have the age-long habit of spending every day what they have earned without thought for the morrow. The occupation of these tappers leaves them a small surplus but owing to their ignorance and improvidence, interest payments on their borrowings convert their surplus into deficits. The tappers sell their product to the local store-keeper almost every day or whenever they feel the pinch for a little money. They sell at low prices and are frequently defrauded in weight.

[11] Report of the Royal Commission on Labour in India, June, 1931, p. 226.
[12] J. Waskom Pickett, op. cit., p. 103.
[13] Ibid., p. 103.

It is necesary for the tapper to hold up his jaggery product and sell it at favorable prices.[14]

AN INADEQUATE MISSION STRATEGY

After one hundred years and more of the presence of modern missions in non-Christian lands, it is time for the Church to be lifting its eyes from the needs of the depressed and indigent Christian groups alone and to be planning with reference to the long-term economic strength and leadership and the future of the whole Christian community as an indigenous and on-going enterprise. Attention must be paid to the development of leaders in practical affairs as well as to the winning of higher-caste families and, through them, bring to bear new skill and economic power for laying the material groundwork of an independent church.

The growth of the Christian movement in the West is, in large part, due to the mobilization of the leadership and resources of the great number of Christian laymen who have consecrated their material possessions, no less than themselves, to the upbuilding of the Church. This partnership of spiritual and material resources has created the foreign missionary enterprise throughout the world.

If we are really seeking to create Younger Churches which will be more than financial wards of Europe and America, we must cease to plan only for their spiritual and institutional leadership. One is impelled to ask, where are the resources both in large funds and in competent lay management to which the indigenous church must look for its future growth? What practical steps are the missionary societies taking to meet this situation among the churches of the many fields for which they are responsible? The description of Dr. Hu Shih of the necessary partnership of the spiritual and material resources for the advancement of mankind may be applied to the progress of the Kingdom of God and His Church: "The spiritual and material forces are the two wings of the bird which, to rise from the earth in flight, depends upon the control and harmonious action of both wings."

There are baffling conditions to be met and obstacles to be overcome in the development of leadership in economic and public affairs among a small Christian minority in the midst of non-Christian and often hostile communities. In India the large

[14] Survey made by the American College under the direction of J. S. Ponniah, 1938.

commercial and banking houses have been in the hands of powerful families, cliques, or guilds for generations. With few exceptions these groups are not friendly to the foreign religion, and opportunities for promising young men to take junior positions are reserved for sons of families who support the national faith. The constructing, engineering, and skilled artisan trades and enterprises are the monopoly of closed guilds from which would-be Christian apprentices are excluded. The Christian businessman or artisan is often subject to boycott and persecution from competitors. He finds that a business run upon Christian principles, with Sabbath observance, and in competition with the low wage scales in vogue can be made to pay a profit only with the greatest difficulty.[15]

An outstanding exception to the business weakness of the Christian communities of India is found in Travancore state where the Syrian Christians have, for generations, been among the leaders in banking, transportation, large scale production and trade.[16]

A major obstacle for the Christian young man who would develop a business or factory of his own is lack of capital. He needs premises for operation, tools, furnishings, a stock in trade and can find no patron or money-lender from whom he can secure the required loan of money except at ruinous rates of interest. He is surrounded by hostile competitors and must create a clientele in an often unfriendly community. In these ways the Christian youth, in embarking upon a practical career in any but the lowest brackets of activity, finds all the cards stacked against him. Rarely can a Christian young man break through this formidable array of obstacles into the world of practical affairs.

On the other hand, the Christian movement, including the church leaders, the membership, the training schools and missionaries, is not equipped to help him. There are many mission-founded industrial schools in various fields which are training boys in trades and handcrafts but seldom is any instruction provided except in the simpler forms of cabinet work, metal work, machine work and printing. There is no training given in practical buying, marketing, modern building, architectural drafting, estimation of

[15] E. C. Bhatty, "The Economic Background of the Church in the United Provinces."
[16] See: P. C. Joseph, "The Economic and Social Environment of the Church in North Travancore and Cochin," Chapter II, India College studies prepared for the Madras meeting, 1938.

costs and the procedures required for taking contracts. In 1938, a mission industrial school in south India that had celebrated its centenary had not produced a graduate who was able to build the extensive school, hospital, and residential buildings of this great Christian center. Such responsible contracts and even the repairs upon mission buildings had been given to Hindu or Roman Catholic builders and contractors. Here is a field of strategy which has been neglected by the Protestant missionary enterprise in many parts of the world.

The comparatively high economic standards to which Christian Indian young men become accustomed in mission institutions is a further handicap in securing positions with commercial firms or in establishing themselves independently. In this connection Bhatty asks:

How can the Indian Christian community demand higher wages than the non-Christian groups possessing the same educational and technical qualifications? The non-Christians readily adjust themselves to the economic changes that have taken place, because no material change has occurred in their standard of living. But the case is different with the educated Christian Indian. . . . If the Indian Christian community is to make its contribution to the life and body politic of these provinces it must adjust itself to the economic and social changes . . . otherwise a situation may arise which will deal a staggering blow to the development of Christianity in these provinces.[17]

ILLITERACY

One of the most formidable and widely spread obstacles to the independent growth of the Christian Church is illiteracy. The Church faces this handicap on all but two or three of the mission fields of the world. In spite of heroic efforts on the part of many governments and not a few private agencies to enable the people of non-Christian lands to read and write the percentage of illiterates remains appallingly high.

Frank C. Laubach in his *Toward a Literate World*[18] lists the following percentages of literacy:

[17] E. C. Bhatty, *op. cit.*
[18] Columbia University Press, New York, 1938. (For the World Literacy Committee of the Foreign Missions Conference of North America, 156 Fifth Avenue, New York.)

Dutch East Indies (1920) 5%   Philippines (1935) 65.85%
India (1930) 8%   Guam (1920) 78.2%
Egypt (1915) 10%   Gilbert and Ellice Islands (1929)
Bantu South Africa (1920) 11.42%   94%
Siam (1920) 21%   Samoa (1925) 95.8%
Brazil (1920) 24.5%
Mexico (1920) 37.8%   Bulgaria (1920) 44%
Cuba (1920) 47.6%   Portugal (1918) 45.4%

It is not generally known that several of the Christianized island races of the south Pacific rank in literacy with the United States, Canada, and France in a general ratio of between 93 per cent and 95 per cent (1930).

The ability to read and write is a first step toward the economic improvement of the individual in the modern world. More and more the people of the countries of the Younger Churches must deal with relationships which demand literacy as a requisite of self-protection and self-help. Bills of sale, rental contracts, post-office and banking requirements, purchase of railway tickets, traffic and travel regulations, government and police rules, health and sanitation measures, agricultural improvements, newspapers and the world of books, including the Bible, except through the help of an intermediary, are all sealed to the man who cannot read.

During a visit in Dornakal, India, in 1937, we met an illiterate Christian landowner who came in from a district in the dominions of the Nizim of Hyderabad to report the loss of his land through deception. He had agreed to rent his farm at a fixed annual rate and had placed his thumb mark upon the document in lieu of signature. At the end of the first year, he discovered that what he had taken to be a lease contract actually was a bill of sale and that he had ignorantly sold his land for one-twentieth of its real value. The transaction was registered in the district recorder's office with the man's own personal seal upon the paper.

On the platform of a railway station in central India, we came upon a little family group quietly weeping on the stone floor. They had paid for railway tickets to a point 150 miles further on, the ticket agent had fraudulently substituted tickets to the nearer station at which the family had been put off the train, and he had pocketed the difference.

In the lofty central corridor of the Andes, the Indians of Ecuador,

Peru, and Bolivia, who are from 95 to 99 per cent illiterate, have been losing their lands systematically for generations through fraudulent claims and seizures by the large estate owners. Where land owner, police, district courts and registration offices are all in collusion to defraud the illiterate Indian, he has no alternative but peonage or revolution.[19] Many of the *haciendas* and some mining companies keep their peon workers in permanent indebtedness through the manipulation of accounts of purchases and records of working hours. Serious as are the limitations imposed by illiteracy upon personal liberty, justice, and economic advancement, illiteracy equally cripples a man for mental and spiritual progress, including an adequate understanding of life, of himself, the world in which he lives and his relation to it and to his fellow men.

ILL HEALTH AND LOW VITALITY

A barrier to the development of a vital and indigenous Christian movement which, in many fields, is not fully recognized is the condition of endemic disease, undernourishment, low vitality and short expectation of life of the masses of the non-Christian populations. Here is a problem in which the Church makes common cause with Government and secular agencies for rehabilitation.

The enormous drain upon the producing power of the nation and the cost of ill-health is discussed by S. M. Herbert in his study entitled, *Britain's Health*. He estimates that the cost of illness in the United States is ten billion dollars annually, in Canada $300,000,000 and in England and Wales the expenditure on health promotion and preventive services is £113,000,000.

Similarly India's ill-health is a great economic liability. For example, of the four million pounds sterling spent on medical and public health work in 1942-43, two-thirds was spent on "patching,"—a disease policy rather than a health policy. . . . And this takes no account of the work lost through illness. It takes no account of the very large part of the population whose lack of fitness makes it impossible for them to lead full and useful lives. . . . No man can be a positive asset from either an economic or health point of view when he has to struggle perpetually with a general lack of interest in all that goes on around him. Worse still the whole outlook on health is distorted until a very low average of health has come to be regarded as normal.[20]

[19] Moisés Sáenz, *The Peruvian Indian*, pp. 72-75. *The Strategic Index of the Americas*, Office of Coordinator of Inter-American Affairs, Washington, 1944.
[20] S. M. Herbert, *Britain's Health*, pp, 19-21. Penguin Series, 1939.

The high incidence of such parasitic and germ diseases as hookworm, malaria, enteric and dengue fever among the Asiatic, African, Latin American and Pacific Island races is almost beyond belief.

The recent surveys made for the Medical Department of the United States Army[21] record the estimates of the incidence of hookworm and other parasitic and germ diseases in the countries of eastern and southern Asia and the islands of the Pacific.

India: "It is thought that at least 210,000,000 of India's people are infected with hookworm. It is estimated that the incidence of infection with hookworm in the whole country will vary from about 40 per cent to as high as 70 or 80 per cent."[22]

Burma: "Throughout almost all the rural areas of Burma infection with various types of intestinal parasites actually was the rule rather than the exception."[23]

Ceylon: "Estimates of the infection with hookworm in the native population vary from 90 per cent to 99 per cent."[24]

China: "In Manchuria and the northern part of China the infections are mild. . . . Approximately 60 per cent of the farming population of the province of Kwangtung have infection with hookworm; 80 to 95 per cent of the people of Hainan Island are reported to be infected."[25]

Korea: "It is estimated that 25 per cent to 30 per cent of the people are infected with hookworm."[26]

Thailand: "Almost every native Thai who lived outside a large community or a city was said to have intestinal parasites. In the examination of 2,410 stools in 1936, evidence of hookworm was found in 52.8 per cent."[27]

Cook Islands: "In 1926 it was said that 90 per cent of the population was infected with hookworm."[28]

Fiji: "The former 93 per cent incidence of hookworm has been reduced through preventative measures to 60 per cent."[29]

Dr. L. Mottoulle, medical director of the Union Minière Corporation of the Belgian Congo reported in 1932 that the average

---

[21] *Global Epidemiology*—A Geography of Disease and Sanitation, Vol. I. J. B. Lippincott Company, Philadelphia, 1944.
[22] *Ibid.,* p. 12.
[23] *Ibid.,* p. 9.
[24] *Ibid.,* p. 26.
[25] *Ibid.,* p. 55.
[26] *Ibid.,* p. 150.
[27] *Ibid.,* p. 192.
[28] *Ibid.,* p. 226.
[29] *Ibid.,* p. 241.

health quotient of the scores of thousands of Bantu applicants for labor in the copper mines was about 60 per cent. No man was accepted who could not show a vitality of 70 per cent or over. Ninety per cent of the men who applied for work in the mines were rejected as too weak and too ridden with parasites and germ diseases to qualify as miners. Dr. Mottoulle was justly proud that the average vitality quotient of the miners who were discharged at the end of three years had risen by 18 per cent.

A man who suffers from a 40 per cent deficiency of vitality and who is ridden with intestinal parasites, hookworm, dysentery, enteric and malaria can hardly be expected to be more efficient as a farmer or as a church member than as a miner.[30]

Hookworm is but one of twelve common varieties of intestinal parasites with which the rural populations of the world are infected. A large proportion of the people are simultaneous hosts to several of these parasites and over and above this formidable drain upon their vitality are subject to malaria and other debilitating tropical maladies.

It is estimated by a specialist in African intestinal diseases that hookworm hosts suffer a 25 per cent to 40 per cent loss of vitality from this parasite alone. From this an idea of the heavy aggregate health handicap under which the rural worker labors may be obtained.[31]

The Indians of the Andean regions of Peru, Ecuador, and Bolivia have a life expectancy of from thirty to forty-five years. The infant mortality among these Indians ranges from 250 to 750 per 1000 births.[32]

The report of the Government of Puerto Rico upon health conditions in the Island in 1939 estimated that 70 per cent of the people were suffering from either malaria, intestinal parasites or hookworm. Many were afflicted simultaneously with all three maladies. In some areas and in certain occupations the incidence of these diseases rose to 90 per cent.

A student of the health of the farmers of Japan reported that in 1937, 3,243 Japanese towns were without any medical help whatever and that ill-health was the greatest source of loss to the Japanese

[30] Madras Series, Vol. V, pp. 91-92.
[31] Dr. L. Mottoulle, Medical Director, Union Minière Company, Elizabethville, Belgian Congo.
[32] Findings of the Commission to the Indians of the High Andes, 1945.

worker. It was estimated that a million Japanese were sick in bed all the time and that a large proportion of resulting social and economic loss could be avoided by simple hygienic and preventative measures.[33]

The Christian Church through its medical services has a supreme opportunity to demonstrate to the social order the feasibility and beneficent results of a self-sacrificing health program for the people. In nearly all of the lands of the Younger Churches there are no health services for the rural areas. Vast masses of rural people are born, live, and die without the help of a doctor and without access to any clinic or medical center for treatment or advice. The doctors and the hospitals in these great lands are massed in the cities. A country medical practice is almost unheard of since the city-trained doctor is reluctant to live in the country because of difficulties of transportation, living hardships, and the inability of rural folk to pay remunerative fees for services.

If the corporations which are seeking, for material ends, to exploit to the fullest the physical resources of the tribal African take great care to condition and strengthen their workers, the missionary societies which are seeking to establish progressive churches and vital Christian communities may well pay equal attention to the vitality and health of their people.

LACK OF CHRISTIAN SOLIDARITY

The individualism of Christian teaching and experience meets practical difficulties when it seeks to adapt itself to communal forms of society in the fields of the Younger Churches. The Church has been built up in the main by the process of detaching individuals from their natural social groups. They are thus obliged to give up the solidarity of the old brotherhood and the family system for a spiritual brotherhood that too often does not and cannot provide them with economic and social security. The Church should be aware of this dilemma and not shirk the responsibility of creating a new brotherhood which can provide economic security and mutual assistance. Otherwise the convert must either become a ward of the mission or seek practical fellowship and help in the old brotherhood.

From observations in various fields,[34] it is clear that stronger

[33] Quoted by Felton in *The Rural Church in the Far East*, p. 208, from S. Kimoto's article on Health Mobilization in *The Japan Times*, 1927.

[34] Notes preparatory to the Madras Conference from correspondence with fifteen leading missionaries in India.

practical backing of Christians by the Church and by their fellow Christians is needed. The alleged inefficiency and unreliability of Christian servants and workmen cause impatience among Westerners and even among missionaries. "The Christians expect more consideration and special treatment than do non-Christians; they are lazier and less teachable, less competent and trustworthy; they let you down in a tight corner where a Mohammedan or Hindu would not," are frequent criticisms heard in India. A missionary superintendent in the Punjab writes, "The real problem seems to be the lack of push and initiative on the part of the Christians as well as their lack of business integrity. We try over and over again to employ Christian workmen but lose heart over the job. They find it hard to get contracts in the open market and when the mission wants a piece of work done they charge exorbitant prices. Such men are not employed a second time. For this reason many of our Christians are out of work."[35]

From Bijnor comes the comment, "I have seldom seen Christian artisans, but when they have been good workmen they have been employed and secure permanent work. However, their work is usually inferior and their demands for payment unreasonable."[36]

A missionary in Meerut says, "It is true that Christian artisans, builders, servants and general laborers are seldom employed by missions, Christian institutions, and families, but for a very good reason: they are not capable."[37]

One is impelled to ask, is it good strategy for the church or missionary to abandon the inefficient, unreliable Christian artisan or servant? Is it not part of the task of the Church to do its utmost to enable the Grace of God to shine forth in first-class craftsmanship and trustworthiness in the converts it has won? How weak the witness of the Church becomes when these qualities are lacking in its members.

The need for Christians to stand by each other and to support Christian enterprises is also brought out by correspondence from other parts of India.

Our Christians are not too good at working together and helping each other. They often pull each other down instead of supporting the one Christian business firm of the community. The Christian business manager apparently does not have the initiative to ask for orders. The Indian Christian community, instead of supporting its own weaving industry which employs Christian widows, gets cheap but not durable goods from the bazaar. Instances of this nature could be multiplied.[38]

In spite of the generations of emphasis upon Christian ethical and industrial training by the Church in India, we have yet to hear of a Protestant Christian contractor or builder who is employed by missions in large scale construction. The fact that mission industrial schools are not able to prepare their students for taking large responsibilities indicates a lack of statesmanship and strategy within the missionary movement.

THE LOSS OF CHURCH YOUTH

An obstacle to the growth of the indigenous church that has been mentioned more often than any other among the pastors of nearly every mission field we have studied is the loss of the children and young people from active church membership. Out-marriage with non-Christians is named as a major cause of this loss. Especially where the Christian community is very small, the forming of unions with young people of other religious faiths is an inevitable source of retarding the growth of the church. The difficulty is increased by the fragmentation of the Christian forces of a community into several denominational bodies which frequently are not on friendly or social terms with each other.

The pastor of a Methodist church in Mexico described a method he has used to meet this problem:

I often take my congregation to spend a whole day with some other congregation. We have no prearranged program, but mingle together, play, worship and sing together and talk over our problems and experiences informally. Last month thirty of us chartered a bus and went to Vera Cruz to visit the Presbyterians. Each paid his own expenses and carried his own food so as not to burden our hosts. We had a happy day together and widened our acquaintance and sense of Christian brotherhood. This plan not only overcomes denominational barriers but brings together socially the young people of different Evangelical groups who otherwise would never meet and increases the chances of their marrying within Protestant circles.[39]

[38] *Ibid.*
[39] J. M. Davis, *The Economic Basis of the Evangelical Church in Mexico*, pp. 96-97.

In some city fields the young people themselves are leading the way toward Christian fellowship and solidarity. Federations of young people's societies bring together the youth of different denominations to a degree which their elders never realized. This is done in Sao Paulo and Rio de Janeiro, Brazil. The young people of the Methodist and Baptist churches of Puebla, Mexico, meet once a month for mutual acquaintance and fellowship and four times a year the two groups join in interchurch bazaars and picnics.[40]

Not only out-marriage but leaving home for higher education and commercial and business careers and the absorption into the non-Christian circles make serious inroads upon the youth of the Christian community. There is a constant shrinkage from these causes which calls for a study of the problem and the devising of effective measures to meet it.

It is not usually understood that the growth of the church may be assured through conserving the natural increment of its member families. In a study of a Mexican village congregation which had started fifty-eight years before with a group of eight families and thirty-five members, it was shown that had only two and one-half children per family been brought to maturity and themselves become the heads of families, the natural increment during the fifty-eight years would have yielded between four and five hundred members to the Protestant community. This estimate was on the basis of population growth alone and did not include accessions by baptism or letter. Contrasted with this estimate of possible growth the church, after fifty-eight years of life, enrolled only 124 members.[41]

A further serious loss of the youth of the Christian community is caused by the failure of the Church to understand the natural craving of young people for recreation, activity, and social good times and to provide suitable outlets for these normal instincts. It is not a hardship for the first generation of Christians to give up the forms of recreation of the non-Christian community. The break with the old environment is too recent and complete while the fervor and inspiration of the new faith tend to fill the convert's horizon.

[40] *Ibid.*, p. 97.
[41] *Ibid.*, pp. 94-95.

However, it is a different matter for the second and third generation Christians who have not undergone the violent social and cultural dislocations or the deep spiritual experience attending their parents' conversion. With the modern generation of youth there is a natural urge for self-expression and recreation which cannot be denied without peril of alienating them from the Church. Church leader and missionary should discover through adaptations of drama, pageantry, music, decorative art, and social and recreational activities the joys and beauties of life which youth instinctively craves and should be able to find within the sanctions of the Church.

WORLDLY SUCCESS

Closely related to the centripetal forces which are detaching youth from the Younger Churches is the influence of worldly success upon the Christian community. The pressure upon church members, especially of the second and third generations who have come up from humble backgrounds to positions of business, professional or official success, is peculiarly strong. This is a frequent experience among families which have risen to a middle-class status. Parents who have prospered materially through the practice of self-discipline are eager to give their children the advantages which they themselves were denied. Academic and professional goals are held before the second generation which attract the children to different social and economic levels from those which their parents knew. This puts a heavy strain upon the loyalty of the young church member. When he begins to enter circles of society which are critical of and sometimes violently opposed to the Christian faith he must decide whether to keep his close relationships with the little group of Christians or lose the patronage and good will of the wider community.

DAVID IN SAUL'S ARMOR

The Western Church has made the mistake of girding the Eastern David in Saul's armor and putting Saul's sword into his hands. Under these conditions the Church on the mission field has made a brave showing, but it is reasonable to expect that it will give a better account of itself by using its own familiar gear and weapons.

H. Kraemer, in his *The Christian Message in a Non-Christian World,* discusses the importance of using indigenous thought-forms:

. . . the necessity of making a creative and critical but free and courageous use of existing and serviceable indigenous social forms and of methods of fostering spiritual life for the building of the Church. This is so, not because indigenous forms and methods are always the best and invariably the most serviceable to Christian life, but because the indigenous has the right to be considered seriously and sympathetically as the vehicle of life-expression before any other possible vehicle. Just as a man expresses himself best in his own language, however many other languages he may master, so communities and social groupings express their life best in forms congenial to their temperament and tradition better than by the imposition of alien forms. The criterion for adoption or rejection lies in whether it serves to express or to frustrate, and this criterion applies alike to indigenous forms and methods and to alien. It ought to become a fundamental law in missionary work that alien forms and methods of spiritual and ecclesiastical life (which are to the Western missionary the indigenous ones) are viewed with the same scrutinizing criticism as indigenous forms and methods are usually subjected to.

Of course, there may be many cases in which the Western forms and methods are exceedingly serviceable, but the creative and critical use of the already existing and congenial forms must be stressed with all possible strength, because the natural aptitude of man, and of the missionary, and the indigenous leader too, is to find the accustomed denominational forms the proper ones.[42]

In 1927, one of the most thoughtful of the Oriental delegates to a conference of the Institute of Pacific Relations, in the discussion of the problem of East and West working together, said, "I wonder if you Anglo-Saxons have thought of the handicaps that we Orientals experience when we work with you in an international gathering. The research program which determines the subjects we are to study is largely framed by Western members; the conference agenda is set up on Western lines,—parliamentary procedure, committees, commissions, round tables,—and its timetable has a Western tempo. You choose the game we are to play and then decide the rules of the game. Moreover, you have the choice of the weapon with which our battles must be fought on the conference floor,—the English language—which we use imperfectly but which is your mother tongue."

It is difficult for the Westerner in the East—whether he is a

[42] Kraemer, pp. 421, 422. Harper & Brothers, New York, 1938.

scientist, manufacturer, diplomat or a missionary—to sense the extent to which he and the interests he represents determine the conditions and decide the program upon which an enterprise will be based. The East has played the rôle of pupil to the West for so long that the acceptance of the Western way of doing things has until recently been largely taken for granted and acquiescence on the part of the Oriental is mistaken for approval.

Malinowski, in his *The Dynamics of Culture Change,* stresses the dominant rôle of the representatives of Western culture in their initial contacts with the people of the African continent.[43]

The Western Church was brought over from Europe and America and set up in much the same way as the Western bank, factory, college and ship-building plant. From the pressure of economic needs and cultural standards these secular institutions have had to adapt themselves to their surroundings. The Church alone, both by reason of its tradition and its foreign subsidy, has not been obliged in the same way to adjust itself to indigenous standards and has been slow in making adaptations to the culture and economy of its environment. It is probable that the heightened spirit of self-determinism among the non-Christian people in the post-war age will insist upon church buildings and equipment which are more in harmony with the genius and economy of national culture. The growth of congregations financially independent of the foreign mission, and the pressure to devise types of construction that are within the economic means of the members, and which do not entail considerable expenses for upkeep and repairs are factors which will gradually alter the type of church construction on mission fields. With the passing of the first generation of native Christians and their prejudice against everything connected with the old religion, a new appreciation of the art embodied in the old temple structures will gradually appear and adaptations of Eastern designs to Christian buildings will be made. This trend has already been seen under Western initiative in the imposing buildings of Yenching University, Ginling Women's College, and the Peking Union Medical Center. What has yet to be brought about, however, is the fusion of Eastern and Western architectural types fashioned in the mould of an Oriental mind rather than by the taste of Westerners enamored of Oriental art.

[43] B. Malinowski, p. 64. Yale University Press, New Haven, Conn., 1945.

India furnishes several beautiful examples of the embodiment of national art motives and Christian aspirations in ecclesiastical architecture. The Cathedral at Dornakal, built upon purely Indian lines by Christian artisans under the direction of the late Bishop Azariah, provides a spacious and beautiful temple of Christian worship in harmony with its surroundings. The church of the little Christian community at Bethlehem in the Punjab is a product of the planning, artistry, and love of the congregation. Into its lines and decorations these Punjabi peasants injected the spirit of the vast plain upon which they lived. Their ideology found its way into the walls, cornices, and decorations of a unique building which is not readily recognized by a Westerner as a Christian church.[44]

The problem of the upkeep of Christian institutions such as colleges, hospitals, and asylums is not yet solved on mission fields. This is where young David frequently is overwhelmed by Saul's gear. The responsibility for the upkeep of such public services has never been carried by the people but by governments. Privately endowed institutions are extremely rare in non-Christian lands and a great educational, medical, or social service project provided from the West in a majority of cases must continue indefinitely to look for financial assistance from abroad. One or two generations of culture contact with the West does not suffice for developing a sense of public responsibility for social needs in a society in which the family has had the responsibility for the care of its own unfortunates, nor has the economic strength of the Christian community yet developed to a point where it can assume the entire cost of its own institutional services.

LACK OF TRAINING IN GIVING AND IN CHURCH FINANCE

A major obstacle to the growth of an indigenous church in mission lands is the failure to train missionaries and native pastors in the business management of the church, the organization of its finances, and the emphasis upon sacrificial giving together with

[44] The reader is referred to two rare collections of Oriental and African interpretations of Christian art and architecture edited by Daniel J. Fleming. In his *Heritage of Beauty,* (1937) he has selected types of Christian architecture embodying the art motifs and designs of the African, Chinese, Indian and Japanese inheritances. His later book, *Each With His Own Brush,* (1938) portrays the Oriental and African concepts of familiar incidents in the life of Christ from His infancy to manhood. (The Friendship Press, New York.)

the assisting of church members in the demonstrated techniques and methods of giving. The study of the status and practice of hundreds of Younger Churches and the policies of many mission boards in these matters lead one to conclude that here we have a blind spot in the strategy of the missionary movement.

An analysis of the reasons for this amazing situation and suggestions for meeting it are outlined in other chapters of this book. It is difficult to understand why, when more than four-fifths of the 55,000 Younger Churches in the world are being supported wholly or in part by the missions which brought them into being, adequate steps toward remedying the situation have not been taken. The concept of a church as a spiritual society has so absorbed the attention of a majority of mission boards that the reality of a church as a corporate human society, which thrives or languishes in the degree that it uses the means which God has provided for its economic and social well-being, is obscured. Nor is the relation clearly understood between spiritual health and the economic and social welfare of the corporate church body.

Many mission boards appear to accept the fact of an assisted church as inevitable and the problem of long-protracted subsidy as insoluble. However, the presence of self-supporting churches on nearly every field and of a few great groups of churches which are entirely independent proves the feasibility of independence among the Younger Churches. Why has not the experience of these churches been studied and the methods they have employed been utilized? In the training of their missionaries and the education of their native pastors the great majority of mission boards do not provide practical courses of instruction which would enable their workers to help put the mission-dependent congregations upon an independent basis.

An independent status to be secured by a congregation, as by an individual, must be worked for. It will not happen by chance or by leaving it to Providence alone. It will come about by patiently following definite policies and by putting definite methods into operation with practical instruction and training of church leaders and members. If mission boards are unable or unwilling to recognize these principles and put them in action, it would be an honest procedure to cease talking about the goal of a self-supporting church and acknowledge to the mission-supporting constituency that their gifts are required for an indefinite period to keep alive the churches they have organized since there is little hope that they will stand upon their own feet.

THE STATUS OF THE PASTOR AND OF PASTORAL SUPPLY

In many fields of the Younger Churches a basic obstacle to the development of self-support is the weakness, lack of resourcefulness, and qualities of leadership of the ministry. It requires a man of unusual courage, vision, and ability to overcome the inertia of traditional dependence that is the inheritance of great numbers of churches.

As C. W. Ranson points out in his report of "A Survey of Theological Education in India,"[45] the problem of enlistment of able pastors is in the nature of a vicious circle. A weak dependent church does not attract high-spirited and efficient young ministers, but only through the leadership of such superior men can the Indian Church be lifted to a position of greater spiritual and economic power. Thus a mediocre or weak ministry is reflected in a mediocre and dependent church and conversely a weak and dependent church attracts weak leadership.

In a majority of the fields, there is a serious shortage of young men who are applying for the ministry. While conditions widely vary in mission lands, in those countries which are being organized upon a modern basis, with government and educational services, with growing commercial, industrial, and banking activities and professions, the pressure upon Christian young men and women to avail themselves of these opportunities for employment is a most serious obstacle to the growth of a trained ministry. The salaries which secular positions offer to well-trained graduates of mission colleges are very much larger than those which the young minister can hope to receive from a church; thus, great numbers of promising young men who have been educated for the ministry are lost to church leadership.

The problem is far too complex to yield to a simple solution. Young people frequently are educated through the sacrifice of family or friends and on graduation feel an obligation to pay back the loans which their schooling has necessitated. This cannot be done on a pastoral salary. The ambition of parents that their

[45] National Christian Council of India, Burma, and Ceylon, Nagpur, 1944.

children should have a measure of worldly success which they themselves have never known is an additional influence which turns the children away from the Church as a career. Within the Christian movement in lands like China, India, and Brazil the Christian colleges, hospitals, and supplementary services are able to pay salaries to well-trained young people that are far larger than the ministry can offer. Trained doctors and educators command salaries three to four times those which the trained pastor can ever expect to receive. An inevitable result has been that many of the ablest and most creative minds of the Christian movement are found elsewhere than among the church pastors, and the ministry is often obliged to recruit its candidates from second-rate material.

A missionary of long experience in south India expressed concern as to the effect on the morale of pastors in a district where it was proposed to open a large Christian hospital. It was felt that the salaries which this modern institution would pay its Indian staff would be on a scale so much higher than that of the trained ministry that it would place this latter group in a social and economic class quite distinct from that of the hospital staff.

Another factor is the insufficiency of the pastor's income for maintaining himself and his family upon the scale of living and amenities which his years of contact with the Western surroundings and culture attending his education have taught him to crave. From the bare support of his family, there is no margin left for books, journals, travel, nor for the higher education of his children. It is with great difficulty that the pastor and his wife can even dress in a manner suitable for mingling with the upper-class people of the community. The outlook that the ministry offers to the pastor, his wife, and his children is one of perpetual struggle and self-denial.

Unlike Western lands where the ministry is a traditional and highly respected profession with a long history of leaders of national renown, in a majority of mission lands the pastorate is yet in its infancy, without a recognized status and with few outstanding representatives who, by their personal gifts and community influence, appeal to the imagination of Christian young men who are eager to serve society. Finally, the dependence of a majority of pastors of the Younger Churches upon mission funds for a considerable part of their support is distasteful to high-spirited youth in the increasingly nationalistic mission lands.

THE PATTERN OF THE URBAN CHURCH

Closely related to the foregoing named obstacle to the growth of the indigenous church in mission lands is the urban orientation of the Christian movement. In most mission fields the first Christian churches were city churches, the preparatory and theological schools were, and still are, located in urban surroundings and the pattern of pastoral training has been suited to the leadership of the city church. With the increasing growth of rural churches, which now in a majority of fields far outnumber the urban organizations, the theological students still receive a type of preparation which has the city church as its primary objective.

Few seminaries offer a curriculum which provides the specific orientation and training which would prepare the student for the specialized demands made upon a rural pastor. The uniqueness and significance of the country church field as a life work is rarely stressed in the training offered by the seminary, with the result that the rural ministry too often takes a secondary place in the interest and respect of the prospective pastor.[46] An added emphasis to this trend already mentioned is the definitely lower economic basis and cultural standard of the rural community with the almost certain prospect for the pastor and his family of an inadequate income and a ceaseless struggle with poverty.

Strong Christian rural communities, such as exist in parts of south India, Korea, and Burma where many hundreds of families are enrolled in a single church, create exceptions to the principle just discussed. The head of a leading theological seminary in south India states that rural charges are sought by the graduates because of their comparative stability and economic strength.

THE TURNOVER IN CHURCH MEMBERSHIP

There is continually taking place an alarming turnover in membership in many of the Younger Churches. In a small city church in central Japan, within a five-year period between 1931 and 1936, forty of its sixty members had moved to other localities, a number had dropped their connection from dissatisfaction with the pastor, some had died and others had lost their faith. In spite of a few ac-

[46] Frank W. Price, "The Training of Rural Ministers," Nanking Theological Seminary. Agricultural Missions Foundation, 156 Fifth Avenue, New York. Mimeograph Series No. 14.

cessions during the five years the Church was but a shadow of its former self. While this may be an extreme case, it illustrates a tendency that is apparent in thousands of congregations on mission fields. A stream of people are entering and leaving the Christian movement. The process is more evident in industrialized centers and cities than in the rural areas, but even the rural church suffers a severe depletion of its strength from the moving away of a large proportion of its young people who seek education or employment in the urban areas. The devastating and recurrent droughts which have driven out the population of great areas of northeastern Brazil have extinguished or reduced to a minimum the life of scores of the rural Evangelical churches. Their members have emigrated as families to distant parts of Brazil and only occasionally have found new church connections in the districts to which they moved.[47]

In a large port city of Cuba the pastor of a church of one hundred and fifty members reported that during its twenty-five years' life, the names of seven hundred members had been entered upon its rolls. He said, "Possibly five per cent have died in this period and ten per cent more may have moved away, but there are several hundred former members of this church who are still living in our city who, for various reasons, have been lost. If we could hold our members we would have one of the strongest churches in Cuba."

THE ECONOMIC PRACTICE OF THE OLD RELIGIONS

A deep-seated handicap to the economic stability of a Younger Church is the totally different philosophy and practice in the support of religious institutions in which the convert has been reared from that of the Christian church which he enters. Buddhist temples with their priesthood are usually supported by the income from temple lands or endowments which provide for their upkeep. The approaches to Buddhist temples in Japan are lined with great numbers of wooden tablets on which are inscribed the names of deceased followers with the amount of the votive offerings which the families have contributed to the temple in honor of the departed spirits. These publicized gifts aggregate very large sums and are a continual source of income.

The handful of rice placed by devout Hindus and Mohammedans

---

[47] J. M. Davis, *How the Church Grows in Brazil*, pp. 131-132.

in the bowl of the mendicant monk or holy man is familiar to all who have visited India and other Asiatic lands. The religious levies for services rendered by the priesthood is a traditional source of income not only among non-Christian religious organizations, but with the Roman Catholic Church in Latin American lands. The religious fiestas of the scattered Indian communities of the Andean republics are occasions in which thousands of pesos are collected regularly by the priest for baptisms, marriages, funerals and masses for the dead.

The pattern of Protestant Church finance based upon regular free-will offerings for the general upkeep of a church and the support of a pastor is new to the experience of the people and the genius of their culture. In many mission fields the demands for payment of the religious ministrations of the priesthood are so heavy and ubiquitous as to encourage the poorer classes to get along without the services of the Church. Under such conditions the contrasted financial practice of the Protestant Church becomes a practical excuse for not a few to change their religious allegiance. This trend has been furthered in some mission fields by the accepted slogan, "Salvation is without money and without price."

It is not surprising that with such a religious background there has been reluctance among Christian Church leaders to emphasize the obligation of the new convert to support financially the church and its pastor. From these causes the discipline and practice of regular and generous giving has been neglected from the very outset in great numbers of the Younger Churches.

CHAPTER VII

RESOURCES FOR SELF-SUPPORT

THE Church possesses within itself and its environment resources which, if understood and used, are sufficient to give it stability, independence, and an enlarging life.

The history of the Christian movement in many mission fields demonstrates the fact that the way of life which Christ has taught and the Church which has arisen from the fellowship of believers is adaptable to the conditions and resources of every type of human society. No social or economic group is so humble or primitive that it is incapable of organizing its life upon Christ's teachings and the Christian institution of the Church, and eventually of maintaining that Church. God does not intend His way of redemption to be so complicated and expensive that it is beyond the powers of His children to support it—however simple an economy and culture they may have. Each group possesses its own peculiar store of powers. But the resources of the Younger Churches are elusive and not easy for the mission-sending churches, the missionary, or the leaders of the Younger Churches themselves to recognize, to assess at their real value, and to use in building the Christian movement.

The missionary who has a knowledge of the economic basis, social structure, and ways of life of the people, such as their use of the land, their sources of income, spending habits and motivations is in a strong position to recognize and use the resources of the Younger Churches.

Such knowledge would enable him to put the poverty of the people into its true focus within the frame of their actual income and expenditure.

Such knowledge also would quicken the missionary's imagination and form a basis of judgment with regard to the type of church and overhead expenses which would meet the needs of the people and be within their economic capacity to support.

One incurs the charge of presumption in suggesting sweeping changes in a great movement such as modern foreign missions whose history goes back for a century and a half, which has developed such well-defined and long-tried policies, and which with success has established the Christian Church among such widely variant peoples. However, two factors impel the writing of this chapter: One is the extreme weakness of so great a number of the Younger Churches in the midst of the available resources of their economic and social environment. The other is the conviction that, if foreign missions are to enter the unoccupied fields and the spheres of service awaiting them, they must take account of stock and use these resources as well as the new aids to their work which the modern age offers them.

Bearing these factors in mind, the following considerations are presented in the belief that it is possible to surmount some of the obstacles and get away from some of the assumptions which stand across the path of the largest growth of the Younger Churches in the second half of the Twentieth Century.

The Land. First of all the available resources of a very large majority of the Younger Churches is the land. Civilization has its roots in the materials and resources of the earth. But the greatest material resource of all is the soil. More than two-thirds of the world's population make their living primarily from the land. All the great mission fields are from 75 to 85 per cent rural.[1]

It is true that the Christian movement in many mission lands was anchored in the churches and institutions of the great cities. These centers became its first home and they continue to provide much of its economic strength, its trained leaders, and the general headquarters for its national program. But the place of the city in the national life must be kept in perspective. It has been created to serve the needs of the vast and scattered rural areas. It could not exist without these areas, and it is built up and constantly replenished by the rural populations which are the reservoirs from which the strength of the city is drawn.[2]

The rural church rests squarely upon the land as its economic base and an intelligent integration of its life with the fructifying

[1] Kenyon L. Butterfield, *Christianity and Rural Civilization,* Report, Jerusalem Meeting, International Missionary Council, Vol. VI.
[2] *Ibid.*

power of the earth provides a guarantee of continued existence. A church whose economy is rooted in the soil, either through the dedication of the produce of a part of the members' land or the dedication of a portion of their time or their income, is economically secure.

Among the congregations of the Younger Churches studied, the unused resources of the land were nowhere more evident than in Cuba. A majority of Cuban Evangelical Christians have access to land in small plots, but it is rarely used for supplementing their diet or income. In many parts of Cuba, we saw rural housewives buying garden produce at the public market or from peddlers at the door which, with forethought and a little labor, they could have grown in their own patios or backyards at a small fraction of the market price. A Cuban pastor commented upon the unused resources of his countrymen: "I have repeatedly seen a family out of work and virtually starving, with a patio of unused land big enough to raise food to feed the entire household. We need practical training in agriculture for our Evangelical youth far more than the courses in arts and sciences at present given in our schools."[3]

At Los Pinos Nuevos, we were shown the individual kitchen gardens personally tended by the faculty members of the West Indian Mission Bible Institute. In an average garden measuring only 25x50 feet were growing a wide variety of vegetables, berries, melons and ground nuts. The garden was a perennial source of food and, together with five or six fruit trees and the canning of surplus crops, the annual needs of the family for fresh vegetables and fruit were met. Fowls also supplied eggs.[4]

A few years ago, the members of a small rural Mayan congregation in Yucatan were able to raise the entire debt incurred from the building of their church by jointly cultivating a tract of unused land to wheat during a series of harvests.[5]

Methods and practices in the use of the land which are being followed by the Younger Churches are described in a later chapter.

The Social Structure. A second resource for the Church of Christ

[3] J. M. Davis, *The Cuban Church in a Sugar Economy*, pp. 91, 92.
[4] *Ibid*. p. 92.
[5] J. M. Davis, *The Economic Basis of the Evangelical Church in Mexico*, Reported by Mr. D. B. Legters, Dzitas, Yucatan.

in non-Christian lands is found in the social structure of the people. With few exceptions some form of collectivism is the pattern of non-Christian societies. Whether it is the caste-bond in India,[6] the extended family of China,[7] the tribal structure of Africa,[8] or the *comunidad* of the Indians of Latin America,[9] a grouping together for mutual stability and defense in ties of blood or dialect, common traditions or ancestry is the framework of the racial culture. This also is the pattern which shapes the thoughts, feelings, and actions of the individual.

It is difficult for the individualistic Westerner clearly to grasp the nature of the collectivist way of life or the extent to which it controls the non-Christian community. The collectivist social philosophy and the concept of society held by a democracy are as far apart as the poles. The Anglo-Saxon tests the worth of a civilization by its capacity to enhance the freedom, development, happiness and prosperity of the individual citizen. The collectivist philosophy, on the other hand, values the individual by his ability to contribute to the prosperity and solidarity of the family or larger group of which he is a member.[10] Each act, decision, and movement of the household or group member is of concern to all the other members. The fear of weakening the larger social unit by the action of the individual has had a profound effect upon the growth of the missionary church and has been a basic obstacle to the acceptance of the foreign religion. Nowhere has the instinct for group action and solidarity been more strikingly illustrated than in the mass movements toward Christianity in parts of India and Sumatra, and the islands of the Pacific.[11]

A study of collectivism as a resource of the Church would be richly rewarding to the missionary for within the social structure

[6] J. Waskam Pickett, *Christian Mass Movements in India*, pp. 26-33 and W. H. Wiser, *The Jajmani System*, Lucknow Publishing Co., 1936.

[7] Ta Chen, *Emigrant Communities in South China*, Chapter VI, "The Family," pp. 118-147, Institute of Pacific Relations, New York, 1940.

[8] Edwin W. Smith, *The Golden Stool*, pp. 188-190, Edinburgh House Press, London, 1930.

[9] Moisés Sáenz, *The Peruvian Indian*, Chapter II, "The Indian Comunidad," pp. 26-36—(The Strategic Index of the Americas) and Eyler N. Simpson, *The Ejido—Mexico's Way Out*—Chapter 18, "Collectivism vs. Individualism," pp. 316-334. The University of North Carolina Press, Chapel Hill, 1937.

[10] J. B. Condliffe, *China Today: Economic*, pp. 51-52, World Peace Foundation, Boston, 1932.

[11] J. Waskam Pickett, *op. cit.*, and J. M. Davis, "The Batak Church," pp. 19-21.

of the people he would find sanctions, disciplines, and values which are of the essence of the Christian teaching and way of life and which could be used as natural foundations for the Church of Christ.[12]

The *Biradari,* or caste brotherhood, of the depressed classes of India is a notable example of a social pattern which should be studied by the Christian Church. The *Biradari* is a guild or closely knit society which defends the rights of the caste group, champions the cause of the individual member, enforces obedience to the caste code of mutual service, judges cases of infraction of caste rules and exacts penalties and fines. The local instrument of the *Biradari* in the Indian village is the *Panchayat,* or council of five wise men, which controls the conduct and practical affairs of this group.[13]

It is not a long step from the *Biradari,* with its defense of its members' rights and its enforcement of standards of conduct and discipline, to the Christian brotherhood of the Church, with its teaching of the bearing of one another's burdens, its concern for the welfare of each member, and its creation of standards of Christian public opinion and church discipline. The importance of utilizing the existing customary sanctions of the Indian *Biradari* for enforcing Christian discipline is felt by national leaders and missionaries.[14]

In another part of the world the *comunidad,* or ethnic community of the Quechua and Aymara Indians of the high Andes, is organized upon the principle of reciprocal help. Family work teams, or *minga,* are exchanged between households to assist in ploughing, planting, harvesting and in the building of houses, roads, irrigation ditches and bridges. These teams consist of three or four persons, usually two adults and two half-grown children; a work account is kept between the households,—the labor of two children being reckoned the equivalent of one adult,—and a shortage on a team is made up upon the next exchange.[15]

[12] J. W. Burton, Madras Series, Vol. II, Chapter 5, pp. 79-80. "The Methodist Church in Fiji."

[13] E. C. Bhatty, "The Economic Background of the Church in the United Provinces," pp. 72-90, India College Studies, prepared for the Madras meeting, 1938.

[14] Raymond A. Dudley, Notes on "The Use of Foreign Money in Assisting the Church of South India," Seminar on Stabilizing the Younger Churches in Their Environment, Kennedy School of Missions, Hartford, April, 1945.

[15] *The Handbook of South American Indians,* Vol. II, Bureau of American Ethnology, Smithsonian Institution, Washington, D. C., 1945-1946.

Such disciplines prepare people for working together as a church group and with other church groups, and they may be utilized with advantage from the very beginning of corporate church life.

Psychology. An appreciation of social psychology may be invaluable to the missionary. Psychology tells us that the average human being habitually uses only a small part of the physical, mental, and spiritual energy with which he is equipped. This startling conclusion, with its implications for every sphere of human activity, is pertinent to the foreign missionary enterprise.

The primitive human being exists on little more than a subsistence level not only in the spheres of livelihood and bodily exertion but also a subsistence level in the realms of his brain and his nervous energy. Progress in any sphere can only come when a degree of exertion and a use of latent capacities are stimulated to lift the individual above the level of bare subsistence into that of creative effort. Redemption of the individual should certainly provide for the exercise of all his powers and enable him to call upon and organize these potential reservoirs in his personality.

The assumption of the incapacity and economic helplessness of the national Christian has often led the missionary into the pitfall of doing things for him which he might better do for himself. There would be more justification for this assumption were the members of the mission-founded churches children or people inexperienced with life. But many of these "younger Christians" are mature men and women who have made a more or less satisfactory adjustment to their economic and social environment. They may be "babes in Christ," but they are shrewd people of the world, able to drive close bargains and accustomed to derive a practical advantage from every situation.[16] The experience of a missionary in Argentina with a church member who for years had been "too poor" to give any support to the church was illuminating.[17] The missionary on a Monday morning met the man who explained his absence from church the day before by the fact that he had attended a sale of land and had bought two lots toward which he had been saving for some time.

[16] J. M. Davis, *The Economic and Social Environment of the Younger Churches,* Chapter IV, "The Psychology of Self-Support."
[17] J. M. Davis, *The Church in the River Plate Republics,* Reported in questionnaire return, Survey of Evangelical Churches.

The sense of ownership in an enterprise, responsibility for its upkeep and direction, and the desire to exercise ingenuity and effort for carrying out what one has planned are difficult to arouse in a project which not only has been introduced by foreigners but which apparently has an endless supply of money for its promotion.

The First Presbyterian church of Curityba, Brazil, had outgrown its Sunday School rooms and was in need of an extension. The mission declined financial help and the pastor went to the United States to try to raise the funds. He failed to secure the money and on his return called his people together and told them that this was their church, the children of the Sunday School were theirs, and if they really wanted a new building for them, they must work and give to get it. After three years of effort in which the whole church—including the children—took part, they completed a beautiful, well-equipped building costing $8,500. In the meantime there had developed a need for a parish house for the growing activities of the young people. The church members again set themselves at the task and in two years the second new building was finished, paid for, and occupied.[18]

The missionary in one of the poorest districts of the Batak Church of Sumatra commented upon the capacity of the people to raise funds:

Even the poorest of these Christian groups can collect money to do the thing they really want to do,—mind you, what *they* want to do,— not what the *missionary* wants them to do. For example, a group of less than 400 families of a village in my territory decided that they must have a clock on the steeple of their church in time for Christmas. There was only one other tower clock in the whole district. Every man, woman, and child was determined that they must have one. In two months, they had collected and made a payment of one hundred guilders[19] towards a two hundred guilder clock, gave their note for the balance and the clock was installed before Christmas as a gift to the church.[20]

Nationalism. Another potential resource which is often over-looked by the missionary church is the factor of patriotism with the natural pride of country and race. In not a few fields, the for-

---

[18] J. M. Davis, *How the Church Grows in Brazil,* pp. 106-107.
[19] One guilder is equal to $.38¼ U. S. Currency (1945)
[20] Madras Series, Vol. V, Chapter 22, p. 409.

eign mission is looked upon by the upper classes as a denationalizing influence and a species of foreign cultural penetration. The mission compound and its imposing institutions built and maintained by foreign funds, the mission-paid evangelists and Bible women, and the native churches largely supported by foreign money, open the whole movement to the suspicion of alien cultural and even political imperialism. Mission-supported nationals and members of mission-paid churches in China have been termed, "the running dogs of imperialism." Money speaks with a deafening voice in Oriental circles and where money is known to pass from foreign to native hands in a religious enterprise, but one conclusion is reached and the religion is discounted.[21]

The native self-supporting church is looked upon in a different light. The story of Uchimura Kanzo's church in Tokyo is an example in point. Uchimura, a high-spirited pastor of Samurai descent, had worked in the employ of an American mission but decided to cut loose from foreign funds and influences and develop an independent church in the nation's capital city. Uchimura's unusual personality and abilities, his patriotism, and aggressiveness won a following of high-class Japanese,—academic men, government officials, and army and navy officers. Here was Japanese Christianity, and freed of the apron strings of the American or British Church. At the height of his influence, Uchimura's church numbered several hundred Japanese men of affairs. He preached the Gospel of redemption from sin through the power of God in his son,- Jesus, and Japanese leaders listened and gave their hearts to the "Japanese Christ." Members of the Imperial household heard of Uchimura Kanzo and summoned him to appear before them to expound the Bible and explain Christian doctrines.

Ideology, Inner Motivations and Thought-Forms. In every mission field there is the challenge to the missionary and the national Christian leader to delve deeply into the racial philosophy and ideology and to explore the possibilities of utilizing the basic motivations, aspirations, and thought-forms of the people as vehicles to the acceptance of the Christian revelation.

As stated by Ernest Hocking, "If a new idea is to take sturdy

21 Charles Allen Clark, *The Nevius Plan of Mission Work in Korea*, p. 26, Christian Literature Society, Seoul, Korea, 1937.

root, it should make a maximum use of whatever kindred ideas have been there before."[22]

H. Kraemer, in his *The Christian Message in a Non-Christian World*, says,

Yet the situation in the case of building the Church is the same as in all problems of indigenization. In the case of indigenizing Christianity by expressing it in thought-forms and terms congenial to the environment, we found the rule that the radically religious and theocentric conception of Christianity as contained in Biblical realism gives freedom and courage to use the heritage and to use it creatively and critically . . . provided the impelling and primary motive is to express the Gospel and its invariable essence. This is the most energetic way of being Christian and indigenous . . . the free and courageous use of existing and serviceable indigenous social forms and methods of fostering spiritual life for the building of the Church is at once self-evident, and stringent. This is so, not because indigenous forms and methods are always the best and invariably the most serviceable to Christian life, but because the indigenous has the right to be considered seriously and sympathetically as the vehicle of life-expression before any other possible vehicle.[23]

One of the deepest instincts of the Japanese people is the feudal inheritance which centers in the passion of fealty to an overlord. The desire to serve a superior who will communicate some of his nobility, skill, and strength to him is still strong in the heart of the Japanese.

Okamoto san had been in our employ for ten years without an emotional outbreak but finally left us because he discovered that his master, whom he had believed to be a superior being was, after all, only an ordinary man. I had ordered him to get my dress linen laundered in twenty-four hours. He protested that the time was too short, but I was to dine with the United States Ambassador and the linen had to be ready. When Okamoto san failed to produce the laundered shirt, I gave him my first severe scolding in ten years. The next day he resigned with the words, "During the years I have served you, harmony has prevailed in this household. Yesterday that harmony was broken." I responded that I wished to reestablish the *status quo ante* by apologizing for losing my temper. Okamoto san said, "You do not understand. Either Danna

---

[22] *Re-Thinking Missions—A Laymen's Inquiry After One Hundred Years*, p. 30. Harper and Brothers, 1932.
[23] Kraemer, pp. 420-421. Harper and Brothers, New York, 1938.

san lost his temper over a trivial matter or I have failed as your servant. In either case, harmony has been destroyed and I must leave you." This son of a farmer was responding to a profound Japanese instinct. When he discovered that his master, in whose nobility he had believed and whom he had contentedly served, was only a common man the mainspring of his devotion snapped.[24]

Three hundred years before this modern incident, another peasant's son, Toyotomi Hideyoshi, "the Empire Builder of Japan," followed the same racial instinct.[25] In rapid succession he attached himself first to a robber chieftain, then to one feudal prince after another. In each case, he discovered the innate corruption, cupidity, cruelty or cowardice of his lord and he argued, "If I follow this man, I will eventually become like him and no better a man than he. I will find a lord whose true greatness will make me great," and so he left his service. Finally, as a skilled warrior, Hideyoshi entered the ranks of Oda Nobunaga, Lord of Hikone, one of the outstanding feudal chieftains of Japanese history. He was attached to Lord Oda's bodyguard and served him with such devotion and ability that he was finally appointed commander-in-chief of his army. In this position Hideyoshi led the campaigns which eventually consolidated the many feudal kingdoms of Japan and opened the way to the formation of the Iyeyasu Shogunate and the later reestablishment of the Imperial power.

Peasant cook and peasant warrior each sought to attach his wagon to a star: the one was disappointed but the other by persevering, himself became a star of the first magnitude in the Far Eastern heavens.

For one who would present the claims of the Lordship of Christ to the Japanese,—a race which is only eighty-five years removed from the feudal era,—the implications of these two stories are profound.

J. Leighton Stuart describes China's ideological values:

The basic characteristic of Chinese philosophy and life might seem to be the effort to become *adjusted to the environment,* to accept it and come to terms with it, instead of attempting to master it and subjugate it so that it will yield more comfort and pleasure to human life as is

---

[24] J. M. Davis, *The Economic and Social Environment of the Younger Churches,* pp. 50-51.
[25] Walter Dening, *A New Life of Toyotomi Hideyoshi,* The Kyobun-Kwan, Tokyo, 1904.

true of the West, or of persuading ourselves that it is all an illusion from which to escape, as is the case of India. This dominant quality is at once the strength and weakness of all Chinese life. It explains the marvelous plasticity of social and moral conceptions, the mutuality that is called for in all human relationships.

Another element of the Chinese heritage is the ineradicable belief in the moral order of the Universe. Despite all the vagaries of their metaphysics, all the villanies of their life, all the vicissitudes of their economic struggle, the people . . . have clung to this conviction through the millenniums since their earliest sage-kings first taught and lived it. It is their supreme possession. One big contribution of the Christian movement in this country ought to be a share in preserving the moral emphasis, the cosmic idealism and the spiritual conviction which have come down from its earliest history and in helping to recover for all Asia and the West that which is in serious danger of being crushed.[26]

The people of every mission field possess ideological foundations which are awaiting understanding and use on the part of the Church. Some of these foundations, such as the Analects of Confucius and the Sacred Books of India, have long been the objects of Western study. It may be questioned whether or not a comparable attention has yet been focussed upon the implications of elements in these cultural heritages for the approach of Christianity and their possible use in presenting the Christian faith and way of life. The recent formation of the Institute for Research into China's Religious Heritage by the National Christian Council of that country may prove to be an important step in this direction.[27]

The Constructive Use of Leisure. A potential resource of the Christian community in non-Christian lands is the leisure of the people and that portion of their time which was formerly devoted to gambling, drinking, and loafing. In colder climates, when winter interrupts agriculture for a large part of the year, there is little to occupy the rural household and leisure may become a liability. During the disturbed conditions in north China, the unemployed farmer finds it a short step from idleness to banditry. While the women are occupied with household duties and the care of children, the men have time upon their hands.

[26] J. Leighton Stuart, "Conflict of Cultures in China," *The Chinese Recorder,* August, 1929, Vol. LX, No. 7, pp. 485-486.

[27] *Bulletin,* National Christian Council of China, Recorded in Overseas Newsletter No. 13, Canon G. F. Allen, Chungking, September, 1943.

In Latin American lands, the Roman Catholic Church fiesta is responsible for absorbing a very large part of the working year of the lower classes, particularly that of the Indians. Redfield, in his vivid description of the Indian villages of Tepoztlan in central Mexico, describes forty-six local and national festivals which are observed annually by the people of the district.[28] Between preparation for the festival, its celebration and the aftermath of recovery from its effects, a single fiesta may absorb from four to seven days of the peasants' time with an aggregate of one hundred days during the year given to fiesta celebrations.

The Quechua Indians of Ecuador and Peru spend from twenty to twenty-five per cent of the year in the observance of their local and national fiesta programs and in the drunken impotence which accompanies them.[29]

A considerable charge upon the time of the rural dweller of Buddhist lands,—notably China and also various Moslem countries,—is the religious pilgrimage. Once or twice a year, in the slack working season, the people travel long distances on foot, railway or boat to provincial or national holy places. Weeks are often consumed on the way and considerable sums are spent in travel costs and votive offerings. These pilgrimages provide the relaxation of an outing, a change from the drudgery of work, as well as an outlet for religious devotion. Even in lands where the climate permits year-round cultivation, there are unused margins of time which could be used for constructive purposes.

While it would be a doubtful blessing to introduce the pressure of Western life into lands of a slower tempo, the time factor is an asset which the Christian Church can help its members and the community to use in constructive lines. Cottage industries and handcrafts, literacy classes, lending libraries, village improvement projects, visual entertainment, discussion groups on village problems such as water supply, health, sanitation and prevention of malaria, classes in dietetics, baby care and home economy, evangelism and laymen's training institutes are among the activities which the church could promote.

An aim of the church in every land should be to assist the people

[28] Robert Redfield, *Tepoztlan, A Mexican Village,* pp. 97-132, University of Chicago Press, 1930.
[29] Quoted from notes of a conversation with the Indian Supervisor, Saraguro, Ecuador, Andean Indian Commission.

who are struggling for a bare existence to rise from a subsistence economy to the level of a marginal economy. A family which is bound to a subsistence economy cannot move forward or upward. Progress comes only when there is an increment of time or money, of crops or hand products, of strength or health or spiritual energy which can be invested.

Expensive Habits. An economic resource of thousands of Younger Churches which has been widely overlooked is the savings effected by the Christian convert upon giving up non-Christian and extravagant habits. In different fields studies which have been made of this phenomenon reveal astonishing results. Among the Huastica Indians of central Mexico, tax collectors, storekeepers, and missionaries estimate that from thirty to sixty per cent of the average Indian householder's annual income is spent upon social, religious, and personal extravagances. The aggregate cost of hard liquor, prostitution, gambling, witchdoctor fees, church and local fiestas, Roman Catholic Church taxes and fees for personal services is a formidable charge upon the Indian family.[30]

This picture of the non-Evangelical Mexican Indian is more or less typical of the masses in a majority of mission lands. The weight of the vices, and social and religious obligations of the environment, keeps the individual and the family from rising in the economic scale and robs them of the financial margin which is needed to lift them above the subsistence level to a point from which they could support their church.

It is time for Protestant Church leaders, and the rank and file of the church members, to face realistically this whole matter. What becomes of that very large proportion of the income which was formerly spent in the upkeep of the habits and customs of the non-Christian environment from most of which the family is now freed?[31]

An obvious reason for neglect to organize this potential source of support of the new church among Roman Catholic constituencies is the rebound from the commercialized basis upon which the older church places its services. In contrast to the Roman Catholic charges for masses, baptisms, burials and marriages, and the heavy

[30] J. M. Davis, *The Economic Basis of the Evangelical Church in Mexico*, pp. 89-91.
[31] John Ritchie, *Indigenous Church Principles in Theory and Practice*, Chapter VI. Fleming H. Revell Co., New York, 1945.

levies upon families for leadership in church fiestas, the Protestant tradition has held that salvation and the ministrations of church and minister are freely given.[32]

This emphasis has been accepted by great numbers of Protestants without a countervailing emphasis being placed upon the duty of stewardship and self-sacrifice in the giving of self and substance to God in support of the new church.

A similar case cannot be made with respect to the use of the large sums of money which were formerly squandered by the convert before he entered the Christian life. Some of the savings of this nature are undoubtedly used for the education of children, for better and more food, and for raising the general standard of living of the family.

The possibilities of applying a part of this margin of money, time, and nervous energy to the support of the church are challenging. Here is one of the untapped reservoirs of power which, psychologists tell us, are available. It is not reasonable to expect that the Christian should pay toward the support of his church the equivalent of what he previously squandered, nor to base standards of church support upon mathematics, but even after discounting by one-half the estimate of a fifty per cent spending of the non-Evangelicals' income for non-Christian practices, and dividing that amount again in half, the remaining twelve and one-half per cent of income, if devoted to the support of the average church by even one-third or one-quarter of its members, would lift it to independence.[33]

Speaking of this potential source of church support, a missionary to the Mexican Indians says,[34]

These new Christians need quickly to be taught the necessity and joy of giving generously to the church as a thank offering. They could readily spare a tenth of their income out of the large savings which their conversion has effected. Unless these habits are early formed in the new Christian life, they are later formed with difficulty, if at all. On the other hand, the Indian's escape from Roman Catholic and community obligations is one of the potent reasons which attracts converts to the Evangelical church. It is in the nature of a pitfall and, unless conversion is accompanied by a recognition of deliverance and the volun-

---

[32] J. M. Davis, *The Cuban Church in a Sugar Economy,* pp. 80-81.
[33] John Ritchie, *op. cit.,* Chapter VI.
[34] John T. Dale, The Mexican Indian Mission, Tamazunchale, San Luis Potosi.

tary return to God of a substantial portion of the accrued income, it may prove a curse rather than a blessing.

A further reason why such savings of an Evangelical have not been more largely drawn upon for the upkeep of the church is the intimate nature of the problem. The pastor shrinks from inquiring into the personal habits of expenditure of his people and finds it distasteful to stress their obligation to support the church.

The traditional customs connected with fiesta leadership, weddings, and burial ceremonials are not only an immense financial burden upon non-Christian society but, in many mission fields, they are also a major drain upon the financial strength of the Christian community. As already described these customs are a direct source of the indebtedness that dogs the farmer and rural villager through a lifetime. The heavy cost of a Chinese wedding frequently is borrowed and may take years to pay back. The expense of an elaborate funeral in the style that is dear to the heart of the Chinese may represent his earnings for a year.[35]

The Andean Indian Commission in 1943 were told by the supervisor of Indians in the town of Saraguru, Ecuador, that the family which is given the honor of entertaining the parish guests during the days and nights of a Catholic Church fiesta will spend the savings of half a lifetime upon the quantities of food and drink that are supplied the many hundreds of merrymakers during the celebration.[36]

The British Indian low-caste villager is peculiarly subject to the penalties of extravagant expenditure. In north India the marriage of a son or daughter is an occasion upon which all consideration of economy or of cutting the garment of expenditure to the cloth of income is thrown to the winds. The cost of weddings often is in excess of the earnings of an entire family for a whole year. India college research studies reveal that the poorer the family, the greater is the discrepancy between income and expenditure. Indicative of the social pride which stimulates such disproportionate expenditures among the very poor are the words of an old Indian Christian in

[35] Ralph A. Felton, *The Rural Church in the Far East*, pp. 8, 9.

[36] Moisés Sáenz in his, *The Peruvian Indian*, p. 65, quotes Castro Pozo's *Nuestra Comunidad Indígena* that "there are Indians who work the entire year to pay for the fiesta; it is estimated that as a general average each *encargado* must buy around fifty soles' worth of candles and that the general expenses amount to some 250 or 300 soles, not counting the daily wages that he has to forego."

the Narowal area of the Punjab: "Though we are poor, yet we marry our sons and daughters in a manner that would bring credit to us. Even if we cannot afford it, we *must* spend."[37]

H. Brian Low in his study of 15,316 Chinese farms in 144 counties computes the average cost of special family events in Chinese currency as follows:[38]

	$ C.N.C.
Weddings	127
Funerals	102
Dowries	96
Birthdays	63
Birth of sons	30

When we consider that the income from the average farm is not over Mex. $400 per year, the huge burden which these family events put upon Chinese farmers is apparent.

The Christian Church has an obligation through its preaching, teaching, and example to bring a new freedom and a saner, healthier living to its members. This would also mean new financial strength for the Church itself.

In various fields, efforts are being made by nationals to curb extravagant trends and to simplify the cost of social life. A group of Christians in the Sialkot district of the Punjab have pledged themselves to limit the expense of weddings to Rs.6 instead of the usual Rs.100 to Rs.200. This example is spreading to other parts of India. The Bo Hie Dong parish in south China has a Cooperative Burial Society in which each member is assessed $1.00 at the death of a fellow member and the total amount collected covers all the expenses. The funeral paraphernalia are owned cooperatively and the cost of ceremonies and processions is rigidly controlled.[39]

The Use of Laymen. So much has been written upon the subject of the use of laymen in the work of the Church that the brief treatment to which a handbook of this nature must be limited cannot begin to do the subject justice.[40] Our discussion will deal with only

[37] E. D. Lucas and F. Thakur Das, *The Rural Church in the Punjab*, p. 36.
[38] Quoted by Lossing Buck in *Land Utilization in China*, p. 468.
[39] Felton, *op. cit.*, pp. 9, 10.
[40] Madras Series, Vol. IV, pp. 149, 150, 196, 197, 209, 211, 213, and "Education for Service in the Christian Church in China," The Report of a Survey Commission,

a few of the practical aspects of lay effort in relation to the Younger Churches. It is becoming increasingly clear that the strategy of lay effort for the stability and expansion of these Churches cannot be overstated, nor the methods which have been employed with success be too often emphasized. Before speaking of the training and organized use of laymen by specific churches, we will mention a few conditions governing the most successful laymen's activities as they have been observed on different mission fields.

Unless the latent energy and motivations of a congregation are aroused, the powers of a majority of the members may never be discovered nor harnessed to the progress of a church. Ironically enough, an active deterrent to lay activity in a younger church may be the energy of a missionary or national pastor. The missionary or pastor finds awaiting him in a church many challenging tasks which need immediate attention. It is difficult to see how he can relate his laymen to them. He himself has been trained to do these things, he is full of ideas and plans, and so he tackles them. The urgency of the situation, the apparently unpromising material in the church members, and the slow process of training stand in the way of putting his people to work.

In most mission lands, there is no pattern of lay religious activity such as many Western congregations possess. The priest, the holy man, the fakir and the mendicant monk are professionals. Religion is their business and is not the responsibility of the layman. The concept of a church as a brotherhood and a fellowship, in which each member has responsibility and duties, is new.

The most vital organized lay work in the Younger Churches which has come under our observation has been led by national pastors. Many of the city churches of Brazil have notable programs of lay work. The Congregational church in the northern city of Campina Grande[41] enrolls 800 members and has the most active

1935, Chapter VII, "Training for Lay Service in the Church," The Christian Literature Society, Shanghai.

Charles Allen Clark, *op. cit.*

J. M. Davis, *The Economic and Social Environment of the Younger Churches,* Chapter VIII, "Lay Leadership," pp. 120-135.

Felton, *op. cit.,* Chapter VII, "Lay Preachers," pp. 216-233.

Alice E. Murphy, "Training and Guiding Lay Leadership in the Village Church," An Account of an Experiment in North China in Training Lay Leadership for Village Church and Community Service. Agricultural Missions, Inc., New York. Mimeograph Series No. 157.

[41] J. M. Davis, *How the Church Grows in Brazil,* p. 80.

men's missionary society which we have met in any church. At the monthly meeting of this society 100 men—the backbone of the church—were present. The chairman of the society owned the largest general store in the city; the secretary was a cotton broker. The monthly reports of the society's seven missionaries were read and discussed in detail. Each man's progress was noted, with the difficulties, methods, and results of his work. These men had accepted the responsibility of evangelizing the eastern part of Parahyba state as their job. The mission was run on the same principles and the work of their missionaries was checked with the same care as that of their own business projects and their own salesmen. In seven years six churches—two of them self-supporting—and twenty-one preaching places, each the nucleus of a congregation, had been formed. The Campina Grande church and its denominational body have never had the financial help or the direction of a foreign missionary society. The able Brazilian pastor of the church kept his hands off the management of the society and was an interested member only.

There are many active Younger Churches in mission fields whose laymen are working as evangelists and teachers in depressed or outlying districts of their cities and there are other laymen who work without pay as evangelists in a rural field. National groups of churches frequently have organized missionary societies for reaching their own countrymen with the Gospel. Campina Grande, however, is the first local church we have met where the laymen have undertaken as their responsibility the evangelization of their State.

An outstanding example of a national Christian movement which has been developed through the training of its lay members is that of Korea.[42] The field is notable for the speed with which the Church has grown, the central place of the Bible in the church program, the large number of unpaid lay workers, and the unusual degree of self-support achieved by the churches.

The Bible was early translated and systematically taught. Individual Korean leaders became proficient Bible students and teachers.

For more than a generation, special Bible training courses have been held each year in church centers all over the country. These

[42] Charles Allen Clark, *op. cit.,* Chapter XIV, p. 275.

continue for from five to twelve days and have had an annual attendance of over 100,000 members. In this way, the rank and file of the church have been inspired and trained as teachers of other Koreans and as lay evangelists. The cost of these Bible schools is met by the people who pay their own travelling expenses (largely walking) and provide their own food. In the mission stations, longer Bible Institutes are held annually for from one to two months over a period of five years. These courses introduce the students to the major portions of both the Old and New Testaments. Thousands of other Koreans are enrolled in correspondence Bible study courses.

The leadership of village congregations by the unpaid lay preacher or teacher has made possible the care of large circuits by the paid ministry and the placing of seventy-five per cent of the Korean churches upon a self-supporting basis. This training in evangelism of virtually an entire church membership is unique in the history of missions.

Government and Secular Cooperation. In many fields official or private programs of rehabilitation of the people are coming to be a possible source of strength for the Christian movement. Such programs frequently have been modelled upon the work of the foreign mission, often parallel it, and sometimes conflict with it as in cases where the government seeks to standardize and control all educational and medical activities.

More and more, the governments of non-Christian lands are endeavoring to strengthen and build up the people's life upon modern standards. They are promoting medical aid and sanitation, education, better housing, farming, cooperatives and hand industries. The Christian mission has been a pioneer in many of these fields. Its medical and educational leaders have established very high standards for government endeavor. Missions have been called upon to carry the burden of educational work by such governments as those of India,[43] the Dutch East Indies, the Belgian Congo, the British protectorates of South Africa and many British colonies.[44]

[43] Post-War Educational Development in India ("The Sargent Plan")—Report of the Central Advisory Board of Education, New Delhi, 1944.
[44] Imperial Reconstruction and Social Welfare Commission for the Colonies, Colonial Office Publication, London, and British Information Services, 30 Rockefeller Plaza, New York.

The recent decades have seen an awakening among governments to the gravity of the depressed social and economic conditions among their peoples which has not been matched by many of the missionary societies working in the same areas.[45] In some fields the churches have been slower than governments to understand that, upon foundations of undernourishment, a high mortality rate, bad housing, indebtedness, illiteracy, narcotics and illegitimacy, no virile, progressive church or nation can be built. The Church is aware that these factors are obstacles to building a strong, indigenous Christian movement but governments in many instances have outdistanced missionary vision and action in these rehabilitation spheres.

In this connection, the experience of the Church with official social welfare activity in Jamaica, Puerto Rico,[46] and Trinidad is important. Eight years ago a social welfare organization—Jamaica Welfare Limited[47]—was formed by civic leaders of Kingston. The project was financed by a self-imposed tax of a half penny a stem upon bananas exported from Jamaica by the United Fruit Company. Trained social workers were employed to promote cooperatives, youth activities, home visitation, adult educational classes and recreation among the population of depressed Jamaican negroes.

The pastors began to see new centers of public activity arising in their villages where the church had long been the chief community interest. When their young people were drawn into these activities, some pastors were alarmed and assumed a non-cooperative attitude. None of the pastors and few of the missionaries in Jamaica had been trained in rural sociology and the techniques of social welfare or economic rehabilitation. Although the new project was dealing with basic conditions which were retarding the progress of the churches, pastors were inclined to look upon the newcomers in their communities as interlopers and competitors. It is slowly dawning upon the Jamaican Church that the social and economic stability of the community is also its own concern

[45] "Mass Education in African Society," Colonial Office, Advisory Committee on Education in the Colonies, Colonial No. 186, British Information Services, 30 Rockefeller Plaza, New York.

[46] Reports of Puerto Rico Reconstruction Administration, U. S. Departments of Agriculture and Commerce. Washington, D. C.

[47] Reports of Jamaica Welfare, Ltd., British Information Services, 30 Rockefeller Plaza, New York.

and that in ministering to it the secular agency is making common cause with the Church.[48]

In Puerto Rico, the United States Federal Government has established expensive services for soil conservation, rural reconstruction, the rehabilitation of broken-down farms and for rehousing and resettlement projects. The extension offices and demonstration projects of these services are scattered throughout the Island and are accessible to a large number of the people. In 1941 there was ignorance on the part of church pastors and many missionaries as to these rehabilitation programs and few Protestants were benefitting by the government program. The reasons for this Evangelical detachment from government efforts were:[49]

1. The widespread impression that the rehabilitation program overlooked the peasant class;
2. Pastors and church members were reluctant to expose themselves to the rebuffs of district officials who held an anti-Protestant bias and often discriminated against Evangelicals in the reconstruction program;
3. Church leaders had not acquainted the members with the provisions of the rehabilitation program nor encouraged them to avail themselves of it;
4. Pastors were untrained in rural sociology and economics and felt unable to cooperate intelligently with trained government workers.

With the greatly increased demand for social and economic rehabilitation which will follow the war, and the growing recognition by governments of the necessity of helping their people, missions will find a new requirement for cooperation with secular agencies and programs and for this will need among their staff members a specially trained personnel.

A practical step toward such official cooperation is to place the church facilities and equipment at the disposal of the secular program. In many places the church provides a convenient meeting point and a center for ministration to the many-sided needs of the people the like of which does not exist in non-Christian lands. The post-war era preeminently will be one in which, through community service in conjunction with government and other secular

[48] J. M. Davis, *The Church in the New Jamaica*, pp. 82, 86-88.
[49] J. M. Davis, *The Church in Puerto Rico's Dilemma*, pp. 62, 63, 68, 69.

agencies, the Christian movement will be able to demonstrate that its ministry includes the whole of life. However, to make this effective, the pastor must be acquainted with the principles and some of the methods of social rehabilitation so that he may efficiently cooperate with official programs and cooperate intelligently in community activities that emanate from his church.

The Unexplored Powers of Youth. An unmeasured resource of the missionary church lies in the powers of devotion, self-sacrifice, and the response to calls to heroic adventure and ideological causes which are latent in the young people of the community.[50]

This great reservoir of power has been recognized by some of the Younger Churches and has been drawn upon for upbuilding the Christian movement. However, the pastors of ninety per cent of the hundreds of churches surveyed by the Department have stated that the failure of the Church to hold its youth was a major source of weakness. Many pastors placed this as first among their problems.

It is unfortunate that a negative attitude toward the recreational side of life has so widely prevailed upon mission fields and that so few satisfying and constructive substitutes for the proscribed youth activities have been provided. Attendance at church services, Sunday School, and prayer meetings and work upon evangelistic teams, while essential for the spiritual growth of youth, are inadequate to meet the normal craving of every boy and girl for social activity, recreation, and fun. For the church to discourage dances of all kinds, attendance at the theatre and cinema, and anything but conventional religious activities on Sunday and still not to provide opportunities for the young people to meet socially, or to express themselves in art, music, and drama, in games, outings, and athletic competition is to court disaster. It is also a sure means of repelling the youth of the non-Christian community.

The Southern Baptist Convention of Brazil has met this problem through a special Youth Department under trained leadership in the central organization.[51]

The Methodist Church of Brazil has decentralized its youth activities through Young People's Societies in its local churches. Such societies are organized in one hundred and forty churches and

[50] Madras Series, Vol. V, Chapter 27, pp. 503-511.
[51] Report of Youth Department, Southern Baptist Convention of Brazil.

groups for intermediates in thirty-six churches, with the belief that this decentralization offers the young people more opportunity for self-development and avoids the tendency toward adult direction of unified programs.[52]

Chorus singing, orchestral work, discussion groups, dramatics, social evenings for games and recreation in Christian homes, organized athletics, excursions and vacation training institutes are some of the activities that are used by both Churches in their youth work. These youth departments have published, in Portuguese, handbooks of games adapted to the use of Brazilian young people which include not only American and international games, but parlor and out-of-door pastimes used by Brazilians. Both Churches also are specializing in youth literature and publish attractive magazines for young people and books by Brazilian authors, as well as translations of foreign titles.

However, over and beyond such efforts to enrich the social life of Christian youth of the Younger Churches, there remains a road to the heart of the young people that has not been explored. This is in the field of public and community service rather than of self-culture or spiritual interests alone. The Christian Church frequently suffers in comparison with communism, socialism, and other ideological and revolutionary movements because it has not called out the uttermost of devotion and sacrifice from its young members. When nations like China and India are faced with staggering economic and social issues such as the struggle for political freedom, the dead weight of illiteracy, poverty, undernourishment and land serfdom, unless the Christian Church commits itself both by preaching and by programs of action which will challenge the idealism and heroism of its youth, youth will rally behind the banners of other more dynamic organizations.

In 1937, at Nanking, the young director of the Government Bureau of Economics of the Ministry of Finance, formerly an active church member, in explaining why he no longer attended Sunday church services said, "The saving of my country has become my religion. To this end I am working sixteen hours a day, seven days a week. I have no time or interest to attend a church which lacks social vision or program and listen to a sermon which has nothing

[52] W. C. Barclay, "Christian Education of the Methodist Church of Brazil," 1930-1943. Methodist Board of Foreign Missions Joint Committee on Religious Education in Foreign Fields, 150 Fifth Avenue, New York.

to say upon the economic and social ills that are strangling my country."[53]

An example of the response of Chinese youth to service of this nature was the Lichwan Project in Kiangsi Province, southwest China, 1934-1936. Under the leadership of George Shepherd of the American Board mission, and as a part of the government movement for reconstruction of war-devastated areas, young men and women from Christian colleges enrolled for a two-year term of rehabilitation service. They lived in the war-torn villages, shared the hardships of the farming population, helped to rebuild homes, established sanitary services, distributed clothing, seed and implements, nursed the sick and counselled with broken and destitute families. Lichwan was a distinctly Christian service project and gave the working teams of young people an outlet for their eagerness to minister to the desperate plight of scores of thousands of their fellow countrymen.

In rapid succession the Lichwan Project started programs in education, health, agriculture, transportation, village improvements, cooperatives and financial stability. After three years of work by these Kiangsi rural service centers, a measure of prosperity and stability was brought back to the vast farming population.

The Lichwan Project stimulated the Church to help create a new social order with the result that Christianity today has the goodwill of the people in a wide area of southern China and the spirit of sacrifice and the social passion of the young men and women have become a part of Chinese tradition.[54]

The Christian Church is losing many of the ablest and most courageous of the younger generation because it does not speak with a clear voice or take a practical stand on many issues that are matters of life and death to the people. This is a terrific challenge to the ministry and the missionary program. It cannot be adequately met by the traditional type of pastor and the concept of the church ministry and program alone to which he has been trained.

Education. The Christian mission possesses in education a remarkable resource for culture change. In every field of the Younger Church, streams of Western and Christian culture have been flow-

---

[53] J. M. Davis, *The Economic and Social Environment of the Younger Churches,* p. 44.

[54] Condensed from the report of George Shepherd, Director, Lichwan Project, 1937.

ing from schools, colleges, and universities established by the missions. Extending over the course of several generations, this has exerted an incalculable influence upon the peoples of mission lands, an influence which non-Christian nationals are among the first to affirm.

Japan has illustrated how, in seventy years, an intensive, ultra-nationalistic educational system can develop a nation from a semi-barbaric people to the status of a highly militarized and industrialized world power. In forty-four years democratic education has prepared a new generation of Filipinos for self-government. In a yet shorter period, the Soviet system of education has transformed an illiterate population of serfs into efficient citizens.

By the use of the same instrument the Church can help to direct the course of the young life which it trains and can permanently mould the culture of that portion of the social order which it touches. This opportunity is nowhere so evident as in the case of the rural community. Governments, as well as the Christian Church, are facing the question: How can the leadership of the great country areas, and through it, the quality of rural life, be built up?

The rural young people of the non-Christian lands, as everywhere, are caught in the current that flows strongly from country to city. The most promising boys and girls in the primary schools go on to the secondary schools and the most successful of these enter the higher schools to prepare for professional, commercial or political careers. Few graduates of the secondary schools, and practically none from the higher schools, return to their rural communities. They are drawn into the maze of business, political, and professional activities of the towns and cities. Country life is not organized in a way to demand or to support the services of educated men and women, and the lack of amenities and opportunities in the rural field closes the door to a career. Through government and mission education this process of selection and of alienation from their normal environment of the picked young people of the rural areas has been going on for so long that there is a tendency to rationalize it as a part of the inevitable pattern of modern life.

A system of education which considers the primary grades of either a rural or urban school as the first rung upon the ladder which leads to a successful urban career inevitably results in the loss of potential rural leaders and the disillusionment of the ambitions which have been aroused in the student. To the extent that it holds such an educational philosophy, it is an open question whether the Christian movement does not actually disintegrate and weaken the rural community. By what concept of education may the tide of youth, which sets from country to city, be guided so as to retain able leadership for the rural areas?

The practical training provided by the farm schools of American state universities has greatly improved rural life and conditions in many communities. However, especially in non-Christian lands, the source of the difficulty lies deeper than the preparation of highly trained agriculturalists. It inheres in the popular assumption that urban life is of a higher order than rural life, that there is something inferior and even degrading in working with and living upon the soil. Education is looked upon as a means of escape from, rather than a preparation for, the activities and conditions of rural life. It is a kind of vicious circle for education, as now set up in many non-Christian lands, is leaving the great rural areas in a more or less static position, with primitive methods, inefficient organization, and backward standards. If this is to be changed and the rural areas are to go forward, they must have the trained services of many of their own ablest youth.[55]

The Christian mission through the schools which it establishes may contribute powerfully to the strengthening of rural life. By reorganizing its primary and secondary education, it can prepare the pupils to return to their homes with an understanding of the dignity and importance of the vocation of farming and possessed of practical skills to help them to lift the agricultural and social level of their communities. This cannot be done by the Christian schools alone. The orientation of the Christian movement needs to be shifted from its present center in the city toward the country areas. This calls for the growth of the conviction that agriculture is a rewarding and dignified vocation and that it is the foundation of the nation. Theological students must be convinced that the country parish is not only a stepping stone to a city field but offers a satisfying lifework. It calls for an enrichment of

[55] (a) B. Malinowski, *The Dynamics of Culture Change*, pp. 58, 60. Yale University Press, 1944.

(b) T. J. Jones, *Education in East Africa*,—Report of the Second African Education Commission, pp. 35, 36. The Phelps-Stokes Fund, New York, 1924.

the life of the village and the farm home, the betterment of sanitation and health, improvement of traditional farming methods, the bringing of literacy, literature, and recreation to the village, the introduction of cottage industries and new handcrafts and experimentation with cooperatives.

A clue to the content of the reoriented primary and secondary education is found in the comprehensive needs of the rural village and farm household. A curriculum devised to prepare rural young people for leadership in the lines indicated would lead not only to the rehabilitation of village life, but it would in itself be a liberal and practical education for the young people. It would build up the economic, social, and spiritual standards of the country areas and would strengthen at its source the life of the national Church and of the nation. A great incentive toward this rural reorientation of life would be the transfer to the rural environment of some of the educational institutions which have centered in the cities. With this would go the removal of the residence of the educational staff from city to village. The personal demonstration by missionaries and national leaders of the possibility of living a rewarding and expanding life of service in the countryside would go far toward creating the new emphasis.

An example of the possible reorganization of a mission educational system upon the discovery of the primary needs of the people in the adjacent countryside was described at the Rural Missions Workshop in 1944 by the Rev. G. Gordon Mahy, Jr., of Warren Wilson College, at Swannanoa, North Carolina. Following the disbanding of a large government middle school after the occupation of Shantung by the Japanese, the missionaries and Chinese leaders at Weihsien decided to start in its place a Bible school for lay workers. This school assumed the responsibility of going into nearby villages to preach, teach the Bible, and hold evangelistic meetings and to carry on Sunday Schools. This work began in churches and preaching stations but rapidly expanded by entering many new villages and organizing work there until over sixty villages were being reached each Sunday and over a hundred and fifty school girls and boys were participating.

It soon became apparent that many things besides the Bible and Sunday Schools were needed in these villages and the curriculum kept changing progressively to meet these needs. Students became

especially conscious of health conditions, and courses were introduced in hygiene in relation to the lack of sanitation, to smallpox,
trachoma and other common diseases. Courses in agriculture were
also added because the students saw its practical relation to the
life of the people to whom they ministered, and there was such a
demand for literacy classes that a course in phonetics was added.
Thus the whole curriculum of the school revolved around the actual
needs which were discovered during the field work and the experiment served to integrate so closely the evangelistic, educational,
and medical forces in the mission that they were strongly desirous of
making it their primary educational task.

The Solidarity of the Missionary Enterprise. The resource of
solidarity among the Christian forces is still far from being realized
in the foreign missionary enterprise. The divided front of Protestantism in its missionary program is contrary to Christ's injunction
to His disciples.[56] It violates the principles of social progress; it
runs counter to the laws of sound business management; it is bad
faith with "the younger Christians" to pass on sectarianism to
them; it opens a most vulnerable point of attack to the enemies of
Protestantism. It weakens and retards the Christian movement and
renders remote the possibility of winning to Christ the nations
among whom the Church has been planted. The strategy of the
many Protestant foreign boards at work in non-Christian lands may
be likened to an army of occupation composed of many divisions
fighting under different flags, issuing different orders, having
different plans of campaign, and with different disciplines and
manuals of arms.[57]

The National Christian Councils have brought about an encouraging measure of cooperation between many denominational
bodies in various mission fields and in doing this have taken a long
step toward the realization of a united Christian front. Although
the National Christian Councils are, as yet, far from their objective
of including all the mission church groups in their membership,
they have made good progress in effecting the pooling of resources
in specific areas and for specific projects.

[56] John 17:21, 22.
[57] *Re-Thinking Missions, A Laymen's Inquiry After One Hundred Years,* pp. 92-
94. Harper and Brothers, New York, 1932; also, Madras Series, Vol. V, pp. 230-233.

The difficulties in the way of actually uniting churches and of securing a coordinated direction of the whole Protestant missionary movement seem insurmountable. The missionary churches were started and have been developed as denominational projects. Large bodies of national Christians and imposing institutions have been built up and carefully nurtured in a denominational tradition, and they have been supported by great groups of churches in the mission-sending lands, churches in which denominationalism is strong and whose members have a traditional pride in the growth of Younger Churches of the same affiliation. A hasty attempt to merge these great sectarian bodies would result in confusion, in the fragmentation of National Churches, the widening of existing cleavages, and a possible loss in the total strength of the world-wide Church. The movement among the National Churches on the mission field for drawing closer together and doing many things together is being paralleled by similar movements among many of the churches and mission boards at the home base and is a first and important step in the direction of an organic solidarity of the Church of Christ for which increasing numbers of His followers are looking.

Several conditions under which a definite pooling of strength and unified direction appear to be feasible are *first*, where the national Christians themselves take the initiative as in the formation of the new United Church in Japan;[58] *second*, where the missionary forces upon the field jointly with National Churches have taken the initiative as in the history of the Church of Christ in China and the movement toward Church Union in south India;[59] *third*, in specialized activities which are of concern to all denominational bodies such as work for students, the producing and publishing of Christian literature, literacy movements, and evangelistic campaigns; *fourth*, in the pooling of denominational strength in the institutions,—educational and medical,—theological seminaries, colleges, universities, hospitals and nurses training schools; *fifth*, the pooling of resources and personnel to meet the peculiar social and economic conditions occasioned by modern industry and the massing of labor in new areas. An example is the United Missions

[58] The *International Review of Missions*, Vol. XXXII, No. 126, April, 1943, p. 121.
[59] *Handbook of the South India United Church*, The Christian Literature Society, Madras, 1918.

in the Copper Belt of Northern Rhodesia which was formed in 1935 by the joint action of seven British missionary societies;[60] *sixth* is the missionary approach to a new field or to a field which is peculiarly difficult or is inadequately occupied such as is represented by the Board of Christian Work in Santo Domingo,[61] the United Mission in Mesopotamia,[62] and the United Andean Indian Mission recently organized.[63]

The state of weakness and confusion in devastated areas with which the churches will be confronted at the end of the world war will be unique in the extent of destruction of church buildings and institutions, and in the dispersal of Christian populations, and will present an unrivalled challenge to the Christian statesmanship of mission boards and church leaders. The opportunity which the post-war era will offer for the reestablishment of Christian work on broad and enduring foundations of comity and union will not come again during this generation.

Another aspect of the lack of Christian solidarity upon the mission fields of the world, for which denominationalism is responsible, is the fragmentation and isolation of the Christian groups in the local community. In a city in which the combined membership of the churches of several different denominations constitutes a tiny minority in a hostile or indifferent population, an absence of spiritual or social fellowship and of a sense of the brotherhood of believers between sectarian groups is a calamity of major proportions.

We have visited communities in which the Christian movement had a precarious foothold, where the members of some of the various denominational churches were not only unacquainted with one another but were even antagonistic and suspicious. Each congregation was weak and was struggling to maintain its position in the city; all were in danger of being neutralized, if not swallowed up, by the pagan forces about them, but in this position of peril they denied themselves the source of strength which would come from pooling their interests and joining hands in Christian fellow-

[60] Annual Reports 1936-1944, United Missions in the Copper Belt, Edinburgh House, 2 Eaton Gate, London S. W. 1.

[61] The Board for Christian Work in Santo Domingo, Committee on Cooperation in Latin America, 156 Fifth Avenue, New York.

[62] The United Mission in Mesopotamia, 156 Fifth Avenue, New York.

[63] The United Andean Indian Mission, Committee on Cooperation in Latin America, 156 Fifth Avenue, New York.

ship in their common cause. While prejudices and rivalries among local pastors and members are sometimes responsible for such divisions among Christians, the ultimate responsibility goes back through missionary representatives and traditions on the field to the mission-sending organizations. Here is a waste of one of the intrinsic resources of the Church of Christ and a neglect of basic strategy in the missionary movement.

CHAPTER VIII

SOME OUTSTANDING SELF-SUPPORTING CHURCHES

IT is not an easy matter to make a selection for special reference from among the many outstanding Younger Churches which have attained financial independence. Principles that have guided the selection are, so far as possible, churches which the writer has personally visited and studied; churches representing a wide variety of fields; churches from among both advanced and backward racial groups and communities, and churches which illustrate the use of special methods and policies.

An effort has been made to make clear the peculiar weaknesses and penalties as well as the rewards and elements of strength which have accompanied the achievement of financial independence.

THE BATAK CHURCH

We will first look at the Batak Church—that great body of Christians in the highlands of northern Sumatra, about which very little is known outside Dutch and German missionary circles. The Toba Bataks are an aboriginal race numbering 1,200,000. Primitive in culture, aggressive and cruel, these people were notorious for their cannibal practices and were avoided by their Malay neighbors. Among their mountains and lakes, blessed with a salubrious climate and fertile soil, these virile people developed a strong personality, independence, and devotion to their tribal traditions.[1]

---

[1] The material of this section has been compiled from the following sources:
  (a) J. Rauws, H. Kraemer, F. J. F. Van Hasselt and N. A. C. Slotemaker de Bruine, *The Netherlands Indies,* World Dominion Press, London, 1935.
  (b) J. M. Davis, "The Batak Church," International Missionary Council, New York.
  (c) J. S. Schapiro, *Modern and Contemporary European History,* Chapter XV. Riverside Press, Cambridge, Mass., 1931.
  (d) H. Enser, "A Brief History and Critical Analysis of the Rheinish Mission among the Bataks of Sumatra," Hartford Seminary Foundation, 1945

Missionary work was opened in Batakland under the Barmen Mission of Germany in 1864 by L. Nommensen, thirty years after the abortive attempt of the American Board missionaries, Munson and Lymann, to enter the country and their subsequent murder by cannibals. Nommensen entered Batakland single-handed and by the magnetism of his personality, his passion for evangelism, genius for organization, understanding of the people and the wisdom of his financial policy, he laid the foundations of one of the greatest independent Younger Churches of the world.

The founding of the Batak churches coincided with a decade of straitened financial circumstances of the Barmen Mission. The political and financial tensions in Germany, due to the wars with Denmark, Austria, and France in which she was involved between 1864 and 1871, seriously reduced the strength of all the missionary societies. The mission's inability to supply funds in aid of the first Batak groups of Christians left them with no alternative but to rely entirely upon their own resources, and it set the financial pattern of their independence which has marked the Church throughout its whole life. These circumstances, rather than the voluntary withholding of funds, determined the financial policy of the mission.

In this way it came about that from the beginning the Bataks took care of their own pastors, built their own churches, and received no financial aid from the mission. A circumstance which aided this Spartan policy was the later recognition and support by the Dutch Government of the church schools started by the mission. The Batak Church organized its eight hundred congregations under the teacher-preacher system whereby the local church shared the services of its pastor with the local school. A major part of the salary of the teacher-preacher was met by Government who paid him for the time which he devoted to the school. Under this arrangement these churches cannot strictly be called self-supporting, but they have been truly independent of mission financial aid. It is important to note that one hundred and thirty of the Batak congregations received no government educational grant on account of being unable to meet the official requirements for a recognized school and that many of these congregations which supported entirely both church and school were among the smaller and weaker groups of Christians.

The churches were organized into circuits of from twelve to

fifteen congregations under the care of an ordained pastor. Lay presbyters carried the major responsibility for parish work, each presbyter having oversight of from fifteen to twenty families. The general affairs of the Batak Church were administered by the Council of the Great Synod, made up of both Batak and missionary members. This body cared for the central funds of the Church, directed the theological and normal school, conducted the missions and evangelistic work and initiated the business of the Great Synod.

The finances of the local church were of two categories: One-fourth of all gifts was sent to the Central Church Fund, to maintain the pastor-teacher training school, the missionary work of the Church, the Church paper, building fund, poor fund, travel budgets and to assist weak churches. Three-fourths of the gifts of the congregation were used for the upkeep of their own church, their share of the salary of the teacher-preacher, and a proportion of the salary of the ordained pastor of their circuit.

On the death of a pastor or teacher-preacher, every church leader in Batakland was assessed for the support of the widow. A mutual benefit insurance plan helped the pastor's widow and met the funeral expenses. Each minister also gave one guilder a month to a pension fund from which he received the equivalent of half salary on retirement. Theological students, in case of need, received financial help up to one-half of their expenses from the Central Fund of the Church, but the student's family provided the balance. The money to erect local church buildings was paid by the congregations to the Central Fund in order that the property might be held by the Batak Church.

The local churches also supported their foreign missions through the Central Fund. The Batak missionary budget was raised by means of church festivals. The churches of a district united in an annual fête to which people brought gifts of produce to be sold at auction. These festivals drew great numbers together for several days of meetings, singing competitions, and social activities. An annual income of 20,000 guilders for missions was realized by these methods.

Two large modern hospitals under mission direction and staffed by Bataks, together with a network of sub-hospitals and clinics were, with the exception of the salaries of the mission doctors, financed entirely from Sumatran sources. Government subsidies, profits from the industrial workshops of the Church, and the fees of European and Batak patients maintained this medical service. The Batak churches have taken the unusual step of providing 2,000 guilders a year for the travelling expenses of their missionaries from the profits of their Church paper. A mission house costing 4,000 guilders was entirely provided by a large group of Bataks who appealed for a missionary to live among them. The Batak Christian community has also helped the mission by subscribing to a bond issue for adding a wing to the Balige hospital.

By these various methods, and by strict economy in administration, self-denial on the part of the missionaries, scaling down expenditure to the supporting power of the people and by the magnificent cooperation of the Bataks themselves, the work of the Batak Church went forward in the face of the complete embargo upon the reichsmark and the cutting off of every pfennig of support from Germany during the Nazi regime except the salaries of the missionaries.[2]

In Batakland great masses of Christians live beside solid "heathen" areas. Of the 800,000 non-Christians, one-fourth are Mohammedans and the remaining 600,000 Animists have been accepted by the 400,000 Christians as their own missionary responsibility. The Bataks are carrying Christianity into the heart of this non-Christian territory. The Church has a vision of the whole Batak race brought under the sway of Christ and is pressing toward this goal. In 1938, sixty Batak missionaries were working in the northern Mohammedan Residency of Atjeh and in the lowlands east and southwest of the Toba Batak highlands. The Batak is a natural missionary. His aggressiveness, energy, belief in himself and in his faith, coupled with his boldness, his genius for colonization, and his tendency to emigrate over the Malay world, are qualities which have fitted him for wide missionary service in the Archipelago.[3]

Factors in the policy of the Rhenish Mission which appear to be responsible for the Church's *strength* are:

[2] The World War resulted in 1939 in the internment of the Rhenish Mission personnel and the appointment of a few Dutch missionaries to assist the Batak Churches. With the later conquest of the Netherlands Indies by Japan, the Dutch missionaries in turn were imprisoned and a curtain of silence has fallen upon Sumatra.

[3] The progress of the Church among a closely allied people on the neighboring Island of Nias has been as rapid as that in the larger island. In 1938, more than 150,000 people, or three-fifths of the Nias islanders, were enrolled in the churches founded by the Rhenish Mission.

The whole responsibility for Christianizing the Toba Bataks was given to one mission.

This made possible a unified plan of occupation, a common program and aim under an organization that included every church member and every school pupil in its territory.

The application from the opening of the work of the policy of giving no financial support to the Batak churches.

The availability of government subsidies for church schools.

The use of the teacher-preacher in the local churches.

The lay-presbyter plan of parish work.

The recognition of the Batak *adat* or tribal customary law in the Christian discipline.

The use of Christian colonies as a means of evangelism.

The adjustment of the Church in its leadership and equipment to the supporting power of the Bataks.

The physical and mental vigor of the people, their isolation and racial solidarity, their animistic religion which has not offered strong resistance to Christianity and has furthered mass movements toward the Church and, finally, their missionary enthusiasm, previously mentioned, are all important sources of the striking growth of the Batak Church.

Among the *weaknesses* apparent in the inner life of the Batak Church are:

The tendency for Christianity, like the *adat,* to become a legal and formal, as well as a spiritual, religion. To sin in the old regime was to break the *adat.* Punishment only followed in cases of detection: there was no provision for repentance.

The solidarity of the clan system resulted in group conversion. Whole villages were admitted too rapidly and without sufficient preparation into the Church. Many of these groups need to be reconverted to Christianity, and the Church is faced with the difficult task of reevangelizing whole communities.

There is a conflict in the inner life of the Church between the superstitions of the animistic background and the claims of the Christian faith.

The young Bataks who go to the large cities for higher education are exposed to influences of modern secularism. This is making inroads among the youth of the Church.

Finally, the paternal system of mission control of Church policies has developed a restiveness within the Church which has resulted in the separating of considerable groups of churches from the Great Synod.

The Batak Church, now left entirely to its own leadership, is facing the most critical period of its history and presents one of the major problems for post-war Christian statesmanship.

THE CHURCH IN KOREA

With a history of only sixty years of Protestant missionary work, the Korean Church is one of the more recent of the large Younger Churches of Asia. The field is notable for the speed with which the Christian movement has progressed, the intensity and singleness of purpose of the movement, the central place of the Bible in the church program, the use of a particular missionary method, the large number of unpaid lay workers and the unusual degree of financial independence attained by the churches.

Until the outbreak of World War II, six principal mission groups were working in Korea. Of these the Presbyterian, comprising four missionary societies, and the Methodist, comprising two, have developed by far the most extensive work. In 1937, these two denominational groups enrolled 215,000 of the 240,000 baptized Christians and catechumens. Of the 475,000 adherents of the Protestant Churches, 400,000 were connected with the Presbyterian and Methodist Churches. The Korean Presbyterian Church alone included nearly three-fourths (72.45 per cent) of the Protestants of the country.[4] Other Protestant societies at work in Korea included The English Church Mission, The Oriental Missionary Society, Seventh Day Adventist Mission, and The Salvation Army.

Korea provides an excellent "case study" of a unique philosophy and method of missionary activity, "The Nevius Plan."[5] In 1890, six years after the opening of the Presbyterian work in Korea, Dr. John L. Nevius of the Northern Presbyterian Mission in Shantung, was invited by the new mission to explain the principles of work he had used in China. These became the working principles of the Presbyterian Church in Korea. They may be briefly stated as follows:

[4] C. A. Clark, *The Nevius Plan of Mission Work in Korea,* Christian Literature Society, Seoul, Korea, 1937.
[5] *Ibid.*

1. Personal missionary evangelism with wide itineration.
2. The central position of the Bible in every department of the work. Systematic Bible study for every Christian under his group leader or circuit helper.
3. Self-propagation: Every believer becomes a teacher, and at the same time a learner from someone better versed than he in the knowledge of the Bible.
4. Self-government: Every group of Christians works under its chosen unpaid leader; these groups are organized in circuits under paid helpers, who are later supplanted by ordained pastors.
5. Self-Support: All church buildings are provided by the congregations; each group, as soon as it is organized, begins to pay toward the salary of the circuit helper or pastor; schools receive a part subsidy, but only in their initial stages; no pastors are supported by foreign funds.
6. Strict discipline, based upon Biblical teaching.
7. Cooperation and agreed territorial division with other bodies.
8. General helpfulness where possible in the economic problems of the people.

We will discuss only those principles of the "Nevius Plan" which bear upon the development of financially independent churches, viz., the place of the Bible in the life of the Church, the training of lay workers for evangelism, group leadership and the policy of self-support, including the building of churches and the maintenance of general Church work.

The Bible was early translated and was sold widely throughout the country. From the beginning, systematic instruction in the Scriptures has been a central feature of the mission's program. Individual leaders became proficient Bible students and teachers. The whole Church attended Sunday School and nearly every member, from young children to grandparents, was enrolled in a class. In 1937, 184,500 people were enrolled in the Sunday Schools of the Presbyterian and Methodist Churches, with an average weekly attendance of 108,931. On the Sabbath the Korean churches were busy from morning until night with their Sunday Schools.

Supplementing this study of the Scriptures was the training plan whereby adult members were prepared as Bible teachers and evangelists. Year by year special Bible training courses were held in centrally located churches. These continued from five to twelve days and aggregated an annual attendance of over 100,000 members. By these means the rank and file of the Church were trained as teachers of inquirers and also as lay evangelists. The cost of this program of study was met by the people themselves paying their own travelling expenses and providing their own food.

In the principal mission stations, Bible institutes were held annually for periods of from one to two and one-half months over a course of five years,—a course which covered the major portions of both the Old and the New Testaments. Thousands of people who could not attend these institutes were enrolled in correspondence courses. The teaching of the Scriptures also was given a prominent place in the mission academies, colleges, and hospitals.

The Church has stressed personal evangelism as the privilege of every Christian. Evangelistic work in hospitals has resulted in the founding of many churches, and student preaching bands have inspired the weaker churches and developed able evangelists among the college graduates. "The majority of the members of the Korean Church today have been won not so much by the evangelism of the foreign missionary as by the personal witness and work of the rank and file of the church members, whose transformed lives, as well as their words, have borne testimony to the saving power of the Son of God."[6]

Great numbers of the village congregations were led by the lay preachers and teachers who were trained in the winter Bible classes. This has made possible the supervision of large circuits by the paid ministry and the attainment of self-support by seventy-five per cent of the Korean churches. It also has resulted in a degree of evangelization of the rural population attained in few lands.

The Presbyterian and Methodist Missions have restricted the use of foreign funds in evangelism, in the belief that the Koreans themselves should shoulder this responsibility. The objective has been to develop the work on a level which the new Christians were able to maintain. The erection of church buildings was left to the congregations who built as they were able. New Christian groups met in the homes of the members. They worshipped for years in straw-roofed dwellings, whose partitions were knocked

[6] Report of The Fiftieth Anniversary of the Chosen Mission of the Presbyterian Church in the U.S.A.

out to accommodate the growing congregations, until the people themselves were able to erect more spacious buildings. The congregations paid the salaries of all ordained pastors. Where single churches were too small to provide the entire salary of a pastor they united in circuits of from two to fifteen churches and the deacons and officers led the services and preached in the intervals between pastoral visits. This self-reliant spirit has not only covered large areas of Korea with churches, but has inspired generous giving to the current expenses and undertakings of the whole Church.

The budget of the General Assembly, together with the expenses of the ten Departmental Boards of the Church, is a charge upon all of the 3,000 organized Presbyterian congregations of Korea. Each local church is asked to contribute five per cent of its income to the combined budget of the following Boards, whose proportionate expenditure is:

Per Cent		Per Cent	
Christian Education	13.0	Special Charities	1.0
Rural Work	1.6	Leper Work	3.7
Foreign Missions	40.0	Christian Endeavor	4.0
Home (National) Missions	29.0	Theological Seminary	1.8
Student Aid	3.9	General Administration	2.0

The heavy cost of the railway fares of the 350 delegates to the annual meeting of the General Assembly is also met by the local churches.

The Departmental Board support is organized under the "Systematic Giving Board" of the Church.[7] Through circulation of literature and visitation among the local churches this Board advertises the work and needs of each department. It also has educated the members in Christian stewardship and in the nature of the wide activities of the Church. A supply of simple pamphlets, charts, and graphs related to the duty and privilege of giving and suitable for Sunday Schools, homes, and churches has been issued. Record sheets, pledge cards and other devices for systematizing giving have been supplied. This literature has gone into virtually every local church and Christian home.

Church-support is related directly to the Bible study of the members. The aim is to identify Christian giving with Christian

[7] H. E. Blair, *Christian Stewardship in Korea*, International Missionary Council, New York; also, Madras Series, Vol. V, Chapter XVIII.

experience. Tithing is a common, though not a general, practice among the Korean Christians. By these various methods there has been a steady increase in the total contributions to the Church. In 1936, the Presbyterian churches of Korea gave a total of 1,765,552 yen[8] for their own work, or an average of 10.75 yen for each member and catechumen. In 1936, for every yen spent by the mission in its school and church work, not including missionaries' salaries, the Korean Presbyterian Church raised six yen. Of the total budget of the six mission hospitals, of 87,273 yen, 79,000 yen came from local sources.

The record of individual giving in the Methodist churches for the same year was even more notable,—the average gift amounting to 15.20 yen (about $5.00 U. S. or £1 sterling).[9] These *per capita* member-giving ratios rank very high among the Younger Churches of the world.

The Korean General Assembly, through its Board of Foreign Missions, has maintained four missionaries in Shantung, China. The Board of Home Missions supported its missionaries among the large Korean populations in Japan, Manchuria, and in the city of Shanghai. Over and above this external mission work, each of the twenty-four Korean presbyteries had its own missionary society for evangelizing its unoccupied territory, 3,000 of the 3,800 churches under the General Assembly of Korea were fully organized and were financially independent, and the remaining 800 were working toward this goal.

THE KAREN CHURCH

A full century ago the desire of a backward yet vigorous people for autonomy in their religious life and institutions, and the reaction of a group of young missionaries from an extreme system of mission subsidy, produced the independent Karen Church of Burma.[10] This Church with 80,000 communicant members and 400,000 adherents, is a classic example of complete financial independence among the Younger Churches of Asia.

The history of the development of the Karen Church is of peculiar interest for a study of self-support in that it illustrates

[8] $608.812 (U.S.): £121,762 (sterling).
[9] A. W. Wasson, *Church Growth in Korea.*
[10] (a) Rev. C. L. Klein, Baptist Mission, Toungoo, Burma.
    (b) Rev. H. W. Smith, Secretary of the American Baptist Mission, Rangoon.

the use of two contrasted principles in the founding of Younger Churches. The first provided for the gradual diminution of foreign aid until it was entirely cut off and the churches bore complete responsibility for their work. The second was the complete financial responsibility of the churches from the inception of the work. The first principle was followed in the Rangoon and Bassein Karen fields; the second was preeminently illustrated by the work that centered at Shwegyin. The use of both principles has resulted in remarkably strong and self-reliant groups of churches, although the Shwegyin group of churches accomplished from the outset, though not without great sacrifice, a self-supporting status which the Rangoon and Bassein groups took a generation to achieve.[11]

The first missionaries of the American Baptist mission, impressed with the small number and poverty of their Burmese converts, gave money to the Church. They also felt that the Grace of God was a free gift and should not be confused with the Buddhist teaching of earning merit. Not only were preachers paid by the mission, but laymen were paid for witnessing and in some cases even children were paid for attending school. The missionary alone could be pastor of a church; nationals were tract distributors and itinerating exhorters. Under this "Moulmein system" the spiritual vigor of the Church failed to grow.

The coming into the Burman churches of great numbers of Karens, the "wild cattle of the jungle," upset mission tradition. There was no provision in churches or schools for the use of the Karen language and the newcomers were considered as inferior by the more cultured Burmese. The Karen Christians presently became restless, dissatisfied at losing their identity, and were eager for church independence. From the outset they contributed liberally to the Church and as early as 1831, they had started to build their own preaching places. In 1838, the Christian group near Moulmein gave Rs.70 for evangelistic work. Four years later the Karens of Newville contributed Rs.200 in materials and labor for their new church. In 1845, a Christian Karen undertook the entire support, at Rs.100 a year, of the preacher of his church.

Under these conditions those who were far-seeing among the early

[11] Chester Leroy Klein, "An Historical Study of Self-Support in Some Karen Missions in Burma," Berkeley Baptist Divinity School, Berkeley, California, 1936.

missionaries to the Karens demanded the right of self-support for all the developing Karen churches in Burma, and in those fields where this policy was adopted, great strides were made. There was a racial willingness since the Karens by nature share their possessions. The "Moulmein system" became intolerable to self-respecting Karen workers. The center of gravity had shifted from a handful of missionaries with a few followers to a growing Church that was considered merely an adjunct to the Burman mission. The Moulmein Karen mission never realized this completely until 1883. Other Karen stations, except Tavoy, had it from the beginning.[12]

Developments in the United States furthered this independent trend of the Karen Churches. The collapse of the land banks in 1839 caused a large deficit in the budget of the Baptist Board and of many other foreign missionary societies. The Karen Christians accepted the challenge of the situation and continued to build their own churches and schools and to pay the salaries of their pastors and the operating expenses of their new movement. They preached Christianity as their own rather than as a foreign religion. The Karen missionaries finally won in the struggle with the traditional subsidy. They introduced the Karen language in Moulmein, built a new Karen station, founded a theological school, developed a system of English education and secured racial and financial autonomy for the Karen Christians. The Karens threw themselves into the work of building the new station, cleared the jungle, erected houses and school buildings and made roads. They also began to give generously for the extension of the Gospel.

In 1853, a majority of the missionaries among the Karens, assured of the loyalty of their people, resigned from the Baptist Society in protest against a policy of closing schools recommended by a board deputation sent out from New York. This secession lasted more than a decade, during which the Karen mission at Shwegyin was founded on the basis of complete self-support. The work was advanced only as fast as the Karens were able to shoulder the load and contribute money to it. There has been complete financial independence in the churches of the district ever since.

Many years later an elder of the Shwegyin Church described its policy as, "No money help from others. Pay your own bills. Lift

[12] From the notes of Chester Leroy Klein, American Baptist Mission, Toungoo, Burma.

the race by education. Give each generation better ideals. Provide endowments for the work. Provide a leadership a little ahead of the members in education. Finally, evangelize new people. It is the duty of every mission thus to develop shoots from the root stock." The elder went on to say that without self-dependence the people would not put their hearts into the work. They would give because there was glory attached to giving, and when that selfish interest was no longer realized they would complain of the burden they had to carry. The Karens have been loyal to the Church through a long period of years because it is their own and they are determined to make it a successful enterprise. With this loyalty there have grown an understanding of Christian stewardship, provision for an adequate ministry, and an enthusiasm for evangelism in home and foreign missions.

The record of *per capita* giving of the Karen Christians shows that the size of the contribution does not depend on the income of the members. In 1927, in the comparatively prosperous Bassein field, the average gift per member per year was $1.37 while in the backward district of Shwegyin where the soil was poor and the struggle for existence was more severe the gifts averaged $3.94 *per capita*. In the same year, C. E. Chaney states in the Forty-first Annual Report of the Burma Baptist Missionary Conference, "When I came to look over the matter of their contributions considering their ability to give, for Shwegyin mountain Karens are not a wealthy people, I do not think they would take second place to any. Their annual contributions average just over ten rupees ($3.66) *per capita*."[13] Along with this high percentage of giving in the Shwegyin field was found the best record of personal work and evangelism of all the Karen churches although their outreach in home and foreign missions was not as extensive as that of some of the other groups.

Included in the self-support as practiced in the Karen Church are the support of the ministry, both ordained and lay, payment of the entire cost of church buildings and current expenses, evangelism of non-Christians by Karens, the total cost of building and operation of schools for Christian and, to some extent, non-Christian Karens and the upkeep of training schools. Except for the salaries of a number of missionaries, no help has been received from abroad.

[13] Quoted by C. L. Klein in "An Historical Study of Self-Support in Some Karen Missions in Burma," p. 40.

Mr. Klein, in describing the practical results of Karen Church independence, points out that it is impossible to tell exactly how many schools the Bassein Karens have in the jungle villages, but they are in excess of one hundred and seventy. All have been built without American money. The value of their high school plant is placed at 700,000 rupees, or about $260,000. There are twenty-six buildings, a steam laundry, steam cooking plant and a gymnasium, all of brick and cement. The finest school and chapel in the province,—the new Ko Tha Byu Memorial Hall,—was built at a cost of 432,000 rupees ($160,000). This building has an auditorium seating fifteen hundred people, a pipe organ costing 60,000 rupees ($22,000), and is lighted by the current from the school's electric power plant.

In 1934, reports for contributions for evangelism and pastoral support from the Moulmein, Rangoon, and Bassein fields exceeded $35,000,—all given by 37,000 members of four hundred and seven churches manned by eight hundred workers and pastors.[14]

The secretary of the Baptist mission at Rangoon sums up the results of this long record of independence:

Among the non-Burman churches I believe that the results have been good in increased independence and in increased zeal and evangelistic effort. This is probably because it has been possible for the people gradually to work up to the idea and because the ideal of self-support appeals to them. Except in towns, the salaries of the Karen pastors are above the income standards of the people. In villages, where most of the people are cultivators, they see very little real money and the pastors there have advantages beyond those available to the village people,— notably an English education for their children. The Karen village churches make payments in kind. The Lord's Acre Plan is used occasionally for the support of schools. There is some tithing among teachers, but little otherwise. Most of the funds are raised by church offerings and subscriptions. There are eleven Karen stations in Burma.[15]

Among the sources of the remarkable record of independence and initiative of the Karen Christians were,

First, the belief that the coming of the missionary and the Bible fulfilled a treasured racial legend. Thus Christianity was in a sense

14 See C. L. Klein, *op. cit.*
15 From notes by Rev. H. W. Smith, Secretary of the American Baptist Mission, Rangoon.

identified with their own inheritance and the Karens were impelled to proclaim their faith and accept large responsibility for evangelizing their neighboring areas. This in turn stimulated the sacrificial powers of the Christians.

Second, the strong personalities of several of the missionaries who opened the Karen fields and their conviction that self-support was not only possible but basic for the development of the Church.

Third, the considerable periods during which large groups of Karen Christians were without missionary direction or oversight placed upon the people themselves the management and responsibility for the upkeep of their own churches.

In his *Epitome of Self-Support*, in the Shwegyin area, the late Mr. Klein—a founder and for the greater part of thirty-one years the missionary-adviser of the Shwegyin Church—states:

The record of the Shwegyin Karens commends the policy followed in the achievement of self-support. Without the aid of large endowments, fertile rice farms, the income from saw mills and rice mills, these people have shown self-support does not depend upon foreign aid, but upon firm character, strong conviction, independent attitude and an intense loyalty to their task and leaders. The policy of nibbling at an achievement of self-support deprives the indigenous Christians of their full share of the burden of the gospel. Self-support should be accompanied by self-government from the beginning. The achievements of all the Karen missions ably demonstrate what ought to be an established mission policy everywhere, namely, self-support from the very beginning. . . . The enlistment and training of native leaders who will inspire their constituency to accept the responsibility of supporting Christian work, because responsibility has been devolved to them, is a major part of self-support. It is obvious, too, that in each of the missions studied, zeal for aggressive evangelism and extension of the sphere of mission operations, were concomitant with the acceptance of more responsibility, or the achievement of a large task and that it was not induced from the outside, but sprang from within the Christian body itself. These are all essential parts of self-support.[16]

THE CHURCH OF CHOTA NAGPUR

There are two large Church groups in the Chota Nagpur District of the Province of Bihar, India: the Evangelical Lutheran and the Anglican (Episcopal). Both Churches are centrally organized and

[16] C. L. Klein, *op. cit.*, pp. 59, 60.

are entirely free of foreign administrative control. Both are working among the aboriginal tribes of Mundas and Oraons, and have had remarkable records of growth in members and in self-help.

The Gossner Lutheran Church of Chota Nagpur was established nearly one hundred years ago and has been selected as an example of the capacity of a depressed people to develop a self-supporting Church. It also illustrates some of the weaknesses that have accompanied financial independence.

Among the 154,125 baptized Christians (1943) of the Chota Nagpur Church,[17] some 13,000 are in Assam. There are 75,728 communicants and 2,000 catechumens. During 1943, 540 catechumens and 3,878 children of Christian parents were baptized. There are over 500 congregations in charge of catechists who work under the supervision of sixty ordained pastors. The area is divided into twenty-two districts each presided over by a minister as chairman. The districts are subdivided into fifty-eight parishes. There are 200 schools including a high school and twelve middle schools. The Theological Seminary with a normal enrollment of sixteen students provides a four-year course, and trains candidates for the ministry.

For the last twenty-six years, the congregational and pastoral work of the Church has been maintained by the gifts of the people. The cost of the educational and evangelistic work of the Church also has been largely provided by its members.

The average annual contribution of the rural church members is about nine annas.[18] The differing ability of pastors in encouraging their members to give results in a wide variation in the size of gifts between parishes. As a stimulus to giving, the Church has classified offerings under various heads such as special communion offerings, thank offerings, harvest offerings, first meal offerings, and birth and marriage offerings. Prior to 1932, the Church received an income from its own lands which netted Rs.1,300, while the daily "handful of rice" gifts of members brought in an income of over Rs.5,000, but under the subsequent agricultural depression, such sources have

---

[17] The material of this discussion is compiled from two sources: (a) A Study of the Economic Condition of the Church of India, Burma, and Ceylon and the Gossner Lutheran Church in the District of Chota Nagpur, by Mr. S. K. Roy, prepared for the Madras Conference, 1938; (b) A Survey of the Chota Nagpur Church by C. W. Ranson, National Christian Council, Nagpur, 1944.

[18] Nine annas is approximately $.18 U.S.

yielded less than half these amounts. The local income of the Church in 1943 was Rs.125,000.

The rule of the Church that pastors cannot engage in secular occupations has had to be waived since the depression following the first World War, and many pastors now cultivate land to supplement their reduced salaries. The large increase of church gifts in recent years has not equalled the rise in the cost of living so that pastors, catechists, and teachers have suffered serious hardships and have been working for whatever remuneration—often less than one-half the minimum salary standard—the Church could give them. Yet during this whole period, candidates with B.A., B.D., and M.A., degrees have come forward to work for their Church.

The Chota Nagpur Church is entirely free of foreign administrative control but in recent years it has sought the advice and cooperation of the All-India Lutheran Federation. Due to the exigencies of the great war, for the last twenty years the Church has had complete responsibility for the support of its pastors and catechists. Since 1931, it has also made a brave attempt to maintain its own institutions, and in this it has been greatly assisted by the Lutheran Churches in America.

The Gossner Evangelical Lutheran Church is the first large Church in India to achieve autonomy. The governing body of the Church is the Annual General Conference or *Mahasabha,* which consists of all ordained ministers together with elected delegates from the twenty-two districts. Each ordained minister cares for a parish with about a thousand communicants and more than 2,000 baptized members. With such an inadequate number of ministers for a community of 150,000 Christians there has been a decline in the quality of Christian instruction and pastoral care, and the large bloc of partly instructed people within the Church is a serious source of weakness.

The inability of the Church to collect the money required for pastoral work from the districts has led to decentralization, each district raising the funds for its own work with a consequent reduction of its contribution to headquarters. While the wealthier parishes can manage their own support, this disintegration of solidarity of the whole Church body results in the severe suffering of the poorer parishes and the weakening of the Church as a whole.

Mr. C. W. Ranson of the National Christian Council staff, to whom we are indebted for his recent survey of the Chota Nagpur Church, urges four remedial measures:

First, the need for a higher quality of leadership. Study and travel abroad for a few selected leaders would help to offset the danger of an isolated, autonomous Church becoming ingrown and narrow in its vision.

Second, the need of a centralized financial system through a central fund and a finance committee responsible to the Church Council. This would draw the weak and scattered parishes together, standardize the payment of the ministry and the upkeep of church institutions, and provide for the extension of the whole movement.

Third, the need for a program of economic improvement. The great majority of Christian families are farmers who would benefit from expert guidance in agriculture and rural improvement and this in time would increase the economic resources of the Christian community.

Fourth, the whole future of the Gossner Church depends upon the strengthening of the quality, spiritual authority, and continuity of its central leadership. With this in view the adoption of an Episcopal form of government, as illustrated in the churches of one important section of the Lutheran Church tradition, is suggested.

THE CHURCH IN ANGOLA

Angola (Portuguese West Africa) offers one of the best examples of a Church that is geared to the supporting power of its constituency, and of a mission which has accepted the responsibility for strengthening the economic base of the people and by this means, as well as by spiritual and educational uplift, creating a solid foundation for a stable, indigenous church.[19]

Protestant missions began their work in the interior of Angola in 1880. The Government census of 1940 returned 286,182 of the Colony's 3,850,000 people as Protestants or 7.5 per cent of the total population. This growth is the more remarkable since throughout their sixty-five years of life the missions have met strong Roman Catholic opposition.

[19] The data in this discussion has been supplied by Dr. John C. Tucker of the United Church of Canada, Dondi, Angola; by Rev. Samuel Coles of the American Board, and by Rev. H. C. McDowell, former member of the Galangue Station of the American Board.

More than 70,000 Protestant natives are enrolled in the churches of the American Board and the United Church of Canada in their Bailundo and Dondi fields. The history of these fields has been characterized by strong educational work, the development of a trained native ministry and a trained teaching staff, a devoted native leadership and a very high ratio of self-support among the churches. The field is overwhelmingly rural and its economic life has been built up by the unusual agricultural emphasis and extension work of the mission.

The agricultural demonstration and extension work of Galangue mission station of the American Board has introduced the use of modern plows and the sowing of improved wheat and corn and has substantially increased the income of many native farmers who have been enabled to pay their taxes without the customary forced road labor. Through the distribution of imported breeds of hogs and poultry, and the cultivation of vegetables the diet and, with it, the health of the people have been improved and the new prosperity has brought larger and better native homes, a quickened demand for the education of the children, and increased ability to support the churches and schools.

This agricultural and rural betterment is being carried into all the districts of the Church through trained African extension agents who accompany the pastors and catechists on their evangelistic tours.

The Portuguese Government has promoted the agricultural methods introduced by the mission and has extended them to every province in the Colony.

One secret of the enthusiasm of African native Church leadership in Angola is that the Church has been about the only sphere of activity and leadership open to the educated native. As expressed by a pastor, "What else is left to us but the Church?"

Over ninety per cent of the four hundred churches are entirely self-supporting. In 1944 this included over and above the salaries of the pastor-teachers, the payment of $56,000 for education, $10,000 for new churches and school buildings, and the support of deacons and deaconesses. Church buildings are entirely built by the members who supply both the cost of materials and the actual labor.

Among the methods that have marked the growth of the Angola Church is the periodic coming together of great numbers of Christians for fellowship and worship. There are a number of such "high spots" in the year:

(1) During the *Week of Prayer* in January, the 300 delegated workers draw up the general plans for the year's work, including the communion rallies, the visits of missionaries to the districts, and the youth camps and training institutes. The programs planned in this annual Prayer Week are carried out by the delegates on their return to the outlying districts.

(2) *Easter Week* is observed with a devotional program at all district centers by the coming together of hundreds of the church leaders and laymen.

(3) *Pentecost* is celebrated at the central Dondi Station as a rally day to which thousands of members from the districts come as a pilgrimage. They spend five days at this annual rally, sleeping and eating in the open, worshipping together, and witnessing the annual ordination of pastors. The practical problems of the people are discussed in special group meetings: catechumens are examined, local finances studied—church by church—the sale of books is reported, school records are examined, offenders are disciplined, the condition of the villages and homes is scrutinized, relations with local officials are explained and improved seed grain is distributed. The problems of the family, of young people, and of children are dealt with in age-group meetings. Questions of housing, gardening, tree planting and grafting, care of stock, business management and debt are all dealt with by trained leaders. The mission medical staff is present and gives instruction in health, diet, hygiene and sanitation. The week closes with a final concert and lantern lecture and a communion service.

The Angola Church work has been geared to the supporting capacity of a constituency who are ninety per cent agriculturalists. Ordained pastors are paid $90 a year by their churches and each pastor has his own farm, fruit trees, and animals. Deacons receive $10 a year from their churches. Lay workers are helped with a small annual grant from the church to meet the government hut tax. The total receipts from the churches are pooled and brought to the central treasury from which the pastors are paid. The Africans themselves control the spending of all the Church money. The missionaries assist in accounting and in guarding the funds in the mission safe but no payments are made on their authority.

Ten years of preparatory study are required of candidates for the ministry before they take the theological course. No one is baptized who has not had at least two years of catechumen training nor who cannot read portions of a Gospel. Local committees govern the schools and select and pay the teachers. The fact that the Africans themselves provide the money for their schools makes them keen to see that their children get "their money's worth." The mission finances the opening of new work in remote places, but this subsidy is withdrawn after four years. The mission also finances the higher schools and religious education, trades and industrial classes, medical work and hospitals and scientific agricultural instruction.

The early missionaries found an efficient system of African village government and with adaptation of details incorporated it in the Church government. The tribal sanctions and rules for the control and discipline of the people have been carefully studied and recognized and have been woven into Church discipline and the Christian way of life. In this way the authority of chiefs and of tribal law has not been undermined.

The founder of the Galangue mission station[20] has analyzed the problem of shifting financial responsibility from the mission to the African churches as follows:

When a missionary enterprise is projected out of relationship to the supporting capacity of the people, it becomes necessary to provide salaries, or parts thereof, of native personnel. Those for whom salaries are provided are likely to be the best trained and most capable,—the men who should develop into leaders of large calibre. Experience demonstrates the fact that financial considerations, however unselfishly and democratically administered, militate against vital leadership and thus the system moves in a vicious circle—efforts and funds are doubled to train native leadership and it is so successful that they require a measure of foreign support for their maintenance, and are thus handicapped ever to become true and independent leaders. Only those who have made adjustment with the supporting capacity of their constituencies are leaders in their own right. It is extremely difficult for native personnel, receiving salaries from afar, to normally develop as leaders, even the conscientious and well-intentioned rarely escape financial inner questionings and mistrust of a system that provides a certain amount and from all indications could easily provide more. The general spirit of growing unrest among natives

[20] H. C. McDowell, "Adjusting the Missionary Enterprise to the Supporting Capacity of the People," May, 1933.

in mission employ has its foundations in the use of foreign funds, and will not be corrected until the enterprise is geared to the country.

THE SELF-SUPPORTING PRESBYTERIES OF MEXICO

One of the most unusual records of attaining financial independence among the Younger Churches of the world is that of the Frontier and Central Presbyteries of the National Presbyterian Church of Mexico.[21] These bodies represent about one-half of the churches of this denomination, but are in a class by themselves among Mexican Evangelical churches in economic strength and independence of mission assistance.

The Frontier Presbytery. This Presbytery was formed twenty-nine years ago as a protest by Mexican leaders against the so-called "Cincinnati Plan." The plan provided for a reallocation of the zones of activity of the various denominational groups in Mexico and was extremely unpopular among very many nationals who felt that Mexican opinion had not been adequately considered. The Presbyterian churches of the northern states of Mexico refused to accept the Cincinnati Plan and decided to sever official relations with the mission, to decline further foreign financial aid and, finally, to create an independent Presbytery.

Although nearly every church in the Frontier Presbytery had been receiving aid from the mission board, in 1916, under the leadership of an energetic pastor, they voted to take the step of independence. The movement was well organized and ably led. Every church in the northern area was personally visited, the situation was explained, the issues stated and the support of both the laymen and the clergy was secured. Thus, without a period of preparation or of reduction of mission subsidy, these churches moved forward at one step from traditional dependence to entire independence of foreign financial help.

Using the principle of the strong aiding the weak, the new Presbytery created a Central Fund for helping smaller churches until they could stand on their own feet, and it assessed a quota to be paid by each church to this fund. It was fortunate for the Presbytery that at this very time an oil boom in the Tampico dis-

[21] J. M. Davis, *The Economic Basis of the Evangelical Church in Mexico,* Chapter VI.

trict enabled the churches to contribute generously to the Central Fund during the first years of presbyterial independence.

Although the Frontier Presbytery came into being upon a wave of emotion and nationalism and without a period of preparation, it has prospered. Well-organized churches are scattered over a very wide field from Monterey to San Luis Potosi and from Matamoras to Zacatecas. The cost of supervising this immense field, in addition to providing aid for the weaker churches, has placed a heavy burden on the Presbytery and has retarded to some extent the extension of churches in more remote districts. The total budget of the Frontier Presbytery, including help to weak churches and the general expenses of supervising the field, is between 45,000 and 50,000 pesos a year. (A peso is the equivalent of $.2065 U. S. currency.)

The leading church of the Presbytery is at Monterey—a prosperous and highly industrialized center of 180,000 people. The Monterey Presbyterian Church, built by Mexican architects and money, is one of the outstanding Evangelical buildings in the country. The church seats 500 people, and an average of 200 of its 400 members attend the Sunday service. The church pays its pastor a salary of 260 pesos a month and, in addition to its own internal activities, maintains several lay workers who are developing chapels and conducting evangelism in outlying areas. Among the members of this strong church are a number of well-placed people, including a family which owns and operates a large factory.

The Frontier Presbytery has organized an "Oasis Society," or pension fund, for retired ministers and the widows of ministers. Though not a large fund, it has provided a degree of security for church workers and has helped the morale of the church. The standard pastor's salary paid by the Presbytery is 120 pesos a month, including a parsonage. In some of the weaker churches the pastors supplement their income by outside activities. Lay workers, usually unmarried, receive fifty-five pesos a month.

The Central Presbytery. The Central Presbytery of the Mexican Presbyterian Church became independent of mission aid in 1928. This group of congregations had observed the progress of their sister Presbytery of the north and had profited by its experience. It includes some of the strongest congregations of Mexico, notably the Divino Salvador and the Coyoacan churches, both of which had been independent of mission aid for a considerable period before the independence of the entire Presbytery.

In the representative character of its membership, its economic resources, its spiritual influence and its outreach in the community, the Divino Salvador church occupies a strong position in the capital city. It also is noteworthy for the way in which it has adapted itself to its environment and for the methods by which it is Mexicanizing its program and services.

The home of this great church is an ancient Roman Catholic structure standing in the heart of Mexico City. It is a long, narrow building rising to a great height. The gilded reredos and altar are unchanged, but the images and statues have been removed and have been replaced by potted palms and scriptural scrolls. The effect is both familiar and strange. It has the beauty and dignity of a Roman Catholic church, but the mystery, the candles, the incense and images are gone and in their place attention is directed to the Word of God. Hundreds of Mexican non-Evangelicals, including barefooted Indians, are drawn to the services in this old, familiar building and many have found a new understanding of God and a new way of life under the powerful preaching of the minister.

The Divino Salvador church has the largest membership and is one of the two most powerful Evangelical churches of Mexico, with between two and three thousand members. The church is well organized, with several strong women's societies, men's committees and activities for children and youth groups which keep the church a beehive of activity from Sunday to Saturday. The church is also responsible for nine suburban chapels and city missions which are served by lay workers. Its financial affairs are in the hands of a strong committee, whose chairman is the outstanding Evangelical business man in the capital, and its operating expenses are not only raised, but considerable sums are given for home missions, city chapels, Christian literature and poor relief. The minister is paid the largest salary received by any Evangelical pastor in the Republic,—more than three times the salary of the pastor of the average Presbyterian church.

The suburban church of Coyoacan, a high-class suburb of Mexico City, is one of the four completely self-supporting churches of the Central Presbytery in the Federal District and is the only Evangelical church in Coyoacan. Of its 140 members, an average of eighty to ninety attend Sunday services. There are more than 100 Evangelical families in Coyoacan and a Protestant community of 500, but an average of only one person per family is a member of the church.

The church is well organized and ministers to an influential and highly intelligent constituency. This, together with the easy access of the Coyoacan community to the metropolis, makes unusual demands of the pastor. The church faces problems similar to those of the American suburban church: the cultural and recreational attractions of the city, the night life and the Sunday social and athletic events which pull the youth away from church attendance and activities, the lack of trained workers and of funds for meeting the needs of the poor and sick of the community, the indifference of many Evangelicals in the community to church attendance, and the half-hearted support of the church on the part of many members who are able to give generously, are problems which could be duplicated in the experience of many city churches north of the Rio Grande.

No description of the independent Presbyteries of Mexico would be complete without mention of the spirit of self-sufficiency that has accompanied their experience of attaining independence. The initial incentive which stimulated these churches to maintain themselves has led them to seek a minimum of contact with other Church bodies, which in turn has grown into a policy of non-cooperation. While individual churches, pastors, and members are free to form their own relationships with other groups of Evangelicals,—and often the friendliest personal contacts exist,—the National Presbyterian Church as a body does not yet see its way to join with other denominations in the work of the National Council of Evangelical Churches, nor to be officially represented in interchurch conferences or enterprises. The resulting situation creates peril for the whole Evangelical movement in Mexico.

SELF-SUPPORT IN THE SOUTH SEAS

Established more than one hundred years ago and enjoying early and remarkable growth, the Christian churches in several of the island groups of the central and eastern parts of the South Pacific have developed a degree of economic strength and power of expansion scarcely equalled in any other mission field. J. W. Burton records,

In Tonga, Samoa, and Fiji, for example, we have well-organized churches which are completely autonomous so far as their own native work is concerned. The Methodist Churches of Tonga and of Samoa and those of the London Missionary Society in Samoa, not only pay all the expenses of the native staff and provide for the erection of all their churches, schools, and colleges, but in addition, they raise the salaries and allowances of all European workers. . . . They have sent forth their own sons and daughters in large numbers to the heathen fields of the western Pacific. One missionary, writing from a tiny island with a population of three thousand five hundred people, states quite incidentally: "On an average two couples annually have been sent for mission work in Papua." And the stream shows no sign of drying up. These churches are, therefore, indigenous, self-supporting, self-governing, and, most praiseworthy of all, self-propagating.[22]

The work of Christian missions in Samoa was organized by the London Missionary Society in 1830. It has been marked by the continuous growth of the Church.

Under the influence of the Gospel the Samoans have become members of a Christian community which is probably unequalled in the Pacific. The work of the training centre at Malua has steadily developed, and has provided pastors and evangelists for the Ellice Islands, the Gilbert Islands, and Papua.

The Samoan Church for many years has been entirely self-supporting. The Samoans build and pay for their own churches and schools, support the European missionaries, contribute to the work of the London Missionary Society in other fields, and, in addition, send donations to philanthropic work in this country, such as Dr. Barnardo's Homes and Schools for the Blind, etc. The Society has now only six men missionaries and their wives, and three women workers, but the Christian community of 31,333 has 233 of its own workers. 8,513 children attend the Christian schools.

The Methodist Mission of Australasia has a large community of 7,300, with 131 native workers, five missionaries and their wives and one woman worker. This work is self-supporting. It maintains four hospitals, and has 2,200 children in its schools. The Roman Catholics, Seventh Day Adventists, and Mormons also have work in the islands.[23]

The Methodist Church in Fiji. Dating from 1835, when the first missionaries began their work, the Church in Fiji has been

<hr />

[22] J. W. Burton, *Missionary Survey of the Pacific Islands,* pp. 16-17. World Dominion Press, London, 1930.
[23] *Ibid.,* pp. 74-75.

chosen as a leading example of an indigenous and stabilized Church in the Pacific area.[24] This Church enrolls the largest body of people who worship in one common language in the South Seas. It has had a continuous development of more than one hundred years; it is entirely self-supporting so far as its institutions and native workers are concerned: it has self-government with its own Synod and church courts; the whole Fijian population is professedly Christian and the Church is self-propagating in that it sends its young people in considerable numbers to other parts of the Pacific,— to New Guinea, Papua, the Solomons, and to the Aboriginals of Australia. It is Methodist in origin and fellowship and is a "District" of the New South Wales Conference of the Methodist Church of Australia. Its European missionaries, however, are still under the jurisdiction of the Board of Missions.

In 1936, the native Fijian population numbered 100,467 with 4,574 persons of mixed blood and 1,616 Melanesians. Of this total 90,552 returned themselves in the census as Methodists and 12,805 as Roman Catholics. Among the 100,000 British Indians in Fiji, scarcely 2,000 are professed Christians. Language, religion, and temperament serve to keep the two races apart although time is overcoming these barriers.

The early missionaries found a strong and stable social system in Fiji, built on a communal basis with a hereditary chieftainship. This greatly helped the early Church and provided mass movements and strong leadership through the conversion of chiefs. The genius of Methodism for employing lay workers lent itself to the social organization of Fiji with the service of stewards, lay preachers, catechists and, eventually, native ministers. Avenues of service were found for every type of ability. In this way, the roots of the Church went deep into native soil and found nourishment there. Because of the large use of native workers the number of missionaries has always been small in Fiji.

From the first, it was impressed upon the converts that it was their duty to proclaim the Good News to their people and to support their teachers and church leaders. There is no record from those early days that Fijian preachers were paid from home base funds. There was gradually created an indigenous lay pastorate

[24] The material in this description is condensed from the article by Rev. J. W. Burton published in Vol. II, Madras Series, Chapter V.

and it seemed quite natural to this communal people that they should themselves support their ministers. The pastor-teacher became part of village life. He was given a house and a piece of land for his garden and a school-church was built by his people so that he might teach and preach. Presents of food and mats were brought him, the school children helped him in digging his garden, and the community saw that his other simple wants were met.

As the Church developed and other expenditures became necessary, annual missionary meetings in the circuits were organized at which presents were made of coconut oil, sandalwood, and other native products which could be converted into money.

With the increase of commerce primitive barter was replaced by a monetary system, and sums totalling over £10,000 sterling annually were given by the people at their missionary gatherings. From these funds, native ministers were paid and general Church expenses such as traveling, support of district institutions, and other non-circuit expenses were met. At one time the Fiji Church tried the experiment of paying not only for the support of its own schools, churches, and ministers, but also the salaries of the European missionaries; but after a few years, the plan was discontinued.

Through the mission schools the entire population of Fiji early became literate. Now after several generations of providing the whole education of the people, the mission has turned over the bulk of the educational task to the government which subsidizes approved mission schools. The training of pastors of sufficient ability to satisfy the demands of the educated Fijians is a major problem facing the Church.

Among the factors that explain the remarkable growth of the Fiji Methodist Church are:

The leadership of the chiefs whereby the people came over from heathenism not as individuals but as tribes and were instructed in masses.

The social organization in which each helped all and all helped each.

The coming of the missionaries before there were serious inroads by Western civilization and before governments had imposed their policies upon the people enabled Christianity to be woven into the social fabric of the race.

The Fijians, with many other South Seas island peoples, have enjoyed an economic basis for livelihood unknown by the masses of India and China. The abounding vegetation and ocean life have enabled the Islanders to develop a marginal economy.

The early translation of the Scriptures into one common language and the teaching of the people to read them have had a powerful and stabilizing effect upon church life.

From the first, the missionaries insisted on the converts supporting their own pastors, and giving the people useful positions in the Church so that scarcely a Methodist family is not in some way or other officially connected with the Church, has had much to do with making it truly indigenous.

On the other hand, some of the very aids to the growth of the Church have also hindered its best development. For example, the early influence of the chiefs has given place to a more or less conventional attitude toward religion, without vital conviction and a lack of personal experience. The later influence of the chiefs has not been helpful.

The early communal system has been increasingly commercialized and this has made acute financial difficulties for the Church in the support of its native ministry.

The incoming Western civilization is having a serious effect upon the people. Liquor, gambling, and venereal disease are ravaging many of the young people and are definitely lowering the spiritual life of the Church. But these influences also are purging the church membership.

THE SELF-SUPPORTING CHURCHES OF BRAZIL

The Evangelical churches of Brazil stand high in the scale of self-support among the Younger Churches of the world. Great, independent churches in other fields have been organized from one caste or race or from the churches of one denomination or one level of economic or cultural development. In Brazil, however, there has been demonstrated the possibility of securing independence on the part of congregations of contrasted racial types, economic and social status, theological affinities and church discipline. This renders Brazil a most rewarding field for an inquiry into the subject of church self-support and lends to Brazilian experience a universal value.

There are notable examples of financially independent churches in all of the principal denominations in Brazil, but several groups, widely contrasted in some respects, stand out preeminently.

The Congregational Union of Brazil. This group of churches has the distinction of constituting the first organized Evangelical body in Brazil, of being founded by lay effort, and of never having had the assistance of a foreign mission board or of missionaries. Under these circumstances, the Brazilian Congregational churches throughout their whole history have been entirely self-supporting.

The Congregational work in Rio de Janeiro was begun in 1885 by a Scottish physician, Dr. Robert R. Kalley who, with a small group of Evangelical families, was driven out of Madeira by the Portuguese authorities.

In 1942 the Congregational Union of Brazil numbered sixty-nine churches with fifty ordained ministers. In the same year, it formed a merger with the thirty "Christian churches" (*Igreja Cristão*) founded by the Evangelical Union of South America, and the united body of ninety-nine churches became one of the larger Evanglical groups in Brazil.

The struggle of these churches for self-support has been severe and although it has somewhat limited the scope of their activities and expansion, it has not adversely affected their vitality. The Church uses the theological schools of other denominations for preparing its ministers, maintains no press or publications, nor is it able to keep up a pension scheme, insurance plan or assistance for widows. Many of the pastors supplement their salaries by outside activities such as teaching or clerical work. Each pastor makes his own financial arrangements with his church. The treasurer brings the annual budget to the congregation and asks for its support. Individual pledge cards are used, the new members and candidates are instructed in the duty of Christian giving to the full extent of their power and the pastor periodically preaches on stewardship.

Both the lower and middle classes and a few well-to-do and influential families are included in the constituency of these churches. The stronger churches contribute to a general fund from which the weaker churches are helped.

There are a number of very strong city churches, two of which each enroll over 800 members. The parent Congregational church in

Rio de Janeiro takes high rank among the Protestant congregations in the capital. Adjoining its large auditorium is a modern four-story parish center, housing Sunday School, day school, young people's activities and the various societies of the church. This outstanding plant was built entirely by the constituency and illustrates what national Christians can do for themselves.

The problem of finance is ever present in the rural churches. From four to seven congregations share the services and support of one ordained minister who usually is assisted by the voluntary work of laymen.

Various methods of raising church money are used. One church owns a farm which is worked by the members and the proceeds are devoted to the support of the pastor. A farmer member of another church offers several acres of his land to be cultivated jointly by the members. The "talent" method[25] is popular among the women's societies.

The Congregational church of the northeastern city of Campina Grande with 800 members holds a high place among Brazil's self-supporting churches, not primarily because of its size but rather because of its remarkable growth from an ordinary church, the dynamic leadership of its pastor, its missionary spirit and the activities of its laymen. The pastor keeps his members so occupied with Christian work that they have little time to get into trouble outside of the church program. His 200 young people are busy with visitation of the sick and poor, with service on evangelistic bands, teaching in eight branch Sunday Schools and holding out-of-doors meetings. The church does not provide recreational facilities for its youth and yet it seems to have no difficulty holding them.

The 110 members of the Men's Missionary Society have taken as their responsibility the evangelization of the eastern portion of Parahyba State. Their seven missionaries have organized and manned six churches and have formed eighteen other small congregations. This missionary society is officered by some of the ablest business men of the city who take pride in its financing, its eficient management, and success.

The pastor has made a special study of church finances; he knows the financial position of each member, and his members are aware of what he expects of them. The pastor bases his teaching of

[25] See Chapter IX.

stewardship upon the Bible, and includes this in the training of each candidate.

The finance committee raises the church funds and each month checks over the giving record of every member. Eighty per cent of the members give to the support of the church and although a majority are poor and many are destitute, one-half of the congregation are tithers. The church is helping to support fifteen member families who are without means of livelihood. The congregation has outgrown its third building and is still steadily expanding. Evangelism is the inner motivation of the pastor and this has been communicated through him to his church.

The Independent Presbyteries. An important group of independent Brazilian churches was formed in 1903 when, as a result of a controversy over Free Masonry and certain doctrinal questions, a large group of Presbyterians left the synodical churches to form a new church body known as The Independent Presbytery of Brazil.

Of the 424 Presbyterian churches with a total of 58,996 members, 274 churches and 43,996 members are in the Synodical Presbyteries, while 150 churches with 15,000 members constitute the Independent Presbyteries. Ever since their organization these churches have been completely self-supporting and their history since 1903 has been one of steady and reasonably rapid progress.

There are four Presbyteries: three in the south and center of Brazil and the fourth in the northeast. The Independent churches suffer from an insufficient number of ministers but the pastorate compares favorably with that of other bodies.[26] Among this large group of Independent pastors are not a few brilliant and devoted men who have led their people in a belief in their own powers and in accomplishing maximum results by relying upon their own resources and their faith in God.[27]

Many of the urban churches of the Independent Presbyteries are among the strongest and most vital Evangelical organizations in Brazil. They are marked by the quality of their spiritual life, the

[26] See E. Braga and K. G. Grubb, *The Republic of Brazil*, p. 87, World Dominion Press, London, 1932.

[27] See story of the Curityba First Presbyterian Church in *How the Church Grows in Brazil*, by J. M. Davis, pp. 106, 107.

devotion of their laymen and women in Sunday School, evangelism and many other forms of service, in the strength of their women's and young people's societies and the loyalty of their members in financial support. However, partly as a means of widening their contacts and service in the community and partly to supplement the income paid them by their congregations, many of the pastors engage in outside activities such as medical and legal practice, journalism, and teaching. In this the pastor is often ably assisted by his wife. These churches are a witness to the power of the Brazilian people to lead and fully to support an indigenous Christian movement.

The Pentecostal Churches. One of the most recent and most rapidly growing church groups in Brazil is the Assemblies of God (or Pentecostal Churches as they are commonly called). The Brazilian Church was organized in 1911 and is still directed by the Swedish pioneer missionaries who have been trained and commissioned in the United States.

The Pentecostal Church has received a wonderful response from the Brazilian masses, and is completely self-supporting and enthusiastically self-propagating. In 1942, the superintendent of the Brazilian Pentecostal Church estimated its total membership at 60,000. Although it has strong congregations throughout the whole coastal area, the most striking growth of this Church has been in the northeastern and northern states.

The Pentecostal Church strategy has been to open work in the seaboard cities and to work from them to the interior. In every coastal capital there are thriving churches with great and enthusiastic congregations whose members are frequently numbered by the thousands. The Porto Alegre church has 2,000 members; Belém, 2,000; and the Recife church enrolls 4,000 members. The secrets of this phenomenal growth and strength are: (1) The membership is recruited from the underprivileged masses to whom the Church appeals as a new source of morale, hope, fellowship and social expression. It forms for the people an entirely new social grouping and brotherhood. (2) The Pentecostal churches, far more than the older Protestant bodies, give scope for expressing the emotion and vivid feelings which are characteristic of the Brazilian people. Great choirs and orchestras of young people take a prominent part in leading the church services, and provide an emotional outlet for the drab lives of the members. (3) Tithing is very widely practiced by the Pentecostals and is accepted as a natural discipline. (4) The leadership qualifications of pastors and workers are not exacting and workers recruited from the ranks are put to work almost at once with a comparatively simple type of preparation. While standards of discipline often are not exacting, the Pentecostal churches are meeting the needs of a depressed stratum of Brazilian society that is not conspicuously attracted by some of the older denominations. Particularly among the great negro population of the northeast, this Church is reaching with the Gospel a large and frequently neglected element of the nation.

The Adventist Churches. No mention of the self-supporting churches of Brazil would be complete without a brief description of the work of the Seventh Day Adventist congregations. The Adventist work in the states of Rio Grande do Sul, Santa Catharina, São Paulo, Matto Grosso, and Minas Geraes is organized into a South Brazil Union, with headquarters in São Paulo. Twelve thousand church members are enrolled in this Union.

The sixty churches of the South Brazil Union are self-supporting. Tithing is accepted as an article of faith and practice when a member joins the church. A very great majority—probably 90 per cent—of the members practice tithing. The members are, for the most part, poor but include many middle-class people and a few families who are well salaried. But all tithe irrespective of financial status. The pastors receive from one to two contos a month ($50 to $100) according to the location and size of their churches, the number of their children, and their own education and ability.

The substantial Porto Alegre church was built six years ago at a cost of 130 contos ($6,500). This sum was raised entirely in Porto Alegre from church members and from city firms by public subscription.

Church leaders were not conscious of serious youth problems, though the loss from marriage with Roman Catholics was sometimes felt in the larger cities. In spite of the generous salary paid their pastors in 1942, the Adventist churches suffered from a shortage of candidates for the ministry. Ten more pastors were greatly needed.[28]

[28] J. M. Davis, *How the Church Grows in Brazil*, pp. 112-113.

PART FOUR

STRENGTHENING THE STRUCTURE

CHAPTER IX

METHODS AND TECHNIQUES USED BY YOUNGER CHURCHES

THE Department's studies of the ways in which individual churches in twenty-two[1] different lands have gained a position of financial independence lead to the conviction that there is probably no Younger Church in any mission field of the world which is faced with a problem of adjustment to its environment that has not been met and, in a measure, solved by some other Younger Church. The experience of the mission-founded churches with the problem of becoming financially independent is vast. In the aggregate it forms a reservoir or pool which is available to every church and to every mission in the one hundred mission fields of the world.

Some aspects of this phenomenon should be mentioned. While it is true that many of the finance principles and methods in use on the mission field originated among the churches of the West, the cases we shall study are those in which these principles have been indigenized and demonstrated by Younger Churches, and represent national rather than missionary initiative. Tithing, for example, though first introduced and taught by the missionary, has become indigenized in hundreds of Younger Churches. On the other hand, several of the methods used by these churches are unique national solutions of old problems.

A large number of the self-supporting churches have reached this position without missionary leadership and have become independent through the initiative of their own pastors and officers. This is a source of very great hope for the future.

A further view of the subject is that church self-support does not depend alone on the economic and cultural status of peoples. This is a principle that has been accepted among primitive or semi-

[1] China, India, Japan, Java, Korea, the Philippines, Sumatra, Angola, Northern Rhodesia, Union of South Africa, Argentina, Barbados, Bolivia, Brazil, Cuba, Dominican Republic, Jamaica, Mexico, Peru, Puerto Rico, Trinidad, Uruguay.

primitive peoples as often as among the more advanced non-Christian communities. Some of the largest self-supporting church groups in the world are found among such people as the Karens of the hills of Burma, the Bataks of Sumatra, the Samoans and Fijians of the South Pacific, and the Oraons of Chota Nagpur, India. On the other hand, a considerable percentage of mission-assisted churches are found among the relatively advanced civilizations of Latin America, viz., Argentina, Cuba, Puerto Rico, and in India, China, and Java. Until the government ban against the acceptance of foreign aid to the Japanese Christian movement came into effect, more than one-half of the churches were receiving financial help from the foreign mission bodies which founded them.

It frequently appears that the more the economic standards and amenities of life of the mission-sending lands are emulated by a non-Christian nation, the greater has been the difficulty of establishing the principle of financial independence of its churches.

Again, self-support has little relation to the age of a native church body or the years during which it has been in contact with the foreign mission. The great Church of the Karens has been financially independent since its very beginning,—one hundred years ago. The Batak Church, numbering 400,000 members, has been entirely independent of the Rhenish Mission during the seventy-five years of its life, although the Dutch Government has supplied more than one-half of the support of the pastor-teachers of the churches. The large group of Korean churches, not yet sixty years old, early attained an unusual degree of independence and since the opening of the Japan-China conflict, has entirely supported itself. The considerable group of churches established among the Indians of the Peruvian highlands by the Evangelical Union of South America has not received outside financial help. From their founding the system of lay leadership in vogue among these churches has made this independence possible.

On the other hand, there are not a few churches now beginning their second or third generation, in fields which were opened a hundred or more years ago, which still receive help from the mission boards that founded them. In many such cases the acceptance of foreign money has not been due so much to the inherent weakness of the congregations as to a traditional dependence and lack of serious efforts at self-help.

ORGANIZATION OF CHURCH FINANCE

Among the fundamental principles in the organization and promotion of the finances of the Younger Churches are:[2]

Member Responsibility. Responsibility for the financing of the church must be accepted and carried by the members. It is fatal for this load to be shouldered by the pastor or the missionary.

The Finance Committee is the cornerstone of the financial organization of the church. The committee should be made up of the ablest, most active and representative members. It should include, wherever they exist, the experienced business men of the congregation and also representatives of the principal church groups such as the women's society and the young people's group. The members of the Finance Committee must be selected with care from among persons of initiative and capacity for leadership. A condition of membership in the committee should be a willingness to accept responsibility and work.

The Annual Church Budget. The whole congregation should be given the opportunity to participate in drawing up the budget. Where the members themselves study the finance problem of their church and share in deciding the amount of money to be raised and the methods to be used, they will more willingly carry a reasonable part of the load. The members should be called together at least quarterly to receive the reports of the Finance Committee. These meetings, however, must provide for more than a reading of the financial report. They should be conducted as forum discussions in which the members are encouraged to take part and their ideas, objections, and recommendations are given serious consideration. In this way the nature of the budget items will be understood by the congregation and the experience and ideas of the whole church will be made available for the committee and potential leadership may be discovered. Most important of all will be a growing feeling among the members that the church is their own affair. They will

---

[2] For a more detailed and a most valuable treatment of this subject, the reader is referred to the Appendix. Here Mr. John Ritchie, a missionary of forty years' experience in Peru, indicates step by step the procedures required for bringing small, dependent churches to a self-supporting position.

begin to see that the life of the church depends on them and will want to help make it a going concern.

The Every-Member Canvass. By the foregoing procedure the membership will be prepared to participate in the every-member canvass to an extent that would be impossible under any other plan. A common method is to divide the congregation into groups which are assigned to the members of the Finance Committee for personal solicitation. In large churches, the Finance Committee is assisted in the house-to-house visitation by members of the congregation who either volunteer or are appointed to this work under the leadership of a team captain. The teams have a friendly rivalry in turning in the largest score of pledges to the church budget.

The Pledge Card. The use of the pledge card in the every-member canvass is reported by many churches. Various Korean and Chinese rural churches use a pledge card which provides for gifts of cash, produce, or days of labor. The following form of pledge is described by Felton:[3]

PLEDGE CARD

Acknowledging God's gifts to me and His claim upon me and upon my time, I hereby pledge to my church:

Weekly Cash Gifts: $............... per week, to be paid, if possible at the time of the regular church service.

Harvest Gifts: $............... to be paid in cash or produce at harvest time.

Labor Gifts: .... days of labor. This labor is to be upon my farm, or on the church farm, or in some village craft, the income of which is to go to my church.

Crops: .... This crop on my farm or on the church farm, raised from my seed or from seed furnished me by the church, I agree to tend faithfully and give the proceeds to my church.

Animals: ....These animals, belonging to me or to the church, I agree to feed and care for and give the proceeds to the church.

Homecrafts: .... These articles I agree to make and give the proceeds to the church.

Signed ....

Date ....

---

[3] Ralph A. Felton, *The Rural Church in the Far East*, pp. 150-151.

The annual budget should make clear the amount of the average *per capita* share of the members. An allowance must be made for shrinkage: Some members will have to give much more than the average to make up for those who cannot or will not come up to the average.

Felton observes that a member's weekly cash offering will be larger if he knows it is to be credited toward his original pledge. The use of envelopes for this weekly offering is too expensive for many rural churches and small cloth sacks are substituted. The sacks are hung on numbered hooks on a rack near the church door. Each sack has the number of the member. As he enters the church he gets his sack from the hook and drops it with his offering on the collection plate.[4]

An even more economical method used by many of the Presbyterian churches of Korea is to furnish the members with small squares of plain paper on which the member's name and the amount of the gift are written and in which the cash offering is folded and dropped into the collection bag.

The Finance Committee of many churches publicly posts in the vestibule a statement of the status of the account of each member. This shows the amount pledged, the payments which have been made to date, and the arrears, if any, of each member.

Another device is to display a large thermometer or clock on which is indicated each week the relation of the total receipts from pledges to the goal of the annual budget. In some Latin American churches, the Finance Committee studies the financial status of each member and from this his fair share in the support of the church is estimated and requested of him in the every-member canvass.

The Finance Campaign. When skillfully led, the organization of the congregation into working groups to raise the church budget or to raise a building fund often secures good results. The 650 members of the Cardenas Presbyterian church in Cuba were divided into twenty-five groups, each with a leader to carry out the every-member canvass. A two weeks' evangelistic campaign which preceded the every-member canvass proved a stimulus to the giving of the congregation. The pastor prepared his people for the campaign by a series of sermons on stewardship and by a week of special meetings.

[4] See Felton, *op. cit.,* p. 151.

Here the various problems of finance, education, and the inner life of the church were freely discussed by the members. By these various means, the church has no difficulty in raising its entire annual budget.

A splendid example of effective organization is that of the First Presbyterian church in Recife, Brazil. Upon coming to this pastorate, the minister found that only a small minority of the 640 members were giving regularly to the church budget through the envelope system. He called his congregation together and showed by a wall chart that twenty-six tithing members were giving 940 milreis a month to church support and that the gifts of 126 other members totaled only 300 milreis. He asked the congregation, "Who is it that is supporting this church of yours?" The answer was obvious and greatly surprised the members. "As a result of this visual demonstration, fifty-four other members decided to become tithers, so that we now have eighty tithing members. . . . At the same time, there was a large increase of ordinary contributors so that now our income is in excess of our expenditures."

The city of Recife condemned this church building in order to open a new avenue, and the congregation was faced with the necessity of raising $25,000 (gold) to erect a new building. One hundred and ten members were divided into ten campaign teams, each with a captain who selected his team mates. The names of the members of the congregation, together with those of friendly non-church members, were divided between the teams for solicitation and each team aimed at the largest possible results. The church is working on a definite program to reach its goal. An annual evangelistic campaign has developed a new devotion to the church and has stimulated gifts to the building project. The pastor described the long-term plan that had been accepted by the congregation and stated that the first essential in this great undertaking was to arouse the consecration and devotion of every member to the point of taking a share in the campaign. "If we succeed in this, the money will come." One of the practical methods adopted by several hundred families of this church was to place in their homes a receptacle for keeping waste paper, bottles, metals and broken objects and to devote the proceeds of their sale to the building fund.[5]

The Evangelical movement of Brazil is rich in illustrations of

[5] J. M. Davis, *How the Church Grows in Brazil*, pp. 113-114.

effective church finance organization in which entire congregations have participated.

Though without funds the members of the Second Presbyterian church of Curityba, Brazil, under the leadership of their pastor, determined to erect a first-class building on a ten-year construction plan. The blue prints were drawn and the budget carefully estimated. Building materials were divided into separate units, ranging from a single brick or a litre of sand at five cents, to a beam or a steel girder. These units were subscribed for by the members of the church and Sunday School and by non-Evangelical friends. The children vied with one another in buying bricks and pailfuls of sand. By all working together, the project began to take shape. After two years, the foundation was laid and one end of the basement was covered with a temporary roof in order to house the church services. Construction progressed no faster than the funds which came in. By giving their spare time to work on the building the members reduced the cost of paid labor. By the eighth year the roof was in place, the tower was finished, and at the end of the next twelve months, the congregation was worshipping in its completed church. It was entirely paid for and is one of the most attractive buildings in this city of 100,000 people.[6]

The pastor of an Episcopal church in Porto Alegre, Brazil, through studying and enlisting the special interests of his members, refurnished the interior of the somber Roman Catholic church building which had become the property of the congregation. Each year he emphasized some special aspect of the church's needs. A new pipe organ was bought; the altar cloth and equipment were replaced; a beautiful lectern was installed and an artistic baptismal font was secured. Finally, a new outfit of church pews was purchased. This Brazilian pastor had an unusual appreciation of beauty and by studying his members, he drew out the artistry latent in them and related it to the practical needs of their church.[7]

An unusual method of raising money for a church project was that adopted by the Batak Church of northern Sumatra in 1938. To provide more beds for Batak patients, an extension to the mission hospital was required. The mission had no funds but of the 80,000 guilders needed, the Dutch Government granted three-quar-

[6] *Ibid.,* pp. 104-105.
[7] *Ibid.,* p. 111.

ters of the amount—60,000 guilders—and the Batak pastors devised a plan for raising the required balance—20,000 guilders—by means of a "bond issue" to which the community was invited to subscribe. The bonds were issued in denominations of from one to fifty guilders each. A one-guilder bond was the equivalent of a donkey-load of boards or of bricks. Throughout the area which depended upon this hospital, these bonds were taken by the church members and the necessary addition was secured.[8]

A plan for assisting Younger Churches in financing new projects was the China Rural Church Revolving Fund, described by Felton. This fund was organized under the auspices of the Nanking Theological Seminary, the College of Agriculture of Nanking University, and Ginling College with a governing body to which each institution appointed three members. The purpose of the Fund was to assist rural churches to float new projects for the strengthening of church life. Its goal was not only to help the churches achieve self-support, but also to help them improve agricultural practices. Loans were made to churches for new buildings and equipment, stock, seed and work animals. Interest on borrowed money was paid yearly at the rate of five per cent. Payments on the principal were made over periods of from one to five years according to the size and object of the loan.[9]

THE LORD'S ACRE PLAN

This principle of church support widely used among farming communities of the United States is admirably suited to the circumstances of rural people in mission fields. Here is a plan that is adapted to the farmer and his way of life everywhere. In communities where cash is scarce and gifts of money are difficult to make, it provides for offerings in kind; it furnishes a training in stewardship for all church members, including children as well as adults. The plan is a spiritual exercise. A man, while tending his Lord's Acre, is reminded that he is working on dedicated ground; that he is working with and for the Lord. His vocation and chief daily activity in this way are directly related to and become a part of his religion.[10]

[8] Madras Series, Vol. V, p. 406.

[9] Felton, *op. cit.*, p. 154.

[10] Dumont Clarke, "The Country Church and the Lord's Acre Plan," The Farm Federation, Asheville, North Carolina.

Under the Lord's Acre Plan the church member sets aside a stipulated part of his land and dedicates the crops raised upon it to the Lord. Or he may give to the church the fruit grown on a portion of his orchard. The Lord's Acre Plan is adapted to the capacity of each member of the family. The father agrees to raise an acre of corn or cotton or a row of sweet potatoes. The mother may pledge the Sunday eggs. The son may raise a pig or a lamb, the daughter may set a hen and give the entire brood of chickens to the church, and a child with a single chick may undertake to rear it as his offering. These gifts are not paid to the minister but to the church treasurer and the proceeds from their sale are applied to the budget and are credited to the donor. This principle has been used by many Chinese churches but it is also practiced by churches in Japan, Korea, the Philippines, Mexico, Cuba and on other mission fields.

The pastor of a church in Fukien Province, south China, has established the custom on Easter Sunday of presenting each child in the Sunday School with two eggs on condition that when they are hatched, the chicks will be given to the church. At the farm of a church member, whose little daughter was a pupil in this Sunday School, the child whispered to her mother that she wanted to show her "Lord's chickens" to the visitors. In a little pen in the farmyard were six hens, with several broods of chicks, all products of the Easter gift of the pastor. The little girl stood erect in front of her flock and said, "Sir, these hens are not my hens; they are the Lord's hens. I am the Lord's hen-keeper." After a few years of this practice, the Sunday School children had saved enough money to build an extension to the church in addition to making a weekly contribution to its budget.

The pastor of the Presbyterian church at Encrucijada, Cuba, reported, "Four of our small boys wanted to share in the support of the church but had no way of earning money. I started a small pig project by giving little pigs to the boys with the understanding that they would care for them and give the profits from their sale, when grown, to the church. After paying back the price of the pigs and the cost of their feed, the boys presented the church with $25.00."[11]

Annually each member of the women's society of a rural church

11 J. M. Davis, *The Cuban Church in a Sugar Economy*, p. 112.

in Yucatan brings to the church a little chick which she dedicates to the Lord. The chick is tagged with a leg band, is raised, sold, and the proceeds given to the society for the support of the church.[12]

The members of the Sunday Schools of the Banes Baptist church, Cuba, have been able by the use of the Lord's Acre principle to contribute to the support of the circuit pastor. A farmer's daughter dedicated a small pig to the pastor's fund; another set aside a hen and gave the eggs, while others gave a part of their crops of pumpkins and fruit.

In various parts of India the Lord's Acre Plan has been used with good results. Teachers at the Daska mission school (Church of Scotland) in the Sialcot District, Punjab, raise vegetables on a portion of their garden plots and give the produce to the local church. A Chrisian land owner in another part of the Punjab has devoted the fruit of an orchard to his church. He has invited the poorer members of the congregation to prune the trees and pick the fruit as their share in the church upkeep.

A Christian layman in Nagano Prefecture, Japan, formed the custom of planting a fruit tree and dedicating it to the Lord at the baptism of each of his children. This was done with the understanding that the produce of the trees should be given to the church. The many children born to this family insured a growing and considerable church income.

The power of organized cooperation on the part of large numbers of humble people is illustrated by the "handful of rice" custom used in Korean and other Oriental Christian households. The commodious Presbyterian church at Masan, Korea, with capacity for seating 1,600 people, was largely built from the handfuls of rice that the mothers of the Christian households daily set aside for a period of years as gifts to the "Lord's house." This daily dedication of rice by hundreds of humble families resulted in the erection of one of the largest churches in southern Korea.

In China and some Latin American lands the Lord's Acre method has been modified through the members of a congregation working together in the raising of crops upon land belonging to or loaned to the church. As related by Felton, "The Disciples church at Ke Tang 'chi, near Nanking, has 15 mow[13] of land which helps

---

[12] J. M. Davis, The Economic Basis of the Evangelical Church in Mexico, p. 64.
[13] One mow is the equivalent of one-sixth of an acre.

the church budget. The Presbyterian church at Li Shu has 100 mow of upland, 14 mow of rice land and 2 cows. The Presbyterian church at Li Yang has 10 mow of land and 2 cows. The Tshtsing church has 3 mow of trees. The Weiting church has 4 mow of trees. The Presbyterian church at Shunwachen has 3 mow of rice land, 24 mow of upland, 5 pigs, 1 cow and 16 mow of peach trees. These trees alone brought in $200 to the church budget in the past summer. The men tended the orchard and the women canned and sold the peaches."[14]

The members of a small Mexican church at San Juan, near Tampico, cleared 1,200 pesos by raising cotton on a piece of land belonging to the Evangelical Cooperative Society of the community. With this money, the congregation enlarged their church building and installed their own electricity. The labor was furnished entirely by the members.[15]

In the rural community of Garrochales on the north coast of Puerto Rico, the Methodist mission bought two and one-half acres of land and built a church and parsonage. With the moving away of several American farmer-members, the church was left in difficulties. Only $120 a year was contributed by the remaining members to the budget. A new pastor began to work with the congregation toward self-support. It was decided to cultivate the church land to sugar cane. The church members—small farmers and peons —undertook the work of land preparation, cultivation, and harvesting. They worked in shifts on different days. One shift cut the cane, packed it in wagons, and hauled it to the mill. A second shift cleaned the field and got it ready for the new crop. The crop from this cane field added from two to four hundred dollars annually to the church income. In 1941, the congregation was planning to buy five more acres of land for diversified farming and dairying in order to become financially independent of the mission board.[16]

A variation of the church farm plan was used with striking results by the members of a Mayan Indian congregation in Yucatan. This project is of importance because it harmonized with the traditional Mexican system by which the joint use of common land is granted to a whole village. It also serves to illustrate a right and a

14 Felton, *op. cit.*, p. 148.
15 J. M. Davis, *The Economic Basis of the Evangelical Church in Mexico*, p. 65.
16 J. M. Davis, *The Church in Puerto Rico's Dilemma*, pp. 54, 56.

wrong way of management. "A few years ago our members cultivated to wheat an unused tract of public land to pay off the 1,500
pesos debt on their new church building. The plan was a success;
the men all worked together and there was an abundant harvest.
Four hundred pesos were cleared. My wife made a huge 'thermometer' to show what was gained and what was yet to be secured.
The second year the members decided that they would not clear a
fresh tract but plant the same piece of land. This time the yield
was less, but it was substantial and the thermometer shot up again.
The third year it was necessary to clear a new tract of land, but
in the meantime a division had entered the church and money was
taken from the treasury to pay outside laborers to cut down the
jungle. That year's profit barely exceeded the cost of labor. Present
prospects are that the church debt will be lifted completely this
coming year."[17]

The Presbyterian congregation of Tungching, China, raised a
herd of water buffaloes and loaned them out to the church members. The farmers were badly in need of work animals. They had
lost their own cattle by rinderpest, famine, and debt. One water
buffalo is ordinarily needed for cultivation by each two farmers.
The farmers were glad to get the work animal and fed and cared
for it in return for its use. These animals calved each year and
when the calf was weaned, it was returned to the church treasurer
to be sold or raised to be loaned. If it was sold, it brought about
$35 (Chinese currency). The receipts from these calves provided
over half the yearly budget of this church.[18]

A most unusual adaptation of the Lords' Acre method as applied
to the building of a church is reported by the Rev. Richard Patton
of the Evangelical Union of South America in the town of Huan-
cayo in Peru. After years of occupying cramped quarters the congregation of one hundred members determined to build a suitable
church. The mission could not help them and though the members
were poor, they decided to go ahead upon their own efforts. The
building materials and labor were divided into various units, each
of a specified value. These units were explained by small sketches
which were duplicated on sheets of paper and distributed among
the members. A picture of the finished church was shown at the

---

[17] Statement by the Rev. David B. Legters, Dzitas, Yucatan, Mexico.
[18] Felton, *op. cit.*, pp. 148, 149.

top of the sheet. Units of various types of material and of labor that were required, together with their cost, were depicted in twelve diagrams. A single brick was priced at nine centavos. The picture of a load of 210 bricks was marked at 10.00 soles;[19] that of a load of earth at three soles; a load of sand at six soles; cement pipes were valued at 2.50 soles each; sacks of cement at five soles; a plastered wall at .45 centavos per foot; planking and joists at .45 centavos a foot; a box of nails at 4.50 soles. Clever drawings depicted artisans each working at his specialty. The mason was shown laying up bricks at a wage of 4.50 soles per day; the carpenter working with saw and plane at the same wage; the hod-carrier and carpenter's assistant at 2.00 soles and the iron worker at five soles per day.

Each church member pledged the cost of one or more units of material or of labor, cut out the design of his selection with his name and the date attached, and gave it to the building committee. This was repeated month by month and in this way each adult and each child was able to donate gifts of material or labor suited to his capacity. After nine months of work, excavation and drainage were completed, foundations were laid, the church walls were three feet above the ground, and more than 4,000 soles toward the 20,000 soles project were in hand.

THE TITHE

The practice of tithing is possibly the most fruitful of all the sources of Younger Church independence. Commonly associated with the practice of the Seventh Day Adventist Church, it is not generally understood that use of the tithe as a method of church support is exceedingly widespread. In the surveys of the Department, it was found that tithing is being practiced in one or more churches of nearly all of the forty or more denominational groups studied. However, in only two of these groups is tithing included in the Church discipline and these two—the Seventh Day Adventist and Pentecostal Churches—have the highest ratio of self-supporting churches among the missionary societies of the world.

Of even greater significance is the fact revealed by our studies that Baptist, Presbyterian or Methodist churches in which a small minority of the members are tithers, invariably stand well above the

[19] The sol is equivalent to approximately $.15 U. S. Currency.

average in self-support. In a Presbyterian church in Recife, Brazil, previously described, the analysis of church income showed that twenty-six tithing members of a total membership of 640 were contributing three-fourths of the whole budget. When this was made clear to the congregation, fifty-four other persons began the practice of tithing, and the church was lifted to a self-supporting position.

Tithing derives its strength as a method of church finance first, because it was used among the Hebrews for the support of the services in the Temple and the priesthood, and is specifically enjoined by the Levitical Law; second, it is a simple, convenient, and definite discipline which is taught new believers who crave concrete advice as to what it means to be a Christian; third, it is a practical and workable formula for achieving self-support. It is based upon the principle that the sum total of one-tenth of the income of ten families in the church will support the eleventh family. Under this formula a pastor theoretically could be supported by a church of only ten families who faithfully tithed their incomes. The supporting power of the tithing system is imposing when it is used by a church of several hundred members.

The Seventh Day Adventist Church is highly and successfully organized upon the tithing system. Each local church sends a tithe of its annual income to the support of the conference office of its district. In like manner, one-tenth of the conference office income is laid aside for the upkeep of the union office of the state or province and in turn, a tenth of the state office receipts is paid to the support of the world office in Washington, D. C.[20]

Under the Adventist teaching of the tithe, the Christian who lays aside his tenth is not dedicating his own money to the Lord, but is giving God what is already His. The real giving of his substance begins after the tithe has been made. On this principle the Adventist Church raises from its members for special contributions and for missionary and administration purposes sums amounting to three-fifths of the total tithes of the church. The giving of this Church in the United States is unique. With a membership of only 190,228 (1943) the total tithe offerings amounted to $11,479,252.80 or $59.56 per member. The foreign missionary offerings totaled

---

[20] Data supplied through the courtesy of the Statistical Office of the General Conference of Seventh Day Adventists, Takoma Park, Washington, D. C.

$4,596,451.92 or $24.15 per member, while gifts to home missions and local church work totaled a further $3,319,124.15 or $17.45 per member. Of the imposing grand total of $19,394,828.87 contributed for all purposes by this denomination, the average member's share is $101.96.

The financial methods, including the theory and practice of the Seventh Day Adventist Church, have been briefly outlined, not necessarily as a model to be copied by others, but as a most striking example of the results which have been secured through careful business management and the enlistment of nearly one hundred per cent of its members in a definite pattern of giving. This church, which ranks sixteenth in the United States in number of members, has an average *per capita* member gift five and one-half times larger than that of any other denomination of which we have accurate records. With more than four and one-half million dollars annually available for the extension of its missionary program, there is small room for wonder that the Seventh Day Adventist Church in proportion to its numerical strength is growing more rapidly than any other missionary church in the world.

The sources of the giving power of the Adventist Church lie much deeper than skill in business management or the use of mathematical formulas: they lie *first* of all in a belief in the authority of the Mosaic and Levitical teachings and practices. These are held to be as binding upon the 20th Century Church and Christian as upon the Hebrew people of ancient times. The amount of the member's gift for the upkeep of the church and its work is not considered a matter for individual determination, but has been fixed by the Word of God. A finality, a weight of authority, a simplicity and a definiteness are in this teaching and provide both a cutting edge and a powerful drive to put it in action.

The *second* principle in general use by this Church is the education of its children and youth in the philosophy and practice of giving to missions. Five minutes of the weekly opening exercises in every Sabbath School is given to the presentation of a missionary project, a short talk by a missionary, a vivid story from a mission field, a new missionary pamphlet or book adapted for children or an interesting picture thrown on a screen. There is also an occasional presentation of a missionary theme by the pupils of the different departments. On each thirteenth Sabbath, a special missionary collection is taken to which all children are encouraged to give. Every third or fourth year, Sabbath School lessons for a whole quarter are devoted to the subject of stewardship. Thus by the time a child has passed through the Sabbath School, he has been thoroughly imbued with the importance of foreign missions.

MISCELLANEOUS METHODS

The following methods of supplementing the income of the indigenous church are described in detail because they are in harmony with the economic power of the poorer members of the community and because they have all succeeded in increasing the giving standards of actual congregations and with this the income of their churches:

The Penny-a-Day Plan was introduced in 1940 by the members of the Mexican Presbytery of the South to raise funds for the missionary work of their churches. The plan was a Mexican idea, initiated and put through by Mexicans, and was supplementary to the regular church contributions. Each pastor and church officer was asked to give one cent a day. In a short time the plan was extended to all the members of the churches in order to support students of the Bible School during the annual four months of field practice work. The mission took care of the students' expenses during the eight months of study and, through the Penny-a-Day Plan, the Presbytery and the local churches where the students worked supported them during the other four months. The plan has met with an excellent response. It is suited to a land of meagre economic standards for it is scaled low enough to be well within the giving capacity of the great majority of church members.[21]

Mite Boxes. A useful source of church income introduced by the women's societies of this same Presbytery is the mite box or "blessing box" as it is called. Into these little boxes the members drop coins to commemorate birthdays and individual spiritual experiences. The offerings are presented at the monthly meeting of the Presbyterian Missionary Union which is partly supported by these gifts. The societies contribute enough in this way to pay for the

21 J. M. Davis, *The Economic Basis of the Evangelical Church in Mexico,* p. 60.

traveling expenses of the secretaries whose salaries are paid by the mission.[22]

Small Business Enterprises. At a ministers' meeting in the Dominican Republic, one pastor told of various ways in which he had helped his members to a better economic status. He had aided a woman to secure credit so that, even on her small salary, she was eventually able to build a house. She rented part of it and from this added income she increased her contribution to the church. Another member opened a small coffee business and a third, who was a carpenter, learned better methods of work. A second pastor had helped his members to improve their earning capacity by showing them how they could make and sell useful articles. One girl in his church opened a small stand in the village where she sold hot, tasty sweet potatoes at one cent each. A man facing bankruptcy went to his pastor for advice. The pastor consulted a banker friend who agreed to take over the man's debts and help him start again in business.

On his trips to the capital, another pastor made a practice of buying small supplies of cheap articles. These he brought back to his poorer members who sold them on a commission basis. In this way, a girl in his church who was a seamstress made $12 a month, over and above her regular work, and she gave $6.00 of this to the Missionary Society and $6.00 to the Young People's Society. Another girl sold notions in her spare time. In two months she had cleared $14 and from this she gave $5.00 to the Young People's Society, bought some clothes, and was fitted with a new set of teeth. Drinking glasses, needles, silverware, dishes and kitchen utensils were sold. The members of the Women's Society of the church earned $70 by selling soap. A carpenter bought green bananas, sold them when ripe, and gave $3.00 to the church. Some of the members collected and sold empty bottles, lard cans, and old papers and gave the proceeds to the church. Women members bought rough toweling and sheeting, made them into finished articles, and sold them at a profit; some even made mattresses from rough materials. A baker loaned a corner of his oven to a poor woman member of the church for cake baking. She eventually built up a small cake business of her own from which she was able to support her family and as well gave regularly to the church.

[22] *Ibid.,* pp. 60, 61.

The women's societies of the churches of Michoacan State, Mexico, made it a practice to buy quantities of grain at harvest rates and retail it later in the season when prices had risen. This plan has provided a good income to the societies. In other parts of Mexico, church societies have made a profit from buying and selling soap.

The women members of a village congregation near Guadalajara, Mexico, determined to have a personal share in helping their church since the cash contributions of the peasant households were all made by the men. After various experiments, they formed a frog-catching-and-selling society. The Guadalajara markets offered cash for selected frogs' legs which were popular with the city people. The women worked in teams; one team caught the frogs, the other sold them in the city. On alternate weeks, the teams exchanged work. By devoting one day a week to the frog-catching industry, the women began to take an active part in the support of their church.[23]

The Talent Method is used by the women's missionary societies of various Latin American churches. Each member of the Women's Society of the First Congregational Church of Rio de Janeiro is given, as a loan, the equivalent of a dollar to invest. This is paid back with whatever profit has accrued from its investment. Some of the women buy woolen yarn and knit sweaters, caps, and shawls; others make dresses to sell; still others make pastry and cake.

Church Bazaars and Fairs. The church bazaar or sale is a finance method rather widely used, particularly among urban congregations. The bazaar provides a way by which the women members, many of whom have time but not money of their own, can help to support the church through the sale of their handwork. The church bazaar also brings the members together for social good times and this, in a measure, takes the place of the fiesta of the Roman Catholic community. The bazaar, too, attracts to the church people who would be reluctant to attend a religious service. "Practically all of our women's societies do sewing and make articles to sell at church bazaars or suppers in order to meet their part of the budget. The Toluca society (Mexico) has a regular sale at intervals of six or eight weeks. They feel that this work is a spiritual under-

[23] *Ibid.,* p. 70.

taking and that the sale and the supper promote Christian fellowship."[24]

A different estimate of the church bazaar and supper, however, is held by a Mexican pastor:

> I have found these methods unprofitable. They tend to waste time and energies, create misunderstandings among members and appeal to wrong motives. As social affairs they may prove helpful, but for promoting spirituality and aiding the finances of a church, they are worthless. The bazaar is a good thing for the poor woman who can only sew for the church, but for the people who expect to get bargains and at the same time fool themselves into thinking that they are contributing their part to the church, I think it is a bad practice.[25]

Processing of Agricultural Products. The canning of surplus fruit and vegetables, the making of grape juice or bean sauce, and the puffing of rice and wheat are methods which have been used in Japan for increasing the income of rural churches.

The pastor of the Furuma Parish in Nagano Prefecture noticed that vegetables and fruits were wasted during the summer and that the people needed to supplement their rice diet during the winter. So he installed a cooperative canning kitchen and the families in his church used it for canning a variety of vegetables.[26]

The pastor of the Iimorino Rural Parish near Kobe, devised a simple project by which the grapes of his vineyard were processed and bottled and the proceeds from their sale added materially to the income of his church.[27]

Another Japanese pastor-teacher at Nishiura, Shizuoka Prefecture, installed simple equipment for canning, making bean curd paste and baking. He shared the equipment with his people and taught them how to use it with the result that these methods of preparing and preserving foods were adopted by members of the farm households.[28]

Methods Used for Sunday School Children. In a town of ten thousand people in Buenos Aires Province, Argentina, is a small

---

[24] *Ibid.,* p. 69.

[25] *Ibid.,* pp. 69, 70.

[26] A. R. Stone, "The Rural Mission of the Church in Japan." An address given to the Emmanuel College Alumni Association, Toronto, September, 1943.

[27] Madras Series, Vol. V, pp. 223-225.

[28] Felton, *op. cit.,* p. 78.

Evangelical church of thirty-five members which with two rural churches and three preaching points is under the care of an energetic pastor. In an old motor bus, he visits his charges and carries groups of his young people to help in evangelistic work. A deacon described how the children and youth of the Sunday School raised funds for the church: The pupils are given three kinds of small savings banks, i.e., a trunk, a house, and a globe. The significance of each is explained to the children: the trunk represents travel costs of the pastor and his helpers in extension work; the house stands for the church building fund, and the globe points to the support of foreign missions. By these visual aids the objects to which their gifts are directed are made vivid to the children.

The "talent" method also is popular with the children. On January first, the pastor gives each pupil a one-peso, two-peso, or five-peso loan, with the agreement that it will be put to work for the church. Some of the pupils buy and sell small goods with their talent; others invest in chickens and sell the eggs; and still others make articles, food or candy for sale. At the end of the year a careful reckoning is made and at a public service each child comes forward and reports to the pastor. Through this experience, the children are trained to have a share in the life of the church.

The dramatic or allegoric method of raising church money is common with the young people. A "competitive race" of Sunday School classes with obstacles placed in the road is held. Classes with a bad year's record are handicapped by "mudholes" in the road, from which they have to be pulled out by a team of horses. Each "mudhole" costs the class a fixed fee which is contributed to the church budget.

A variation of this scheme is the "funeral procession" which passes a succession of cemeteries. The Argentine funeral is required by law to pay a municipal tax for a corpse that is carried through a town which possesses a cemetery. The Sunday School class with a bad record takes the rôle of the "dead man" who has to pay taxes as he is carried along to keep from being "buried."[29]

INTRODUCTION TO NEW FARMING METHODS

The Rev. Samuel Coles, an American negro agricultural missionary of the American Board at Galangue, Angola, observed

[29] J. M. Davis, *The Church in the River Plate Republics,* pp. 55, 56.

that the natives of his district planted grain only in the thin soil of the hillsides and uplands, with meagre yields. The rich bottom lands of the streams—reputed to be the abode of the spirits of the dead—were tabooed for cultivation. The native farmers also were compelled to work on the highways of the colony to earn cash for paying their hut taxes. With a pair of oxen, modern plow, and the use of an improved seed wheat, Mr. Coles cultivated creek bottom lands and, to the amazement of the onlooking natives, was not only unharmed by the taboo but harvested several times the yield of their own fields.

Some of the natives began to follow Mr. Coles' example and to use steel plows and their own draft oxen. At the end of the next harvest, these native farmers appeared at the local Portuguese store with bags of a new strain of wheat on their shoulders that brought a price with which they paid their hut taxes, and so were freed from the conscripted road work. Mr. Coles was invited to explain his methods at provincial official conferences and finally at the request of the Governor-General, addressed the annual conference of all the governors of the territory. In the course of ten years, 1,200 steel plows were in use by native farmers in the Galangue district alone, the government was distributing 1,000 tons of improved seed corn and wheat and the region took on a prosperity it had never before known.

Among the practical results of Mr. Coles' demonstration were the building by the natives of many neat stone houses with two and three rooms, the demand for new mission and government schools to accommodate the children of parents who were now able to give them an education, and the spread of the Galangue farming methods to many of the provinces of Angola. It is not surprising to learn that today a very large proportion of the churches of the American Board in Angola are self-supporting.

Another experiment used by Mr. Coles for improving the livelihood of Angola villagers was the plan of the "itinerant missionary hogs." Imported animals were crossed with native stock and acclimated to the Angola environment. A boar and sow were circulated among the rural communities. The pair of hogs was loaned to a village for a four months' period on the condition that the litter of pigs might remain the property of the villagers, provided they took good care of the parents and returned one pig to the mission. In due time a family of little pigs would be left in the village and the "missionary parents" resumed their journey to the next community where the process was repeated. In this way, at small cost to the mission, a new breed of hogs, weighing from two to three times the native stock and acclimated to the highlands of Angola, appeared in the Galangue district.

CHAPTER X

MORE METHODS

IN the foregoing chapter there has been discussed a variety of principles and methods by the use of which a local church may progress toward the support of its own life. The experience of individual churches in many different fields with these principles and methods was also described.

We will now consider the relation to such a forward step of the various leaders and agencies that are vitally concerned with the welfare of the Younger Churches.

The cooperation of five factors is needed if the movement toward Church financial independence is to be more than a series of sporadic and localized efforts. These factors are: The Church Pastor, The Missionary and the Mission in the Field, The National Church Body, The Mission Board, and The National Christian Council.

THE PASTOR AND THE LOCAL CHURCH

The pastor is the keystone in the edifice of the independent younger church. It is exceedingly difficult for a church to reach a self-supporting position without the active help of the leader who ministers to its spiritual growth.

A pastor who receives a large part of his salary regularly from outside sources will hardly look with favor upon a proposal to shift his support entirely to his parishioners. Such a move would seem to exchange a certainty for a risk, would endanger his economic security, and would place him and his family almost completely in the control of his church members. The pastor has inherited the tradition that his congregation is too poor to support him fully—a tradition that is accepted with equanimity by the church members.

1. The pastor himself must believe in the philosophy and practice

of a self-supporting church. If he has this belief and displays an enthusiasm for the principle, in time he will communicate that belief and enthusiasm to his congregation.

2. The pastor must also be convinced of the practicability of the principle of independence as applied to his own congregation. He must lift the idea of the financial independence of his church out of the realm of theory and relate it to his church members. This will require a sharing of his conviction with his officers, and with the members of his congregation. He must aim to understand the practical situation, the problems of livelihood, and the social and economic position of each family and in the light of this understanding help them to accept responsibility for the support of their church. On such knowledge as a foundation the pastor and his church officers should draft a long-term program of education, suggestion, and demonstration for the congregation, the Sunday School, and church societies.

3. The pastor will need a thorough knowledge of stewardship and should know how to teach it to his congregation. He must be prepared to devote himself to the program that is proposed to the church. He must be willing to share in the sacrifice and discipline which self-support demands of the congregation. He should lead in applying to himself and his household such measures as the Lord's Acre principle, tithing, and the various expedients for individual and household economies which are suggested to his people. While himself not taking the responsibility of raising the finances, which should be carried by the church Finance Committee, the pastor must be ready to inspire and lead his people to action.

4. The pastor must also be familiar with the chief methods through which his church will eventually realize self-support. If these subjects were not included in the pastor's seminary course, he will have to study them through literature provided by his Church body, the National Christian Council or the mission with which he is connected. Attendance at summer institutes where these subjects are studied would be invaluable and he would profit by visiting self-supporting parishes in his or other districts to observe the methods that are being used.

5. The self-supporting Younger Churches which have been studied

by the Department are, with few exceptions, led by pastors who regularly teach that it is the privilege and responsibility of the Christian to support his church. The Biblical basis of giving, the principle of stewardship of time, self, and substance, the practice of tithing, together with an emphasis upon the fact that the church is the possession of the members and that its welfare is in their hands, are some of the topics which the pastor presents to his congregation. The practice of pastors varies from preaching quarterly to once a year on this general theme. Conversely it was found that very few pastors of churches which were being largely supported by the mission boards included these subjects in their preaching schedule.

6. The pastor who is deeply concerned with the development of the financial independence of his church goes much farther than preaching on stewardship to his congregation. He concentrates upon the training of his catechumens in stewardship as a basic principle of the Christian life. The candidate training in stewardship and tithing of the Seventh Day Adventist Church is notable but by no means unique upon the mission field. Pastors of many denominational groups follow this practice and the financial strength of their churches is noticeable.

7. The pastor of a rural church who has only a theoretical knowledge of the livelihood problems of his people is heavily handicapped. If he has never raised a stalk of grain, or a bunch of vegetables, has never struggled with a garden in a drought or had his crops destroyed by cutworm or blight and his animals decimated by cholera, he will find an invisible but real barrier between himself and his parishioners. He can only dimly understand the meaning of the most vital experiences of his congregation. The monthly check which is paid by his mission or the central fund, his strange vocabulary and different background, all contribute to make the pastor appear to his people as someone from another world. Should the pastor work with his hands in the soil and share in some of the livelihood activities of his parishioners, it would not only draw him closer to them, but it would be a wholesome example in a society which considers physical work beneath the dignity of an educated man.

The pastor who cultivates a garden or a patch of corn or keeps a cow or a flock of chickens creates a degree of solidarity with his people; he can share with the church members in practicing the techniques of the Lord's Acre, and he can add substantially to his own income. With a garden, the pastor can diversify the food for his family and by introducing new varieties of vegetables, fruit, and livestock can help the community. Gardening also offers a source of needed physical exercise which may materially contribute to the pastor's health and it is, as well, an activity in which the members of his family may share.

Gardening is not urged upon the rural pastor in order to relieve the church of its responsibility to support him, but rather as an effective means by which he may establish a solidarity with his people and as a contributory measure toward strengthening the rural church.

The congregation is a fluid cross-section of the larger community with old and middle-aged people, youth, and children. Its units are constantly changing. Losses by death and removal to other localities and defections from membership are met by accessions through births, the entrance of Christians from other localities, and the baptism of new believers. If the older church members are fixed in their ways and niggardly in their giving habits, there is always the younger generation coming forward and, under suitable training, their standards may be lifted above those of their parents. With this movement in the membership in mind, education assumes a major place in the work of the pastor.

The Sunday School and young people's groups are the logical and most repaying fields for instruction in those habit-forming practices that prepare for membership participation in the church. The Seventh Day Adventist Church looks upon the Sabbath School as the seed-bed for cultivating the habit of giving to the church. It is the source of very large sums which are raised for foreign missions over and above the tithing gifts of the churches. The Sabbath School systematically teaches the children the principles and practice of giving and follows up this training to adulthood. When a child has been under this training from its earliest years, the practice of tithing is apt to be fixed for life.

The Baptist churches of Mexico hold annual educational contests on the subject of stewardship for the young people of their Sunday Schools. Prizes are offered for the best essays. Two age groups are included—one for children between the ages of twelve and sixteen, the other for older young people. The winners in the local Sunday Schools compete in the district contests. The successful essays in the district contests compete at the annual convention of the Baptist Church and the winning essay is published. An oratorical competition on the theme of stewardship is organized in much the same manner. These contests arouse great interest among both children and adults and have furthered the practice of stewardship and giving among the Baptist churches in Mexico.[1]

An annual "Stewardship Week" is observed by several Latin American churches, notably the Baptist church in Ponce, Puerto Rico, and the Methodist church in Porto Alegre, Brazil. The pastor opens the week by preaching upon stewardship, tithing, and other methods of giving. Literature suited to the various age groups is provided. Each day a special meeting is arranged under the leadership of Sunday School pupils, women's society members, the young people and the men of the church. The Biblical basis of stewardship and the various methods of earning and saving money for the church are discussed and there are demonstrations of handwork, Lord's Acre projects, and other practical devices. The week is closed by a second Sunday Stewardship Service conducted by representatives of all the church organizations including the children of the Sunday School. Some churches use this week as an occasion for enlisting new givers to the church budget and for increasing the pledges of members who are already contributing.

Many of the Presbyterian churches of Mexico hold each year a "Reconsecration Service."[2] At this service a renewal of vows of devotion to the church and its work is made. One by one the members come forward and after a brief dedication of self to God, place an offering before the altar. This practice has been followed especially by the church young people and has served to identify their faith with their practice and to strengthen their loyalty to the church.

"Sacrifice Week" is used widely by the Seventh Day Adventists and also by some other churches. For seven days all of the members of church and Sabbath School are asked to forego some routine expense, luxury or necessity and devote the money saved to the church. Some members reduce their eating to two meals a day;

[1] J. M. Davis, *The Economic Basis of the Evangelical Church in Mexico*, p. 66.
[2] *Ibid.*, p. 66.

others forego the use of sugar, butter, candy, etc., while still others walk to and from their places of business and deny themselves amusements and the cost of various customary activities.

THE MISSIONARY AND THE MISSION IN THE FIELD

The native worker and pastor tend to reflect the stature of the missionary with whom they work and by whom they are trained. The vision of the native leader is often bounded by the horizons of the missionary while the missionary's interests and his estimate of the task of the church are reflected in those of his native associate. If the missionary exhibits little enthusiasm for the development of self-support in the church and puts this problem in a place of secondary importance, there is small likelihood that the enthusiasm or conviction of his native associate will exceed his own.[3]

The rôle of the missionary in promoting the principle and practice of church independence will vary according to the measure of leadership which is required of him, the stage of development of the churches in his field, and the nature of his tasks. Whatever the nature of his immediate tasks, the missionary should never forget that the basic purpose of his mission is to found and develop an indigenous church. This requires of him an acquaintance with the business principles of church management and a clear grasp of the relation of spiritual growth to Christian giving and the stability of the Church. He should be prepared to help his native associates to understand this relationship and should be able to assist the churches with which he is connected to accept the principle of independence and the proven methods and practices which will contribute to that end.

The opportunity of the missionary who is pioneering in new areas to help young congregations without the use of money is difficult to overstate. In a pioneer field no inheritance of subsidy exists and the habit of dependence upon others has not been formed. Such new communities present to the missionary a virgin field for experimentation in laying new foundations. However, the possibility of success in such a situation will be limited by the attitude of the missionary society to which the worker is responsible, the acceptance by the mission on the field of such experimentation,

[3] J. M. Davis, "The Preparation of the Missionary for Work in the Post-War Era," p. 23, International Missionary Council, 156 Fifth Avenue, New York.

and the cooperation of the National Church with which new subsidy-free congregations will eventually be incorporated. The example of subsidized congregations in contiguous areas may prove to be a further practical obstacle to the success of such an experiment.

A *sine qua non* for the development of a church from which foreign financial aid is to be withheld is the conviction of its feasibility on the part of the missionary himself. To gain and steadily to hold such a conviction he will have to be a person of unusual courage, insight, and resourcefulness since he may have to challenge the experience of the mission and the policies upon which its work has been built. For such a conviction the missionary should be equipped with a knowledge of the history of outstanding churches on mission fields which have originated without the help of foreign money, or which have early gained an independent position. He should be familiar with the experience of the Karen Church of Burma, the Batak Church of Sumatra, the Church of Korea, and the churches of Samoa and Fiji[4] and the group of independent churches among the Indians of Peru. Before attempting to emulate the experience of any of these church groups, it would be an advantage for the missionary to visit one of their fields to study the methods used, the obstacles encountered, the mistakes that have been made and the weaknesses that may have developed in the inner life of the churches.

The new missionary should go to his field prepared to lead institutes and discussion groups upon the principles and practices of church management, finance, and self-support. It is not reasonable to expect him to be an expert in all these matters but he should have some familiarity with the techniques of the Lord's Acre, with the principles of tithing, the intensive use of little plots of land, the rearing of small livestock and with the principles of cooperatives. The missionary will need to carry with him practical literature upon these subjects for his own reference and for helping his associates. Before going abroad, he could advantageously establish contacts with sources of authority and of literature on these subjects with a view to assisting the native leaders through adaptations to local conditions and to possible translations of such material into the language of his people.

[4] Descriptions of these Churches and some of the lessons drawn from their experiences are discussed in Chapter VIII, "Some Outstanding Self-Supporting Churches."

As has been mentioned, the missionary and particularly the new appointee to a field is not a free agent in determining his course of action. He is subject to the direction of his mission body and the National Church which he is serving and must accept the type of work which is assigned to him. He should expect to find that proposals for experimenting and for changing established principles and policies will be met with a degree of reserve, if not of opposition, by his more experienced colleagues—both foreign and national.

The new recruit must understand that the rôle of the mission in the promotion of self-support among the established churches of its field is not a simple one. It is limited by the stage of church development, the quality of its leadership, and the degree of its autonomy. Often the mission has to deal with a generation of pastors who long have looked to it as the chief source of their support and with a body of church members who have accommodated their giving standards to the principle of mission subsidy. Arbitrarily and suddenly to cut off financial aid would be disastrous to the life of the churches and to the morale of the pastors. Drastic changes of policy to win the hearty cooperation of pastor and people, must come about through their own conviction and initiative and should be accompanied and, whenever possible, preceded by a period of preparation and education. However, usually some initiative and suggestion will be required of the missionary or the mission.

A striking example of these principles is that of the experience of the Ecclesia Evangelica Peruana, of Lima, Peru.[5] One of the strongest Evangelical congregations in the country, this urban church, after a generation, was still largely dependent upon the mission for its support.

Less than one-half of the members were contributing regularly to the church expenses, in amounts which averaged only ten or fifteen cents a week. The missionary, with the pastor, proposed to the Finance Committee that the congregation be called together to determine the budget for the ensuing year. Item after item was presented, discussed, and finally accepted by the congregation. The budget totalled between three and four times the average annual contributions of the church members. The members then began a

[5] John Ritchie, *Indigenous Church Principles in Theory and Practice*, Fleming H. Revell Co., New York, 1945.

lively debate as to how such a budget could be raised. It was agreed that the money must be secured but opinions differed as to the methods to be used.

During nine successive meetings the matter was discussed. The opinion of each member was invited, his scheme for meeting the budget was heard, and the weakness of the plan was pointed out by the members themselves before it was abandoned. At the ninth meeting when all had been heard the pastor proposed the plan of the missionary. Under this proposal, the total budget was divided by fifty-two weeks of the year and the result was divided again by the number of church members. This showed that, by an average gift of sixty cents a week per member, the entire budget could be met. The procedure was so simple and clear that it won the approval and cooperation of the congregation. An every-member canvass was carried out with the result that the church has continued from that year to be self-supporting. This outcome was made possible only after the ideas and misgivings of every member had been given serious and unhurried consideration.[6]

A principle used by some of the Baptist missions in Latin America is to designate as churches only those congregations which are able fully to support their own pastor and meet the current expenses of operating the church. Congregations assisted by the mission are called "preaching points," or "preaching missions," and do not come into a status of autonomy and self-government until they can fully maintain their own minister. The Independent Presbyterian Churches of Brazil make a distinction between their churches which are helped by the "Regional (or Central) Fund," and those which are completely self-supporting. The latter are called "Churches with Effective Pastors."

THE NATIONAL CHURCH BODY

1. *A Central Organization and Direction of Church Finance and Giving*

The part of the National Church in stimulating and guiding the local congregations in their financial management and practice is basic for the development of the indigenous church. Occasional and intensive effort by local pastors alone cannot take the place

[6] For a detailed account of this incident and the steps in organizing this church upon a self-supporting basis, the reader is referred to the Appendix.

of a centralized policy and action. Nowhere on the mission field has this principle been more successfully demonstrated than by the General Assembly of the Presbyterian Church of Korea. One of the departments of this Church is the "Systematic Giving Board."[7] In forming this board, the General Assembly recognized that the financing of the Church must be well organized and governed by definite principles and practices and that it must be directed by a qualified leader and provided with adequate facilities. Systematic giving in the churches could not be brought about by haphazard, intermittent or unskilled supervision nor by leaving it to local initiative.

The Presbyterian General Assembly placed its Systematic Giving Board under the direction of one of its most experienced missionaries, the late Dr. Herbert E. Blair of Taikyu. To his vision and skill the success of the board's work has been due. Dr. Blair associated with himself able Korean leaders and from his office literature and careful directions were sent out which stimulated the 3,000 Presbyterian churches of the Assembly.

The task of the board was to educate the Korean churches in stewardship and to organize and assist the local congregations in its practice. A further task was to acquaint the churches with the nature of the general work of the Church. Three pamphlets were prepared: "What is Stewardship?", "A Guide to Stewardship," and "The Pastor's Responsibility as to Stewardship." These were used as outlines by pastors in their winter Bible classes. They presented the Biblical basis of stewardship and the practical methods for installing systematic giving in the churches. The pastor's handbook outlined the responsibility of the pastor, the advantages of systematic giving, and methods of putting it in practice. It also provided a list of useful stewardship sermon themes and outlines. Hundreds of these booklets were printed and supplied at cost to the churches.

The Systematic Giving Board also prepared benevolence supplies and materials. It was not enough to teach systematic giving: it was necessary to provide the needed equipment. Pledge cards, envelopes, account sheets and lists of instructions were prepared and distributed. Wherever possible the churches printed their own

[7] See Herbert E. Blair, *Christian Stewardship in Korea,* International Missionary Council, 156 Fifth Avenue, New York.

supplies locally. This enabled the local church to display its name and picture upon the material and to adapt the plan to its particular needs. The preparing of their own supplies stimulated a lively interest in stewardship and its methods among the church officers. Instead of the envelope plan, a cheap pad of fifty-two pages, four by four inches in size, was used. The same number was printed on each page of the pad. The member tore off a page, placed a coin on the back of the sheet, folded it with the number exposed and put it into the church collection bag.

The checking sheets had places for names, numbers, and amounts of weekly pledges and each was divided into fifty-two squares, so that a mark could be inserted for each weekly gift. The records of five members were on each page. The treasurer's accounts were regularly audited by the Finance Committee and the pastor.

The Systematic Giving Board sent out trained men to teach stewardship among the churches. Stewardship lessons also were included in the annual Bible classes. The theological seminary and the Bible institute had special courses upon church finance and systematic giving. Each year the board aimed to publish a new pamphlet upon some phase of stewardship.

The every-member canvass is carried out in home-to-home visitation by the pastor accompanied by an elder and a deacon. The schedule of visitation is announced in advance from the pulpit. The visitors inquire about the members of the family and their spiritual progress. They discuss crops. They discuss the church budget. They go over the giving record of the family during the past year and try to secure a larger pledge from each member for the year to come. Through these painstaking methods churches grow in power as their members are faced with the necessity of honest living and accounting of their stewardship.[8]

Since the organization of the Systematic Giving Board in 1930, the total expenditures of the Presbyterian Church of Korea increased from Yen 1,117,703.03 to Yen 1,913,306.50 in 1937.

The work of the eight special boards of the Presbyterian General Assembly was financed by the annual Thanksgiving offering in the local churches between the end of harvest and Christmas. This special offering added about 20 per cent to the normal church budget and the income was divided on a pro-rata basis among

[8] Herbert E. Blair, *op. cit.*

the general boards. The work of the boards was described in special pamphlets which were distributed among the churches so that the members might understand the causes to which they were asked to give. These boards, with the relative size of their budgets, included Home Missions 33 per cent, Foreign Missions 43 per cent, Christian Education 12 per cent, Christian Endeavor 3 per cent, Leper Work 4 per cent, Theological Seminary 1 per cent, Student Aid 3 per cent and Charity Committee expenses 1 per cent.

2. *Stimulation of a National Group of Churches*

Chile offers a notable example of a National Church superintendent who has dealt personally with each of the churches in his field on the problems of its inner life, including finances. In 1943, there were sixty-eight Methodist churches in Chile which were under the care of twenty-five pastors. The pastors' salaries had not kept pace with the rise in the cost of living. On being appointed to the field, Bishop Balloch found his pastors with a lowered morale, discouraged, and struggling desperately to live upon an inadequate income. The congregations were very poor and only three or four of the churches were self-supporting. Church life was at low ebb and some pastors were leaving the ministry.

The Bishop decided to make a personal, unhurried visit to each church in his field to study its whole position and to introduce new methods, training, and courage. Night after night he met with the congregation, and day after day he called upon each member and family. His aim was to draw out all the problems of the church by the free discussion of the members. They discussed the problems of the pastor, of church support, the position of the church in the community, the spiritual and personal difficulties of the families, their economic struggles and the education of the children. The Bishop met with the women's societies, the young people, the children and the laymen. With pastor and congregation he planned a year's program. This included an evangelistic campaign, an institute for member training, and retreats for deepening the spiritual life and for the study of prayer. He also linked these training classes to the question of stewardship and self-support. He remained with each church from two to five weeks and left the congregations inspired and refreshed, and their pastors with new vision, methods, and goals at which to aim.

The Bishop was prepared to spend two or more years in such visitation since he was convinced that, though a costly method in time and strength, it was the best way to vitalize run-down churches, to strengthen their inner life, and prepare them for self-support.

In the City Church Round Table discussion at the Madras Conference, a system of standards among the Younger Churches was discussed by which those churches that meet the highest tests of efficiency in missionary activity, in Sunday School work, in evangelistic extension, in full self-support, young people's activities and in cooperating with the general work of the Church body would be recognized as "Red Letter" or "Gold Star" churches. Different designations would apply to churches attaining lower standards of efficiency. The plan would offer a special incentive to congregations to lift themselves out of a weak or mediocre status and definite goals would be set toward which each church could strive.[9]

THE MISSION BOARD

The freedom of a foreign mission board to implement new financial policies in its field program is definitely limited by the degree to which the native Church with which it is related is autonomous and self-governing, the commitments it has made to the support of native workers, its financial obligations for the operation of institutional work and the economic strength of the churches.

A further and formidable factor is the traditional policy with regard to financial aid to which the native workers, the church members, the missionaries and the mission board itself have become accustomed. The conviction of the economic helplessness of the people and the necessity of assisting them with mission money has come down from former generations and has created a body of crystallized opinion which is most difficult to change. Further obstacles to the altering of mission board financial policies are the expensive type of building construction and equipment in relation to the economic level of the Christian community and the comparatively high standards of amenities to which the trained native leaders have become adjusted. The whole mission enterprise frequently has been placed upon a level beyond the supporting power

[9] Unpublished findings of a special group on the problems of the urban church which were presented by Dr. E. H. Cressy to the Plenary Session of the Madras Conference.

of its native constituency. On the other hand, with this trend there has not been a parallel emphasis upon training missionaries, national leaders, and church members in the principles and practice of self-support and its relation to the spiritual growth of the Church.

The methods by which foreign mission boards have sought to stimulate the growth of self-support among the Younger Churches fall into several categories:

1. *Subsidy Reduction*

The plan most widely used is the systematic reduction of subsidy to the local churches. An annual decrease of five or ten percent of the board's stipend to an assisted church is made with the understanding that at the end of a stated period the congregation will carry the whole financial load. Sometimes the reduction is based upon the decreased amount of mission subsidy. Dr. Felton calls this "the tapering off plan"[10] and considers it the least successful of all expedients for developing self-supporting churches. A basic difficulty with this method is that it provides the least hope of success with the smaller churches which most need help. Where a large congregation may be able to meet the reduction in subsidy, smaller and weaker churches are apt to lose hope as they look forward to the complete cessation of outside help. Frequent results of subsidy reduction are the cutting off of extension activities and educational work in the church, the decrease of the pastor's salary with the forcing of the pastor to take outside income-gaining work, and the sharing of his ministry and salary with other churches. In many cases subsidy reduction tends to retard the growth of a church, to contract its activities, and to discourage or entirely lose its pastor. A gradual reduction of subsidy often fails of its purpose because the solution of the problem calls for more than the use of a mathematical formula. Spiritual growth, education, psychology and demonstration are all vital factors that enter the equation.

A common reason for the failure of the policy of subsidy reduction to stimulate a church to financial independence is that little or nothing has been put into the life of the church members to take the place of the help that has been taken away and they have not been assisted to meet the problem. A new estimate of the church and of their responsibility for it, a new willingness to sacrifice

---

[10] Ralph A. Felton, *The Rural Church in the Far East,* p. 142.

and a new expenditure of time, energy, and substance somehow must be stimulated in the congregation. This cannot be done alone by the announcement of an annual decrease of help from the mission. In some way spiritual power must be generated in the church to provide the dynamic of decision and effort needed to meet the new financial demands upon the members.

With this in view a period of preparation and of education for developing new power and instilling new habits is required if the vacuum caused by the withdrawal of subsidy is to be filled.

2. *Fifty-fifty Plan*

Another means of stimulating self-support employed by some boards is the "fifty-fifty plan."[11] By this arrangement the mission board matches dollar for dollar the amount provided by the local church. There is a certain incentive to larger giving by a congregation which knows that its contributions will be equalled by the board's gift but, on the other hand, such a church is apt to adjust its giving to the amount of help it receives. The uniform application of the plan in a mission field may prevent jealousies between the churches which otherwise might receive unequal grants. But when rigidly applied, the churches that can pay the least toward their own budgets receive the least help in spite of the fact that they need it the most. Under this plan, in special crises such as the moving away or death of leading members or crop failure, the income of a weak church may be reduced almost to the vanishing point.

3. *The Project Plan*

We are indebted to the Presbyterian Church in the U.S.A. for the data used in this description of the operation of its Project Plan in China. This is one of the most recent and successful of the policies through which the life of the Younger Churches has been vitalized and cooperation in the use of resources of funds and personnel has been achieved between a mission and a National Church.

The plan is described in some detail because of its proved success in demonstrating the intimate relation that the spiritual vitalizing of the churches, together with the enlistment of Chinese

[11] Felton, *ibid.,* p. 141.

Christians in definite lines of service, bears to the self-supporting power of the Church.

The Project Plan has been the means of cooperation between Church and mission in meeting the definite spiritual needs of the churches and encouraging their outreach into their communities. It is recognized that only the Spirit of God working in and through the churches can make them a vital power in a community. Dependence on mission subsidies has, in numerous cases, been found to be a deadening influence on the life of the Younger Churches. The centering of the churches' attention on a study of their needs, the extension of their services to the community with the full use of their available resources, and the making of plans to meet these needs have often been the means of the inflowing of spiritual life and of outward growth.

A project is a piece of work with clearly defined objectives and plans to meet specific needs within a limited period of time. Adequate reports—both narrative and financial—and an evaluation of objectives and results must be given, showing evidence of growth in vital life and usually issuing in an increased measure of self-support. Renewals of grants depend upon satisfactory annual reports. A non-self-supporting church may organize its work around several project objectives but is not given a grant to install a pastor before it is able to assume his support; however, it may temporarily have the part time of a pastor to help it become a unit of a self-supporting circuit of churches.

The work of unorganized groups of Christians may also be eligible for aid in project programs which look to the building up of a self-supporting church or making it a unit in a self-supporting circuit. It should usually be sponsored by a group of reliable Christians or a project committee of a nearby church. Only projects which can give evidence of building up the spiritual life and outreach of a church are helped. All non-self-supporting churches are urged to become self-supporting as soon as possible.

The Project Board usually covers a province-wide or synodical area but occasionally a strong Presbytery has its own Project Board. The board evaluates the project applications and plans presented to it by sponsoring groups and makes grants-in-aid to supplement local effort. The Project Board covers a large enough area to have a wide knowledge of needs and a discriminating judgment on the relative values of projects, and yet be free from local bias and pressure. The board receives reports of the progress of each project before additional grants are made to it. Members of the Project Board may be either Chinese or missionaries but no member of a board may be a beneficiary of the funds administered by it.

A few regions have a Project Secretary who works with the Project Board. His duties are to stimulate the life and activity of the churches and cooperate with local sponsoring groups in organizing and carrying out spiritually worth while projects. He promotes stewardship, religious education, and the training and supervision of lay workers, helps the churches to realize their needs, and shows them practical ways of meeting these needs along the lines of the Project Plan.

The Report of the Project Board of the Wan Peh Presbytery at Nanhsuchow, Anwhei, (1935-1936) covers eleven projects for which it was responsible. The most successful of these projects was that on *stewardship*. Its aim was to investigate, teach, and put into practice the principles of stewardship in order to help the church to an independent and self-supporting basis.

Among the *methods* used were:
A special study of stewardship at the Workers' Retreat,
Preaching on this subject throughout the churches of the field,
A Stewardship Committee for putting the principle into practice,
The study of stewardship in leader's classes, in country sessions, and inquirer's classes. Special emphasis on stewardship at the Annual Meeting,
Two months of one deacon's time was given to promotion through the field.

Among the *results* noted were:
Two hundred and forty-seven members and workers signed as tithers,
A committee formed to supervise tithing, with responsibility for keeping up interest in the subject,
A good leaflet on stewardship prepared to be given to every literate Christian.
The actual cost of the whole stewardship project was only CN$16.78.

Other projects of this Presbytery included:
Hospital Evangelism, A Literate Bible Reading Church, Evangelism in all the cities of the field, Gospel and Bible distribution.

Sample projects of other Presbyteries included:
a) A study of church membership—men, women, children. The rate of increase in members. The effect of a church group upon the life of a village,
b) Visitation of isolated Christians for strengthening them in their environment,
c) Preparation of several rural groups for calling a pastor,
d) Education of a church made up largely of illiterate women,
e) Lay worker training and supervision,
f) Projects for children: health education, vaccination, fruit tree spraying,
g) The intensive cultivation of Christian life among country and city Christians.

Among the gratifying *results* noted in the reports of these projects were:
a) The large measure of responsibility taken by the local sponsoring groups,
b) Careful studies made of the needs of the field as a whole,
c) Defining specific, attainable aims for meeting these needs within the allotted time,
d) Carefully thought-out plans for each project,
e) Cooperation of the entire working force, paid and voluntary, in the several projects,
f) Outside workers used for brief, intensive service,
g) A realistic facing of results and an evaluation of causes of success and failure,
h) An enlarged vision for future projects, profiting by both past mistakes and successes.

In spite of the serious dislocations to the work of nearly all the churches caused by the war, fifteen of the twenty-seven mission stations using the Project Plan reported that it was working satisfactorily, five that it was fairly satisfactory, and seven that it was not satisfactory.

Prior to the introduction of the Project Plan in the Presbytery of south Shantung, the thirty-six churches had all been receiving financial aid from the mission. The new spiritual vitality and initiative aroused by the effort to solve their own felt needs resulted, among other forward steps, in every one of this group of churches lifting itself to a self-supporting position.

At the thirtieth annual meeting of the China Council of the Presbyterian Church, it was reported that, in spite of the war, where it had been consistently carried out, the Project Plan had vindicated its value and all the stations of the board were urged to change to the project basis as soon as possible.[12]

4. Outside Employment

A fourth policy used by some mission boards is to admit the dilemma of local self-support and allow their ministers to take outside salaried employment to supplement their inadequate incomes. This practice is followed among the churches of several denominations in Latin American lands and is occasionally used in the Oriental mission fields.

Teaching, medical practice, and literary work are among the most common extra-pastoral activities while legal practice and employment as interpreters and translators and even small trades are also followed. Such activities sometimes enlarge the service which a pastor can render his church and the general community, and they are justified by some because of the wider outreach and contact with the public which they provide. The added income enables the pastor to give his children a type of education and his family and himself a standard of living and a prestige in the community which would be impossible on the basis of his church income alone.

The pastor who devotes a part of his time to an outside salaried position inevitably exposes his church to the danger of neglect since the supplementary work often makes a major claim upon his interest. While the lightening of their own financial burden is readily welcomed by the congregation, it is too often accompanied by a reduction of their church contributions on the one hand, and, on the other, by the loss of pastoral care and church growth.

Finally, the example of a minister who has to secure a portion of his income from outside employment lowers the dignity of his calling in the estimate of potential candidates for the ministry and runs the risk of discrediting the Church.

[12] Report of the Thirtieth Annual Meeting, China Council, pp. 80-81.

5. *The Nevius Plan*

The Nevius Plan of developing self-supporting churches has been fully described in Chapter VIII, in the section devoted to the Church in Korea. Promoted with great vigor by its originator, Dr. John L. Nevius, in Shantung, between 1880 and 1890, the plan was rejected by his colleagues who claimed that it had failed to demonstrate its power to establish permanently self-supporting Chinese churches. The Nevius Plan is a striking example of the vitality of a philosophy of mission work when transplanted and energetically applied in a different racial and cultural soil. The experience of the Korean Presbyterian mission with the use of the Nevius Plan gives it a very high place among all the methods used by foreign missions in founding the indigenous Younger Church.

Interesting variations of the five methods for stimulating local church self-support listed above are described by Frank Rawlinson in his series of articles entitled, "Western Money and the Chinese Church."[13] These methods are designated, The Emergency Plan, The Pauline Plan, The Half-Time Plan, The Self-Help Plan, The Self-Service Plan, and The First Aid Plan.

Several of the great North American mission boards have created a major office within their organizations known as the *Department of Income Production*. The responsibility of this department is to stimulate and encourage the missionary giving of the local churches of the denomination. The program is highly organized and ably led and has in many instances markedly increased the support of the foreign missionary enterprise.

Paralleling this development the last decade has seen the growth of *Stewardship Councils* within the great Church bodies.[14] Some of these councils have developed an imposing volume of educational material, numbering into the hundreds of items, upon the theme of stewardship and the spiritual basis of giving to the Church and ranging from two-leaf flyers, pamphlets, and posters to ably-written study courses and printed volumes. This material has been used by many thousands of North American churches and has had a marked influence upon the spiritual life and giving practices of their members.

---

[13] *The Chinese Recorder,* Shanghai, Vol. LX, No. 2, April, 1929.
[14] The United Stewardship Council of Hillsdale, Michigan, enrolls twenty-five communions in the United States and Canada.

The Youth Budget Plan of the Presbyterian Church, U. S. A., now entering its twelfth year, is operating in over 2,000 churches and has stimulated the systematic giving of the youth of the denomination in amounts varying from five to twenty per cent of the entire budgets of their churches.[15]

We are impelled to ask why, when such centralized and efficient business and educational measures are considered necessary and have proved their effectiveness for strengthening Christian giving among the churches which possess the Christian heritage of North America, comparable attention has not been given to the strengthening of the weak and struggling churches in mission lands,—churches for which the North American Church is responsible. If such intensive organization and education is necessary for the Christian movement of America, it is surely as necessary for the Christian movement of lands in which the concept of the Church and the practice of sacrificial giving are as yet in their infancy.

We venture the prediction that if, for a full decade, this responsibility of promoting Christian giving and education in stewardship and in church finance were to be seriously undertaken by all the foreign missionary societies in cooperation with the National Church bodies of mission lands, there would result a startling reduction in the seventy-five or eighty per cent of the fifty-five thousand Younger Churches that are now supported in whole or in part by the Christians of North America and Europe.

As pointed out elsewhere in this discussion, such a result would annually release an aggregate of many millions of dollars in the budgets of the foreign missionary societies to be made available for the carrying of the Gospel of Christ to the, as yet, vast unevangelized populations of the world.

THE NATIONAL CHRISTIAN COUNCIL

The National Christian Councils in the lands of the Younger Churches are exerting a potent influence upon the inner life of the Christian movement.

Among the cogent reasons for the appearance of the National Christian Council has been the recognition that the churches of all denominations are facing common problems,—problems which are

[15] The Youth Budget Plan Committee, General Council, Presbyterian Church, U.S.A., 156 Fifth Avenue, New York.

increasing in number and complexity. Many of the issues faced by all mission boards and National Churches not only are identical but demand a specialized treatment which is beyond the power of a majority of mission boards and National Churches to provide separately.

Such matters as education in its many branches, medical work, industrialization, home and family, rural reconstruction, cooperatives, literacy and literature, religious liberty, student and youth activities, narcotics and the liquor traffic can, with great advantage, be dealt with unitedly and they all require trained leadership.

These problems are related to the welfare of the whole nation as well as that of the Church, are integrated with government programs, and require a wider perspective and experience than the individual Church body or mission possesses.

The National Christian Council meets the requirements of the mission field for research, field survey, and the gathering and analysis of facts that are needed by all the churches and missions for formulating policies and devising programs.

The National Christian Council of China for many years has been serving the Christian movement in a wide variety of special lines. As listed in the National Christian Council "News Letter" of April 1st and 15th, 1944, the following commissions and committees are sponsored:

The Commission on the Life and Work of the Church
The Commission on Christian Education and the Chinese Christian Education Association
The Commission for Church and Alumni Work
The Commission on Christian Medical Work
The Commission on Christian Literature
The Commission on Christian Social Service, including the National Christian Council Relief Committee, affiliated with the relief program of the New Life Movement
The Committee on Legal Relations
The National Committee for Christian Religious Education
The Editorial Office, National Christian Council "News Letter"
The Editorial Office, "The Chinese Bulletin"
The Foreign Missions Office

For many years the Commission on Home and Family Life

rendered a most valuable service to the Christian movement of China but it has been discontinued for the duration of the war.

These commissions and committees are served by carefully chosen leaders who are giving largely in time and strength to their respective activities, under the direction of the secretaries of the Council.

The National Christian Council of India is rendering notable service to the whole Christian movement of the country in dealing with many specialized aspects of the life of the Church. The following standing boards and committees of the Council are listed in the 1944 report of the Ninth Meeting of the National Christian Council held at Nagpur, January 28 to February 1, 1944:

Central Board of Christian Higher Education (with its subsidiary
    Committee on Research and Extension)
High School Committee
Committee on Theological Education
Committee on Christian Marriage Act and Divorce
The War Emergency Fund Committee
Famine Relief Fund Committee
Adult Literacy Committee
Committee on Medical Work
Committee on Work Among Moslems
Committee on Christian Literature
Committee on Christian Home
Committee on the "Treasure Chest"
Committee on Smaller Area Tribal Questions
Commission on the Organization and Functions of Christian Councils

Through its Committee on Research and Extension, the National Christian Council carried out and published eighteen studies of the Church and its environment made by Christian colleges in preparation for the Madras Conference.

It has also sponsored important studies of Indian village life, of the religious life and beliefs of college students, of the status of Indian theological education, and of Christian mass movement areas.

Recently two highly qualified secretaries have been added to the National Christian Council staff for special attention to the economic welfare of the Church and the problem of rehabilitating the enlisted men of the Indian Army upon their return to civil life.

The question of the stabilization of the churches in their environment is basic to the whole Christian movement. Problems of the economic basis of the Church, the livelihood of the people, the business management and organization of the Church, Christian stewardship and the support of the corporate religious life are issues which every one of the thousands of Younger Churches is facing. These also are issues that, with great advantage, can be studied and interpreted by the central staff of the National Christian Council. While many of the National Christian Councils have not, as yet, adequate strength for such specialized tasks, there is no group of church problems to which a Council could address itself which would yield more vital or needed results for quickening the inner life of the churches, and insuring their permanent and self-propagating power than this subject of the stabilization of the Church in its environment.

CHAPTER XI

THE COMPREHENSIVE PARISH PROGRAM

The one inclusive purpose of the missionary enterprise is to present Jesus Christ to men and women the world over as their Redeemer and to win them for entrance into the joy of His discipleship. In this endeavor we realize that man is a unity and that his spiritual life is indivisibly rooted in all his conditions—physical, mental, and social. We are therefore desirous that the program of missionary work among all peoples may be sufficiently comprehensive to serve the whole man in every aspect of his life and relationships.[1]

CHRISTIANITY makes the sweeping claim that its Founder is "Lord of all Life," but it is only within recent decades that His Missionary Church has accepted the full implications of that claim. Christ, as Lord of all Life, reflects the comprehensive will of God that life as a whole should be redeemed.

Painfully the Church has been learning that complete redemption of a man or a community cannot take place in one area of human experience, i.e., the spiritual, alone; that the dissection of the life of the man or the social order into spiritual, physical, and economic segments defeats the possibility of full redemption because the basic unity of life is destroyed and the interrelation and harmonious action of natural and spiritual law are ignored. Such fragmentation of the missionary program indefinitely postpones the realization of the Kingdom of Heaven which Jesus taught and exemplified.

Arthur T. Mosher in his, *The Kingdom of God and Rural Reconstruction,* tells us that when part of a mission program pursues economic, social, intellectual and political goals in a secular manner, while another part tries to supplement this by religious

---

[1] *Missions and Rural Problems,* Vol. VI, p. 246, Report of the Jerusalem Meeting of the International Missionary Council, 1928. 156 Fifth Avenue, New York, and 2 Eaton Gate, S.W.1, London.

teaching, the result is an inner conflict in the program. A secular approach and a religious attitude are incompatible. Since extending the Kingdom involves the extension of religious attitudes, we must use a religious approach to all problems. Instead of trying to Christianize a secular rural program, let us see to what Christian rural program the Gospel itself commits us.

Mosher suggests that our Christian rural program should include *four* phases:

First, teaching the Gospel records . . . it is hardly conceivable that a Christian community could be established without an acquaintance with the Bible.

Second, an interpretation of the Gospel in terms of modern village living.

Third, an emphasis on stewardship including health, time, productive resources and personal ability as well as cash in hand.

Fourth, the Christian program must provide for establishing personal and group habits of prayer, study, discussion and expression which will conserve the teaching, support a discipleship, and inspire to the discovery of new implications of the Gospel.[2]

In view of the rapidly growing secularization of all modern life which is defeating the religious interpretations of non-Christan as well as Christian cultures, the comprehensive program of the Church takes on an enormous significance.

Christianity makes common cause with the great ethnic faiths in the face of the world spirit of materialism that threatens to engulf all religions everywhere. More than any other agency the Church itself is responsible for this world trend toward secularization for too often it has cut itself off from permeating the so-called secular areas of life.

There is no greater issue facing Christians in the modern world than the question, "How can we bring under the aegis of the Church education, health, recreation, livelihood and the other areas of life which are now being left to the secularizing influence of government and private agencies?" To abandon these areas to the domination of irreligious forces and to fail to make them

[2] The Christian Rural Fellowship Bulletin, No. 56, November, 1940.

vehicles of the Christian witness amounts to a betrayal of God as Creator of all and In-dweller in all of life.[3]

Mosher, in his "The Spiritual Basis of a Comprehensive or 'Larger Parish' Program," says,

The spiritual basis of the comprehensive program we discuss here is the revelation of God in Jesus Christ. It is a staggering acknowledgment that this program ought to embody and present, not primarily the most modern methods of education, the most advanced programs of public health, the most efficient methods of cultivation, nor effective measures for promoting community solidarity, nor even a well-balanced combination of all of these, but the pure and comprehensive will of Eternal God for people living on the land. The task of our program is not to be a comprehensive omnibus of all good rural programs, but comprehending the Gospel and the nature of rural living, to present the God of Jesus Christ in terms which our generation can understand. . . . To bring that experience to rural people, and to help them express their answering allegiance in effective discipleship, is the purpose of the Christian Rural Mission.[4]

The separate approach of the missionary Church to non-Christian society which trains some people as evangelists, others as teachers, others as health workers, and still others as farm and social work specialists and which concentrates its efforts in preaching, teaching, health work and economic and social service in departments with building units and projects bearing these labels is giving way to a different concept and orientation of the Christian program. Under this approach, evangelization is cure of sick bodies, of broken-down, inefficient, and eroded farms, of illiteracy, of insufficient and unbalanced diet, unsanitary homes, impure drinking water, of a subsistence level of existence, of filthy villages, of the moral, mental, and spiritual stagnation of corrupt practices and conditions. Every effort upon this wide and comprehensive front of Christian service is a part of the Evangel and is required to enable the individual to reach the fulness of the stature which is in Christ.

The task of the Church is not finished when a convert is baptized. It has just begun. There remains the slow and laborious task of creating an environment in which the "smoking flax" of faith will not be quenched and, further, of so equipping the new Christian

[3] A. T. Mosher, "God in the Countryside," Christian Rural Fellowship News Letter, January 18, 1944.
[4] The Christian Rural Fellowship Bulletin, No. 75, October, 1942.

with spiritual, physical, economic and social powers that he can succeed in his struggle amidst hostile surroundings.

The comprehensive parish program not only presents an enlarged concept of the task of the Church but forms a new orientation around which the life of the general community may center. In this wider outreach of the Church culture change, as a reintegration of the old with the new, may take place without serious dislocations, for such a program deals with the basic and traditional interests and problems of the community and at the same time introduces new interests, values, motivations and techniques.

A church program of this nature likewise does not compete with the prerogatives of the established religion, but serves to demonstrate that Christianity is more than another cult since it is concerned with the redemption of all of life.

The comprehensive approach of a church to its community has the further significance that it provides a field for the gifts and an outlet for the energies of every church member. Rather than concentrating primarily upon themselves and instead of functioning as a small enclave apart from the community, the membership will be projected into the community and, through serving some aspect of the public need, will gain a new understanding of the Christian life.

Since nearly every major mission area provides one or more examples of the comprehensive parish program, a selection can be made of a few projects only which, by their unusual success or through the development of special emphases or methods, are of particular interest.

THE COMPREHENSIVE GOSPEL AT PYINMANA, BURMA

The late Brayton Case of the Pyinmana Agricultural School of the American Baptist Foreign Mission Society in Burma for twenty years exemplified in an outstanding way the power of the comprehensive approach to the task of training church workers and developing Burmese churches. In the *United Church Review* of India, December, 1935, he wrote,

People often say, "I don't think there is hope of much improvement in the spiritual life in the villages until there is economic improvement." That is true. At the same time I would say, "I don't see hope of much economic improvement in the villages of Burma unless there is spiritual improvement." The sins of the heart are the greatest obstacles to material progress: Laziness, dishonesty, distrust, deceit, and selfishness ruin crops, spoil trade and spread disease. On the other hand, I have seen villagers get a new Christian faith but because they did not at the same time learn to express the new spirit in a new way of working in the field and home and a new way of living together in the village, they did not grow in spirit and were little better than before. But when they found a new way of expressing their new spirit it was a joy to see their growth in grace. The relation between worship and service is like the relation between food and exercise. One without the other will lead to death.

Our Christian heritage is not only spiritual but also material. We have discovered a way of life in Christ which brings abundant life. . . . Itch, sore eyes, dog bite and broken bones are cured, cholera and smallpox are driven out. The fields yield better and more crops, the pig and the chicken and the cow give more profit. The homes are more attractive and the children healthier, the mind becomes keener and the people sleep more peacefully at night. Even the village dogs wag their tails with a new friendliness. The community is a much better place to live in. It is our privilege to demonstrate to Burma what a wonderful new life the Christian life can be as it is lived in a new relationship with God.

I often tell the villagers if a man becomes a Christian, besides knowing the teachings of the Bible, praying and singing, I should like to require that he grow a garden and eat vegetables, that he know how to milk a cow and give milk to his children to drink, and that he produce more than he spends. I want to help our Christians to live such lives that those who see them will say, "I wish I could be a man like that. I want to hire a Christian laborer because he works better. I want to rent my land to a Christian because he grows better crops and pays his rent in full promptly. I want to buy from a Christian because he gives good quality and honest measure and his word is to be trusted." When I visited one of our village families and found a corner of the house full of plates and bowls, I asked, "Why do you have so many of these here?" They replied, "They belong to the local Buddhist Society for use on their feast days. So many got lost in their own homes they asked us Christians to look after them." These village Christians were valued as good neighbors.[5]

THE MARTANDAM CENTER, INDIA

D. Spencer Hatch in his vivid memorandum entitled, "My Job

[5] Quoted from Agricultural Missions, Inc., 156 Fifth Avenue, New York, Mimeograph Series No. 68.

is Village Reconstruction," clearly states the philosophy underlying the comprehensive program:

We found out as we proceeded with this effort to help those who are
so pitifully poor that there was little good in answering one side of a
farmer's needs. Not much was accomplished by a five-year plan giving
help on health. Hospitals around us discovered that all the time medicine was being given, a good part of the people were so hungry they
could not possibly be healthy. New methods of agriculture, sanitation,
and hygiene were not useful unless a cottage industry filled spare time
and spare hands so that the family had some possible barter or purchasing margin. Moreover, it did little good to teach boys and girls to eat
unpolished rice, sleep with fresh air, and build better houses when
grandmother ruled the house with an iron hand and knew better than
young upstarts. The comprehensive program had to reach out to include grandparents and parents in its fold. Any kind of cottage industry
meant that the young lad had to have the help of mother and sister if
he were to succeed. So we found that not only must we include every
caste and creed, tackle every side of a man's life, but we must also
include the men, women, and children, old and young,—a very comprehensive program, literally all for the good of all.

The purpose of rural reconstruction under our Association is to bring
about a complete upward development towards a more abundant life
for rural people,—spiritually, mentally, physically, socially, and economically.

Among the "twelve pillars of policy" on which the Martandam
project is based, we have selected the following as having universal
interest. The material has been compiled from two printed statements by Mr. Hatch: "My Job is Village Reconstruction,"[6] and
"Further Upward in Rural India."[7]

1. *The Spiritual Basis* is the foundation of the Martandam reconstruction policy. I emphatically include it as an attribute for leading
in India. I doubt whether programmes not including or not based
on things spiritual are fundamental enough to be deep-reaching, or
capable of results lasting enough to be worth the doing. We would
live and do here as nearly as we can as Jesus did when He went
among the villages helping the people upward from all their troubles.
I am sometimes asked if our programme of a maximum of living

[6] The Christian Rural Fellowship Bulletin, No. 98, 156 Fifth Avenue, New York.
[7] Oxford University Press, 1938.

and doing with a minimum of verbal preaching, ever makes any follow Christ Jesus. The answer is, "It does." About a mile from Paraniyam we can show you where one Sunday School grew into a church with a membership of thirty families, who are just now finishing their small church building.

2. Another Martandam pillar is *Self-help with Intimate Expert Counsel*. Rural reconstruction must be a self-help movement, a movement in which villagers are helped to help themselves. Workers must be on very intimate, brotherly terms with the people, willing to go down on their hands and knees to work with the people, not to hand things down from above. These workers must know well what they are trying to teach, so that they can really give expert counsel. But the project must be done by the villagers.

3. Again, *Rural Reconstruction must reach down to the very poorest*. The better-off people with more education and means easily appropriate the benefits and the very poorest who need help the most are often left out. The poorest people cannot afford to be members of the regular cooperative societies, nor do they understand them. We keep ever before us the principle, no man or woman, boy or girl shall be deprived of any of these benefits by reason of poverty. For every project we work out a scheme of participation for those who have no money at all. We sell the eggs from our imported White Leghorns to those who can afford them. But these same eggs must be available to the villager who has no money, so we give him the eggs, but we charge him in our books R.1-2 and tell him that exactly six months later we shall settle with him. Our Extension Department gives him as much help as possible to insure his success and later we buy one of his fowls for Rs.3, the debt is cancelled and the villager has made R.1-14 in cash on only one of his birds nearing maturity.

4. *Post-war Planning must not be for short periods*. The villager is conservative and slow, he has to be shown, and must have his counsellor stand by through his trials during the years. A rural reconstruction center is a life-work, always building, growing, developing. All projects must be tried for years and finally made the people's own before we have accomplished anything permanent. My observation is that the persons who have made a real contribu-

tion to India are those few who have been stubborn enough to resist the demands of the men "at the top" who are running too big a machine with too few personnel and who would jump workers here and there just to keep the machine moving.

5. *A Rural Background for the personnel* is definitely needed. Generally speaking our best rural workers will have been born and bred on the land. I have had city men sent me whom it would have taken the rest of my years of service to transform into useful rural workers. They lacked any sympathetic understanding of rural living. Leaders who have been brought up on a farm are at a real advantage

6. *Simplicity* must be the keynote in all efforts with underprivileged rural people. The worker needs to demonstrate simple habits in his own life, and be willing to teach and help people practice only the most simple and inexpensive methods which they can afford. Rural reconstruction workers need to be rich in the things they can do without. It has been borne in upon us that unless the rural reconstruction movement remains simple it will cost too much and stop short of the millions of needy because enough money will not be available. . . . When a rural worker gets to the place where he hires a car to go where his cycle or the buses go, I count it the beginning of a decline in his value as a worker. . . . So much money is spent on benches in India when simple square mats, placed on the floor, solve the problem of seating. . . . Coats certainly are not required. . . . Every man can wash his own shirt. We have a course in washing and ironing in our Training School and in the making of inexpensive soap.

7. *Work only in those villages where the people want us and ask us to come*. We do not try to improve every village or every family. The success of those who enthusiastically work on projects of their own choosing has such a contagious effect on neighboring families and villages that they soon become interested and desirous of our help.

The introduction of an entirely new product generally fails because the villager lacks anything within his own experience to tie it to. We always find a basis for a new project and try to build on something that is already there. Hand-weaving introduced into an area where there is no weaving or no tradition for it has generally failed although the people may sadly need it.

People must feel that the program belongs to them, is their own choosing and planning and that we are helping them. People are called lazy when they do not work well for a rich employer, but they will work tremendously well and hard on village projects which are to benefit themselves and their village. *A great principle is involved here, we work hard for our convictions and interests but not necessarily for those of others.*

8. *Centres and Extension.* The centre is a place for showing things and methods to people who would come to see and a place for training workers and for experimenting. We chose the poor, rocky soil of Martandam where people were much poorer than in some parts of the state where soil was better and rainfall greater. If we could help people to help themselves under adverse circumstances, other people could certainly copy our methods. A mere centre or government farm will never succeed in getting the people to adopt the improved methods practiced there. . . . It is the addition of an Extension Department which turns the impotent centre into a widespread success. The work of the Extension Department is to get family after family in village after village to take up the helps taught and illustrated at the centre. If a family gets some benefits the neighbors are sure to copy the successful practices.

9. *Leader Training.* When local leaders began to feel the need of more knowledge, Mr. Hatch started a two weeks' summer school. Gradually through the years that simple beginning has grown into the Martandam Practical Training School for Rural Reconstruction. Picked leaders from all over India and from Egypt and China have been coming to study the Martandam principles and methods.

They "learn by doing" through a nine months' course, with long, hard days spent in the field, shop, classroom and in demonstration work in the villages. There also are week-end courses over a period of three months for those who cannot spend time away from their land or their schools. Educational weeks are arranged for whole clusters of villages. Well over a thousand Martandam students have gone out to their home areas to spread a knowledge of the more abundant life to their neighbors.

Among the activities closely related to the life of the Indian peasant which have been taught and promoted by the Martandam Centre are:

Agricultural	Cottage Industries
Poultry culture	Hand weaving
Cattle breeding	Thread and rope making
Goat culture	Baskets and mats
Bee keeping and curing of honey	Collecting and marketing firewood
Sugar from the Palmyra Palm	Palmyra umbrellas
Processing Tamarinds	Fans
Improvement of Cashew Nuts	Lacquer work
Improvement of Pineapples	Christmas and gift cards
Improvement of Pappadams	Fret work

Community Projects

Bore hole latrines	Grading of products
Preparation of compost pits	Apprentice system
Rural sanitation and clean villages	Short-term students
Beautifying the village	Rural Development Association
The rural drama	Cholera and Malaria prevention
Folk dances	Establishing village centers
Literacy classes	Accumulation and use of trust
Folk school for all the people	funds
Marketing and sales depots	Correct weights and measures
Staff training school	

THE ENCRUCIJADA COMMUNITY PARISH, CUBA

One of the few examples of the comprehensive parish program in Latin American countries is that of the Presbyterian church of Encrucijada, Cuba. This small, country town of 5,000 people lies in an extensive sugar-raising district where the livelihood of all the people is affected by the conditions of that industry, including the long months of stagnation in the "dead season."

In 1941, there were ninety-nine members in the church, fifty-eight of whom contributed one-third of the budget, the balance being provided by the mission. Upon the sudden death of the gifted pastor, Rev. J. Ferreol Gomez, Dr. Santiago Adams, a local physician, and a Cuban, whom the late pastor had drawn into church fellowship, led the congregation in founding a memorial institute bearing his name.

The institute is a Christian civic and social enterprise centered in the church and with the purpose of building up the life of the whole community. In addition to the large day school, the playground, the Boy Scout Troop, the cooperative store, and poor relief which had been directed by the late pastor, the new project added a wing to the church for housing a clinic and dispensary service and a varied community welfare program. Dr. Adams is in charge of the medical unit and its extension work and helps the pastor to integrate the whole program of activities with the life of the church and of the community. The J. Ferreol Gomez Institute is directed by a committee of Evangelical and non-Evangelical citizens.

Fifteen young women have been trained locally for home visitation, for helping mothers in the care of young children, in dietetics, sanitation, hygiene and in the care of their homes. Each home in the town is visited by this trained group. Educational campaigns are being conducted against syphilis, tuberculosis, gambling and prostitution and for promoting the use of protected foods and pure water. Suitable literature gives guidance in personal habits, thrift, the use of spare time and the choice of vocations. Evening literacy classes for adults are held in the church school. There are classes for the study of cooperatives and for teaching handcrafts and cottage industries. The young people of the church lead regular services and Sunday Schools in outlying rural centers. The young men have promoted a pure water supply for the town and have paved some of the deeply rutted streets.

Nearly every able-bodied church member and many non-members have found in this wide service program an outlet for exercising their special gifts for serving the community. The project is identified with the church, is inspired by Christ's teaching, and operates in and radiates from the church property. Such identification of social rehabilitation with the Gospel of Christ is new in the Cuban's understanding of religion and the mission of the Church and it offers a powerful apologetic which every citizen can understand.

Two important aspects of this community parish program are, that it was the result of Cuban vision and initiative and, that it has been carried out in a little country town where extremely depressed conditions prevailed.[8] Recent word has been received that the church and the parish program have prospered; the church membership has grown, and its program is now practically self-supporting.

[8] J. M. Davis, *The Cuban Church in a Sugar Economy,* pp. 113, 114.

THE FARM VILLAGE EXPERIMENT, HOPEI, CHINA

The missionaries and Chinese Christians in a typical north China station in Hopei Province had been working for years along the usual lines of evangelistic, educational, and medical work. But some of the results were far from satisfying. A survey of church members showed that one-half were solitary Christians in their families and subject to the tremendous pressure of the Chinese family upon the individual. Christians were thinly scattered in groups of three, five, ten or twenty to a village.

There was a tendency among many evangelists and their "flocks" to think of Christian duty in terms of weekly preaching and listening to sermons. Some of the oldest churches were nearly dead. Christianity did not appear to have taken root in the community and was not attracting the young people. The station work was departmentalized so that some people were being educated, some were being healed and bits of agricultural knowledge, famine relief, and cooperative societies were being scattered among others. China at this time was seriously undertaking the reconstruction of her entire rural life, the help and cooperation of Christians was being sought by national leaders, yet the Church felt unprepared to play an intelligent part in the task of rebuilding rural communities. In view of these facts, in 1933, a little group of two Americans and four Chinese determined to experiment in Christian rural reconstruction.[9]

The purpose of the experiment was to provide a typical village laboratory in which to study all rural problems and, if possible, demonstrate the Christian solution on a community-wide scale but in a manner which would be adaptable to other villages.

THE PRINCIPLES OF THE EXPERIMENT

1. *A correlated program* which would redeem the whole man, and minister to the entire life of the community.

2. *The demonstration method.* Each phase of village improvement, even religion, was approached through demonstration.

3. *Self-help,* with the friendly advice of specialists. The responsibility was put on the village group. All credit went to the local

[9] Agricultural Missions, Inc., 156 Fifth Avenue, New York. Mimeograph Series No. 75.

people. No signs or labels of outside organizations were put up. No program or project was "put over" unless approved and voted by the local leaders. No money was given for local improvements.

4. *Cooperation.* (a) With all departments of the mission station. Twelve mission units cooperated in the sponsoring organization. (b) With all government bodies—local, county, provincial and private agencies of rural reconstruction. (c) With the village—the common good was the chief goal.

5. The experiment had to be *reproducible* and be limited in funds and personnel to what could be readily duplicated elsewhere. The manner of life was to be as near as possible that of the villagers. When change became necessary the new standards had to be within their reach. Plans were to be flexible and capable of revision. Emphasis was to be placed upon the training of local leaders.

6. *Work with three basic groups was stressed:* (a) Village elders; (b) The family unit; (c) Youth. New projects were to be tried on a small scale until expansion was justified by results. A genuine invitation had to be received from a village before moving into it. During the first year the program was to be confined chiefly to one village.

7. *The religious program.* The aim was to change desires, attitudes, habits, hearts, lives. Christianity had to be lived and friendliness shown to every villager. Public preaching was avoided until requested. The workers were frankly Christian in their personal relations and religion was discussed freely in conversations. The best in local religious ideas, culture, and customs was built upon.

CHIEF RESULTS

No quick results were expected. The project was still in its infancy when interrupted by the China-Japan War. Until the standard of living is raised so that people are no longer on the verge of starvation education, health, recreation, and even religion, are in the nature of luxuries not to be afforded in the struggle for bare existence. However, in three years progress was made in the following spheres:

I. Agriculture and Economics

1. Six hundred pounds of "Trice" American Cotton Seed were planted in 1935. In 1936, 260 pounds of No. 82 Millet Seed were planted in thirteen villages with a 35% better crop than from local seed.

2. Eight hundred trees were planted in the village for shade and timber.

3. One hundred peach, pear, and apple trees were planted but only one-half lived.

4. An attack was made on "smut" disease of crops through copper-carbonate.

5. A well-digging campaign resulted in fifty-six wells being dug for irrigation around the farm villages. Thirty more wells were dug in neighboring villages during 1936.

6. A cooperative society was formed in 1935. Total loans for well-digging amounted to $3,883. Five other cooperatives were organized in neighboring villages.

7. A survey of village conditions was begun.

II. Education. (Note: At the beginning of the experiment only one girl in the village had a primary school education and eighty per cent of the men were illiterate.)

1. One hundred and twenty people were taught to read and write in short-term classes.

2. A free school for illiterates enrolled seventy girls and forty-seven boys and won first prize for excellence in the county from the Board of Education.

3. A new room was added to the village school and was provided entirely by villagers in gifts of money, labor, and materials.

4. Three small loan libraries were placed in the village.

5. A weekly lecture program was held with the aid of movies and radio.

6. Daily news bulletins were prepared by the school students and posted in prominent places.

7. The whole educational program was built up around the government village school.

III. Health

1. Through an annual vaccination campaign, four hundred peo-

ple were vaccinated in the first year. This was extended later to twelve villages and several thousand vaccinations.

2. Trachoma was attacked through the village school by means of talks and injections. This was only partially successful due to reinfection.

3. During two years, classes for midwives were held but with only slight success in modifying their methods.

4. Food demonstrations were held twice a year for the women, with exhibits of their own products and a demonstration of better uses of local materials, viz., soya bean milk, cotton seed oil, etc.

5. "Better baby" exhibits with talks to mothers were held semi-annually.

6. Two health workers—a man and a woman—were trained to teach the use of simple home remedies, and each was provided with a medicine kit.

IV. Recreation

Most of the recreational program for adults centered around the New Year's season. Old customs like boxing and lantern parades were revived. Chinese drama was used and in 1936, a three-day continuous series of plays, music, and talks was held. New games were introduced, movies, slide films, and radio included comic and recreational features.

V. Home Work

There was a continual visiting in homes by the women members of the staff and special help in times of illness, death, and difficulty was given. Home meetings were held twice a week. There was a silent demonstration of Christian homes by members of the staff living in the village.

VI. Young People's Work

A Young People's Fellowship was organized both for self-improvement and to serve the village. A weekly Sunday meeting open to the public was entirely in the hands of this fellowship and included debates on current issues, music, stories, jokes and speeches.

VII. Change in Customs

A young couple, in place of the traditional wedding costing hundreds of dollars, had a simple but dignified wedding which cost $10.00.

A cooperative funeral association, greatly reducing costs, was formed.

VIII. In 1934 a "Village Reconstruction Committee" was formed by a group of twenty village leaders to study the needs of their villages and to see what could be done to meet them. Later, this group organized themselves as a "Village Reconstruction Association" with sub-committees on education, health, livelihood and recreation. The following year a Committee on Religion was added.

IX. *Village Government*

In 1935, the head of the Village Reconstruction Association was, by popular vote, elected head of the village. During the same year over $1,000—local currency—was saved to the village over the former year by efficient and honest management. The County Magistrate, who had charge of four hundred villages, frequently referred to the farm village as his "model village."

X. *Extension of Field*

During the three years' period of the experiment, various aspects of the service program reached many surrounding villages, e.g., the vaccination campaign covered twelve villages; well-digging and cooperative societies extended to six. A second village was chosen for a full correlated program and a Village Reconstruction Association was organized but initial progress was slower here.

XI. *Spirit and Attitudes*

The most important result of the experiment has been the increasing spirit of service, sacrifice, and cooperation for the common good. When some poor families could not pay their debts in the annual settlement, men of larger means in the Reconstruction Association, of their own initiative, loaned them $120.

Since the money for well-digging was not enough to go around, the better-placed villagers proposed that they begin with the poorest families and use the money as far as it would go. Twenty-six wells were dug with public funds for the poorest people and thirty more were dug with individual resources.

The farm village received a banner and highest praise from the County Magistrate for its fine work on the provincial road and fortification programs.

Buddhists, Confucianists, and Christians cooperated for the community welfare as the best of friends.

XII. Religion

In the fall of 1935, the Committee on Religion of the Village Reconstruction Association requested the formation of a class to study Christianity. In January, 1936, the head of the village walked into the neighboring city church with his daughter and told the pastor that he wanted to take his stand before the congregation as a Christian. Thirteen family groups, totaling forty-nine persons, took the first step toward church membership in March, 1936.

THE IIMORINO RURAL PARISH

An outgrowth of the visit of Kenyon L. Butterfield to Japan in 1928 was the stimulation of wide interest in rural church methods and the planting of a rural community parish in several widely separated farming districts.

The Iimorino rural parish is of unusual interest because it illustrates the strength of the comprehensive approach of the Church to a conservative farming community, the possibility of bringing a rural parish to complete self-support, and the strategy of relating the training of a theological seminary to the development of the rural church field.

In 1932, Dr. E. M. Clark, of the Union Presbyterian Theological Seminary of Kobe, founded the community parish at Tomiai village, in the midst of an unevangelized rural area of 100,000 farms and a population of half a million people. The Presbyterian mission had worked for seventy years in the great port city of Kobe, close by, but had never approached this great farming district. Dr. Clark asked his mission to try a new policy of self-support in the rural parish since, in the absence of funds, this was the only possible basis on which the field could be entered. Under the plan, 6,000 yen was given in advance by the mission—a sum equal to one-half salary of the pastor for a period of ten years. This money was invested in two and one-half acres of land, in the building of a combination church and parsonage, a barn and workshop, in implements and stock and in fruit trees and seed. The pastor, Rev. J. Horii, was to operate the farm, carry on religious and social work in the community, and develop a Christian church. His support would come from three sources, namely, the farm, the church members, and the mission, with the expectation that, as the orchards and stock developed and the church membership grew, the first two sources of support would increase and the subsidy decrease. At the end of ten years, the project would be brought to full self-support and an independent church would be born instead of a church that would be indefinitely dependent upon the mission.

The pastor won his first foothold in the village through a day nursery for the children of the farmers. This was followed by a Sunday School. Two farm families, whose friendship was secured in this way, became the nucleus of the church. The pastor began systematically to call on the families in his parish. Sunday Schools and Bible classes were opened in five other villages in all of which he preached regularly. The first opposition subsided and non-Christians were attending the church services. Mr. Horii also conducted farmers' institutes with courses on agricultural improvement. He provided public health lectures and arranged for a community clinic. In 1936, the church raised 1,200 yen to build a small infirmary where sick farmers could be cared for. At the end of the first six years, there were four complete farm families in the church and seventy-six persons had been baptized.

The church land was planted to grapes, peaches, and vegetables. The parish owned four hogs, a large poultry run, and many Angora rabbits, the fur from which was spun in the church workshop and sold at a profit. A thriving business was started in the bottling of grape juice. An increasing number of his members worked with the pastor on these projects. The farm income, as yet, was not large since the fruit trees were still young, but it was increasing year by year. At the end of the first six years, church gifts totalled 2,163.63 yen, profits from the farm and industrial work netted 1,307 yen, and the mission had supplied 1,168 yen.[10] Church and farm support had increased 300 per cent, and mission subsidy had steadily decreased. By the end of the seventh year, the enterprise had become entirely independent—three years short of the expiration of the experimental period—and an indigenous, self-supporting church was born.

The second community project was started in the summer of 1936 in a village seventeen miles from Kobe. Six thousand yen was invested by the mission in a small dairy which supplied milk to the

[10] One yen is the equivalent of 1s. 2½d. sterling, or 29 cents U. S. currency.

neighboring city. By 1937, a modern barn, creamery, and separator were set up and three Jersey cows were bought. Twelve other cows, owned by villagers, were stabled and fed, and the milk was sold. The dairy, under the management of a graduate of the Agricultural College of the University of Hawaii, was making a twenty per cent profit on the investment. The earnings paid the salaries of the local evangelists (students from the Presbyterian Theological Seminary), and were also reducing the original loan. This strongly anti-Christian village had its prejudices removed by the opening of the dairy, and a Sunday School and regular preaching were carried on in the village.

The third project was developing toward self-maintenance with a piece of land which had been acquired that adequately furnished a considerable part of the living of the director, and by a small sickle factory that had been developed. However, the director was drafted into the army and, for the duration, the work became a home mission obligation of the Iimorino rural parish. This work was left with a good house, a combined workers' residence and chapel, and a small farm.

In January, 1945, Dr. Clark wrote from Colombia,

I left Japan in the spring of 1942—ten years after the opening of the project. The war had begun to draw heavily on manpower. Rev. Junji Horii, our leader in the whole set-up, had been sent by the National Christian Council to Manchuria to form a Christian village settlement and the work consequently suffered. But fortunately, we had a student graduating who was looking forward to the same type of service. This Mr. Iwazuka stepped right into the situation and was fast winning the confidence and support of the church and community. All expenses of the work were still being paid from local income which had increased to about fifty per cent, from money contributions of church members, and the balance from the sale of farm products. This church group was under the jurisdiction of the Naniwa Presbytery and was called the *Iimorino Noson Kyokwai.*

Underlying the success of the Iimorino rural parish were the thorough training, ability, and vision of the pioneer pastor, Mr. Horii. He believed in the comprehensive approach to this conservative farming district. The project did not start as a preaching point served by a visiting evangelist. It fitted into the economic pattern of the community, and from the beginning, the pastor identified himself with the struggle for livelihood of his neighbors. He discarded his clerical garb for the rough blue homespun tunic and the sandals of the Japanese farmer, and he threw himself into the preparation of his land, the planting of trees, breeding of livestock, and the myriad tasks of the countryman. He established a solidarity of interests and won the respect and confidence of his neighbors by finding ways of serving the physical, social, and spiritual needs of the community. The young farmers were drawn to him, helped him, listened to him and gradually followed his leadership.

KAMBINI RURAL PARISH PROGRAM, AFRICA

The Portuguese East African field of the Methodist Church has made remarkable progress in a planned rural church program very closely integrated with its scheme of training evangelists and pastors. The training school and the rural parishes form the reciprocal poles of a powerful unit of church extension which has produced far-reaching results. Although the unit of supervision is a circuit with a radius of from ten to twenty-five miles the actual working unit is the so-called Christian village of from five to one hundred families, with its field of influence and service extending several miles in all directions.

In a strict sense such a village is not an indigenous unit but an artificial growth centering upon the church and the evangelist. All the scattered non-Christian families of the surrounding areas are urged to send their children to the village school and to benefit by the various village activities. Before the Portuguese Government prohibited schools in the native tongue each village evangelist was also the village teacher.

The native chief dealt with the evangelist rather than with individuals in the village and the government administrator often dealt directly with the village as a unit rather than with the chief. An annual average mission expenditure of $100 for each of the several hundred villages under its supervision has, in the course of years, been cut in half through the program of self-support.

The program within the Christian village includes religious services, Christian instruction, Bible teaching, Sunday School and probation classes, education in primary standards, demonstration of better living conditions with hygienic and sanitary practices, better homes and child care, better diet and agricultural practices, a petty chieftainship authority, recreation, games, singing, etc.

The extension program of the village serves the surrounding country with kraal preaching and Sunday Schools and the village day school is open to all who will attend. The program includes the reading and writing of letters for the people by scribes, midwifery and first aid, entertainment on special days such as Christmas, harvest, planting, etc. The village demonstrates better homes, better building, better agriculture and better use of food and exerts an influence that often extends to the whole area.

The resident agencies that work in and through the Christian village are the pastor-teacher, the unpaid assistant, the village council and the Sunday School superintendent. Visiting agencies include the circuit pastor (missionary or native), the religious education director, the Jeanes demonstrator, the mission superintendent, the native chief and the Portuguese administrator. Occasionally week-end institutes serve the local unit. More general services are given by the Kambini doctor and hospital, the Kambini Training School, and the Hartzell Girls' School.

The Kambini training program is planned definitely to prepare for rural service. It does not consist of agriculture or rural sociology tacked on to a theological or normal course. In the three years of study the students are trained as effective evangelists, but also as efficient leaders of rural life. The course provides a well-rounded, practical education for the man, his wife, and his family. The evangelist's wife is increasingly becoming a vital factor in the rural church program. The future workers are enabled to support themselves during their training by gardening on plots assigned to them and are helped to develop a better village life,—spiritually, socially, economically. The students—both men and women—spend half of the day in the classroom and half in field, shop or home.

The Kambini station offers a very wide scope of training directly related to the needs of the rural parishes that they will serve. It consists of evangelist and pastoral training, boarding school up to the high school standard, training for Jeanes village demonstrators, wives' training course (evangelistic and Jeanes), elementary day school and elementary night school, agriculture, field and handwork, sawmill and light plant, wood working and building, tile, brick making and masonry, tailoring, dispensary and first aid.

Among the *purposes* of the Kambini program are:

1. To develop real religious expression through agriculture
(a) by creating a sense of appreciation for God's gifts upon which agriculture is based;
(b) by instilling the feeling that agriculture is cooperating with God in the use of these gifts which feed mankind;
(c) by setting up such acts of worship as seed-time dedication service, harvest, and thanksgiving festivals.

2. To establish the dignity of agricultural labor and to build Christian character through school, group, and individual projects, honestly carried through.

3. To bring men into a more responsible place in African agriculture through the use of cattle, use of new crops, and use of new methods.

4. To free agriculture from the handicap of superstitious beliefs through instruction and demonstration.

5. To develop an intelligent agricultural system as a basis of self-support—one so simple and adaptable that Africans can and will use it.

6. To control and prevent famine through growing rice and cultivating river gardens; improved methods of storage, use of mandioc, and the adaptation of dry farming and cool season crops.

7. To introduce and test new methods, new crops, and disease and drought-resistant varieties of standard crops.

8. To improve and teach a better use of cattle, goats, sheep, poultry and donkeys.

9. To cooperate with the health program in the greater use of milk, eggs, greens, fruit, etc., and the better preparation and cooking of other foods.

10. To extend the possibility of self-sufficiency through simple allied industries.

The Kambini Rural Parish Program is demonstrating to the African the unity of the Christian life through introducing worship into the daily and periodic practices of agriculture and the work of the people. A book of rural hymns and choral praise has been prepared in the *Tswa* dialect and set to native melodies and chants. These include a wide variety of subjects, such as seed planting, harvesting, digging, cultivating, weeding, awaiting rain, house building, church construction, forestry and timbering, health and strength, food, the love of parents and the care of their children, the blessing of a home and the sustaining love and power of God. They are set in the familiar native style of leader and choral responses and are adapted for the use of children as well as for adults. Typical of these hymns of rural worship are the following:

HYMN TO BE USED AT SEED CONSECRATION SERVICE

Leader: Seed we bring
All: Lord, to Thee, wilt Thou bless them, O Lord!
Leader: Gardens we bring
All: Lord, to Thee, wilt Thou bless them, O Lord!
Leader: Hoes we bring
All: Lord, to Thee, etc.
Leader: Hands we bring
All: Lord, to Thee, etc.
Leader: Ourselves we bring
All: Lord, to Thee, etc.

HARVEST FESTIVAL WORSHIP SERVICE

Leader:	*All:*	
We thank Thee, Lord	We thank Thee, Lord	
We have lived another year	We have lived another year	
You blessed us greatly	You blessed us greatly	
With sun and rain	With sun and rain	*Chorus:* We give thanks, We give thanks.
We thank Thee with seed	We thank Thee with seed	
We thank Thee with corn	We thank Thee with corn	
etc., etc., etc.	etc., etc., etc.	
Lord, receive us	Lord, receive us	
We will serve Thee	We will serve Thee	
All through our lives	All through our lives	

FOR HOME OR CHURCH BUILDING CONSECRATION

Leader: Lord, we thank Thee this day.
All: We thank Thee, Lord.   (Response after each line)
Leader: Thou who art Source of all strength.
Leader: You caused us to build this building.
Leader: Lord, we thank Thee because of the carriers.
Leader: You helped us cut the trees.
Leader: We thank Thee for the building.
Leader: In this house we will remember Thee.
Leader: In this house we will worship Thee.

HYMN USED AT BOTH SEED CONSECRATION AND HARVEST

Leader: The man who works	*All:* He it is who rejoices greatly
Leader: The man who digs	*All:* He it is who rejoices greatly
Leader: The man who plants	*All:* He it is who rejoices greatly
Leader: The man who harvests	*All:* He it is who rejoices greatly.
etc., etc., etc.	

CHILDREN'S SONGS

Leader: I don't forget my father, I don't forget my mother
All: My father, my mother, my parents, I will praise them

Leader: They begin when I am a little child to put me down and take me up
All: My father, my mother, etc.

Leader: They start to teach me, they make me walk
All: My father, my mother, etc.

Leader: Even though I get dirty, they brush me off, they bathe me
All: My father, my mother, etc.

Leader: I will thank him, my father, I will thank her, my mother
All: My father, my mother, I will praise them.

I want to plant, I want to plant, I want to plant a garden.
I will dig like this, I will dig like this, I will dig my garden like this.

I want to weed, I want to weed, I want to weed my garden.
I will weed like this, I will weed like this, I will weed my garden like this.

I want to harvest, I want to harvest, I want to harvest my corn.
I will harvest like this, I will harvest like this, I will harvest my corn like this.

I want to give thanks, I want to give thanks, I want to give thanks to God.
I will give thanks like this, I will give thanks like this, I will give thanks to God like this.

This is a motion song, and the last verse is most effective as they pour out their thank offering in a pile which grows at each gift.[11]

[11] Rural Programme, Central Training School, Kambini, Africa, by J. S. Rea, Agricultural Missions Inc., 156 Fifth Avenue, New York 10, Mimeograph Series No. 18.

PART FIVE

BUILDING IN THE POST-WAR AGE

Part I
Part II

CHAPTER XII

THE TRAINING OF THE BUILDER

I

THERE is no aspect of missionary work today which is the subject of more discussion than that of the qualifications and training of the missionary. Of equal interest and importance is the subject of the preparation of national leaders—both professional and lay—of the Younger Churches.

Leadership-training is related to the central theme of this book, i.e., the task of stabilizing and rooting the Younger Churches in the environment of the new age.

Keeping in mind this frame of reference and the problems it presents to the post-war Christian movement, it should be possible to discover the type of training and equipment the missionary and national worker will need to meet the requirements of the Younger Churches.

The preparation of missionary and national worker, though differing at many points, will be dealt with as one problem since the objective to be gained is the same and to reach it the missionary and national worker must advance together.

In what sense will the post-war period be a new age? What old factors will be left to reckon with? What new factors will appear? The whole fabric of life—politics, economics, the social order and the beliefs of mankind—is being shaken to its foundations. Much of it is being altered and some of it is being destroyed. However, it is a fallacy to expect that missions will start in the post-war age with a clean slate. As long as sin and selfishness remain in the world, the heart of the missionary's task—to make known the redemptive power of God through Christ—is unchanged, but the scope of the Christian movement, the areas of responsibility of the Church, the response of the people to its message and the methods and techniques to be used by the worker are all subject to change. The war has had a profound effect in these spheres, and in many areas it has set a new base line from which to reconstruct the Christian movement.

The missionary in the post-war era, as earlier stated, will find himself in the position of the North American mining engineer who, in Peru, is faced with unfamiliar ore ingredients. The copper metal is the same as that in his homeland, but the processes of separating it from the ore are different. New formulas and techniques are required.

Missions in the post-war age also will face a similar problem. The precious metal will be present but it will be found in combination with new elements that will baffle old methods. With this in mind, the worker should be equipped with insights into the culture and the social, economic, and political conditions of the land to which he goes, together with techniques and skills that will bring results which the old preparation and methods alone could not produce.

OLD FACTORS IN THE POST-WAR MISSION FIELD

First, the *land* is a foundation upon which we can count with certainty to rebuild the Church. The land, in a great majority of mission fields, is a dominating factor. It forms the economic, social, and cultural base of three-fourths of the people of the non-Christian world. It is a factor which war cannot change. Whatever destruction has come upon cities and their institutions, the productive power of the earth will heal the wounds wrought by war and will continue to nourish mankind.

By and large, the missionary movement has not sufficiently recognized the significance of the land and it is not equipping its missionaries, and through them the native leadership, for effectively dealing with a land-based church. The reasons for this are not hard to find. The mission-sending nations have a city-centered civilization with a city-centered church and theological seminary and people of urban interests, points of view, and values. Most theological seminaries are not oriented or organized in a manner to produce effective rural church workers. This trend is directly reflected in the foreign missionary movement.

The importance of the great cities of the non-Christian world to the national life would be difficult to overstate, but their position must be kept in perspective. The cities are glorified market towns, administrative centers, cultural and recreational areas, distribution and shipping points, banking, trading and manufacturing marts. The cities will continue to lead the life of the nations but the rural areas are the reservoirs from which they draw both their population and their economic strength.

The foreign missionary enterprise needs more than a bolstering up and tinkering to make it rural in character. It requires a new examination of its unfinished task, the pattern of national life of the peoples among whom it is working, the forces which have made them what they are, and which, to a very large extent, they will continue to be; and, further, the foreign mission enterprise requires a redrawing of its blue prints in the light of such an examination. Church leaders need to ponder the meaning of the fact that the norm of these vast populations is a *rural norm,* not an urban norm. The cultures of the great non-Christian peoples in Asia, Africa, South America and the islands of the Pacific have all been shaped in a rural mould.

The missionary Church, in nearly every one of the twenty-two fields studied by the Department, is struggling against the tides which, throughout the world, are running cityward from the country areas. The Church, at high cost, is learning that a city-based movement and a city-trained ministry, only with great difficulty, can spread countryward. The city-trained pastor as the city-trained doctor, lawyer, and official finds the economic and social traffic lights to the country set against him. The result, in not a few countries, is a stalemated Christian movement, an inadequately led rural church and, to a large extent, an unoccupied rural field. In many lands, the mission is halted at the threshold of the great rural areas because it has not devised the tools nor the methods which are suited to the task of creating an indigenous rural church.

The Seventh Day Adventist Church, by orienting its educational work in the rural areas, by concentrating its training upon the children of its own constituency, and by careful financial organization is one of the fastest growing mission churches and this, largely, because it has worked *with* and not *against* the tides of human life which flow from country to city.

No missionary candidate or national worker should be commissioned to a land which is predominantly rural in character without having had, at least, a brief introduction to rural life. Some understanding of rural economics, rural sociology, rural psychology, the way of life of the rural family and community and an appreciation of the significance of the Divine processes that are unfolded in the majestic rhythm of agriculture would greatly enrich his ministry.

Some insight into rural life is essential for every branch of missionary activity: preaching, education, medicine, literary work, translation, field supervision, Bible-worker training, evangelism and the training of pastors in the theological seminary.

The struggle for livelihood and for economic security is a *second* factor which will carry over from the pre-war to the post-war age. In many lands the war will have thrown this age-old factor into a new and terrible relief. One of the inescapable demands that will be made upon the Church will be to counsel and assist in the struggle for livelihood. The missionary or church leader will be severely handicapped in the post-war era if he is indifferent to this factor or is unequipped to help the people in their efforts to win economic security. The pressure of steadily mounting populations upon the land, with the fragmentation of farms and the growth of tenancy, the rising cost of living, unemployment and indebtedness are all old enemies that will be present in heightened forms and will condition the possibility of the growth and stability of the Christian Church.

The controlling position of home and family is a *third* factor. The home and the family among non-Christian peoples are so powerful and function in such deeply grooved patterns as to neutralize much of the influence upon the children of the mission or government school. In such societies education or preaching alone, without the rehabilitation of the home and family, is seriously handicapped. More than in the case of Western societies, the home and family have the last word in shaping the lives of the rising generation of non-Christian peoples. They are the guardians of conservatism and the effects of detaching the children for periodic teaching are overwhelmed by the influences which, like the constant pressure of the atmosphere, prevail among them. The high strategy of modern missions in dealing realistically with these citadels of the non-Christian world is apparent.

The family has been undergoing far-reaching changes in all areas directly or remotely affected by the war, and will be in peculiar need of rehabilitation and strengthening. The Church should be aware of these changes and, as never before in the history of missions, needs to be prepared to deal constructively with the family as the base of the new Christian order.

A *fourth* requirement of the post-war age upon the church worker will be the understanding of and some practical training in the problems of the *health, nutrition,* and *sanitation* of the rehabilitated community. The war is leaving a terrible legacy in famine and disease, undernourishment, and lowered vitality and its effects will continue for many decades. The Church must be prepared to take some responsibility for furthering individual and community health in the reconstruction era. Even the small rural church could render invaluable service through its pastor or a layman who had received rudimentary training in first aid, treatment of common diseases and infections, and the use of simple preventive medicine. Public health and village sanitation, also, could usefully be promoted by the Church. Such simple remedial and health work would be a practical measure in opening a comprehensive parish program, but to render it effective the missionary and the pastor themselves will require training.

Illiteracy is a *fifth* and a major handicap to progress which the post-war worker will meet. The Bible and all other literature are closed to the man who cannot read nor can an illiterate function efficiently as a member of organized society. Without the ability to read the newspapers, price bulletins, bus and railway tariffs, bills for professional services, lawyer's and ecclesiastical fees, civil taxes, police and court rulings, a man is in constant danger of being cheated and overcharged.

Teaching church members to read gives them access to the sources of the Christian faith and also enables them to put the Bible into the hands of their neighbors and to extend their spiritual understanding and mental horizons. Of all services for the community that a local church can undertake, this is second to none in importance. Here again, however, the missionary and pastor will need to be conversant with effective methods and techniques.

NEW FACTORS IN THE POST-WAR MISSION FIELD

Among the new factors in the post-war mission field which the missionary will meet are:

The Political Unrest and Uncertainty Pending Post-War Settle-

ments. These will be both national and international in scope and in their effect on the program of missions. The war has let loose tremendous forces of nationalism, consciousness of power, aspirations for freedom from foreign domination and imperialism, including foreign leadership. The philosophy and practice of missions will be deeply involved in the composing of these momentous issues. There are few mission fields in which the status and rôle of the missionary in the control of institutions, policies, and funds will not be challenged, as they were in the case of Japan even before Pearl Harbor. The era will require an ability on the part of the missionary to fit into new patterns of racial, international, and organizational relationships.

The political destinies of India, China, and Japan—not to mention the smaller nations and the great colonial peoples—are awaiting the unpredictable outcome of world issues. The outcome of such issues as the effect upon Asiatics of the Soviets' astonishing success, India's struggle for freedom, and the destiny of the dependent peoples in Asia, Africa, and the islands of the Pacific, will be of profound concern to Christian missions. Mission workers will need, more than ever before, to be conversant with and sensitive to the progress of national and international developments.

Economic Dislocations. The effects of the material destruction and economic dislocation caused by the war will be felt by the Christian movement long after the close of hostilities. Not only will schools, hospitals, and churches be damaged or destroyed, but the homes and the means of livelihood of great multitudes in the areas occupied and fought over by the contending armies will have disappeared. The missionary who has a practical knowledge of the principles and methods of economic stabilization, including handcrafts, cottage industries, poultry and small livestock raising, wood working and building, and an acquaintance with producer, consumer, and credit cooperatives, can help the people to higher standards of living. This will be true of the long future of the rehabilitated community no less than of the period of reconstruction.

Social Disintegration. The Church will be confronted with communities in which families have been scattered and broken up, populations have dwindled and changed, old centers of community life and sanctions of community conduct have disappeared or have greatly weakened. Such conditions will exist not only in lands actually ravaged by battle and by enemy occupation, but in vast areas of Africa, India, and southeast Asia—untouched by actual conflict. The enlistment of hundreds of thousands of men in military service and labor battalions and the enrollment of armies of young people, both men and women, in war industries have broken up countless homes and have introduced great populations to a culture-changing process that will have a lasting effect upon the social order.

Cooperation with Government Relief and Welfare Programs. The Christian Church in the reconstruction era will find new official agencies and programs for helping the people which will attract the attention of the public. Such agencies as UNRRA (United Nations Relief and Rehabilitation Administration), and the British Colonial Development Board, etc., frequently will have resources of personnel and funds beyond those that the Church or the mission will command. The missionary and pastor may well look upon such government activities for public welfare not as rival programs, but as allied efforts in ministering to human needs. The churches should offer their facilities for public service, and the pastor and church officers may wisely cooperate to the full extent of their abilities and identify themselves with every serious effort at human uplift and the relief of suffering. If the Church stands aloof from official rehabilitation programs, it runs the risk of being "by-passed" and isolated at a time when the community is in deepest need of Christian sympathy and help.

New Initiative and Leadership Resources among Nationals. There are the elusive factors of new national initiative, leadership, self-expression and self-help which the war has developed on many mission fields. Unexpected capacities for leadership have been revealed, individuals and churches have risen to surprising heights of self-sacrifice and achievement, and they have discovered hidden powers in themselves for which the war is responsible. The missionary and the National Church leader will face unprecedented situations; they must learn to breathe a new atmosphere, be prepared to understand the extreme delicacy of the issues involved, the significance of the judgments they will form and the decisions they will be called upon to make.

For example, they will be called upon to decide whether to rebuild the disorganized Christian movement upon the old patterns, or to draw new blueprints for the new era. In many places, the war will have provided the opportunity to build anew from the ground up, not only in brick and mortar, but in policies, location, organization and leadership and in the sources of the support of the movement.

The missionary will have to work with a generation of older pastors and Christians who have been trained in the school of mission subsidies and he, himself, may find it difficult to think and plan in other terms than those in vogue in pre-war days.

Growth of a World Consciousness. The war has demonstrated the oneness of human destiny. The distinction between home and foreign missions has disappeared; the superiority of so-called Christian culture has been shattered. The modern world will be saved together or lost together. A religious faith and a Church must be a world faith and a world Church which can effectively minister to the needs of all humanity.

The missionary and church leader will work in this immensely enlarged frame of reference. Without disloyalty to the nation or denomination which has cradled him, he will be called upon to think of himself as the representative of the Christ who belongs to the world and who has power to save the world rather than of a sectarian, denominational or nationalistic Christ. A narrower estimate of himself and of his mission will be increasingly repudiated by the non-Christian peoples in the post-war era.

NEW PATTERNS FOR THE POST-WAR AGE

The demands of the post-war age for new and experimental types of mission activity are so numerous that only a few can be discussed here:

The Coordination and Uniting of Mission Programs. The war has brought to leaders in many lands the opportunity to replan the occupation of both cities and rural areas on the basis of coordinated and united work. The way will have been cleared for a new approach to this problem. The progress of the Christian movement may be set back for generations by many competing and often antagonistic denominational churches, each struggling to rebuild in the same place. There may well be an interim period between the close of hostilities and the final decisions as to reconstruction, pending a joint survey of the areas in question, in which a "moratorium" on building is declared by mutual agreement of the Chris-

tian bodies concerned. These "interregnum" years will be a price-
less opportunity for preparation to face this problem, not only for
the missionary and the National Churches, but also for the mission
board and the Western Churches.

To mission boards which have laboriously built up many local
churches, this argument may seem "a counsel of perfection" or
crass unrealism. However, the stake of the Christian Church in a
nation like China is greater than that of perpetuating sectarianism.
The pattern of a united Church of Christ or one divided into a be-
wildering multitude of denominational bodies may be determined
for a hundred years by the decisions of the post-war period.

The Anthropological Approach. An introduction to anthropology
would give the missionary for the new age an invaluable understanding of the people to whom he goes. The processes of observation, analysis, and evaluation of the social and psychological inheritance and folkways of Social Anthropology introduce the student
to the manner of life, family structure, livelihood, values, motivations, religious beliefs and ideology of a people. In short, that
branch of knowledge which provides many answers to the question,
"Why do people turn away from or accept the Christian message
and the Church?" Social Anthropology also guides in the task of
integrating the Christian culture with the permanent values of the
old way of life.

Man is the object of spiritual healing by the Christian Church as
he is the object of physical healing by medical science. Included in
the preparation for the medical profession are at least two years
of intensive study of the fundamental sciences—anatomy, physiology,
chemistry, pathology and medical psychology. The structure and
function of every tissue and organ are studied in detail, including
the psycho-somatic interrelationships, i.e., the influences of emotional
reaction upon the various organs. Such a discipline is considered
necessary before the student can administer the treatment required
for the injured or diseased member.

However, preparation for the yet more delicate art of spiritual
healing concentrates upon the history, content, and method of presentation of the spiritual message upon which it relies for trans-
forming the object of its ministry. There is little comparable in the
training of future physicians of sick souls to the exhaustive studies
involved in the discipline of the basic sciences for the young doctor.

This gap in the preparation of the theological student is serious enough for his understanding of his own fellow countrymen, but for the missionary who seeks to heal the spiritual ailments of men and women of a completely different culture, such an omission in his preparation is a vital weakness.

To a considerable extent Social Anthropology fills this gap and acquaints the missionary with the spiritual anatomy of the people he seeks to transform and with the forces that neutralize the effectiveness of the measures he adopts.

The Comprehensive Parish Program. The war's close will offer a unique opportunity for the Church to demonstrate that Christianity is not just another cult, but is a faith concerned with the whole of life, viz., better health, cleaner homes, villages and cities, happier families, sturdier children, better crops and stock, less malaria and parasites, pure water, more energizing food, literacy, recreation and education. These things are all included in the Glad Tidings which Christ gives to mankind and are inescapable aspects of the work of building the Kingdom of Heaven on earth.

The comprehensive parish program provides a task of Christian service for every member of a church. It demonstrates that religion consists of more than preaching and more than weekly church attendance; that worship has to do with "the daily round, the common task," and with the simplest duties and basic human relationships. There is a contradiction between Christ's concern for giving more abundant life to men and a Christian Church that is indifferent to the conditions of its environment. The missionary will need to acquaint himself with the comprehensive parish program and be prepared to teach and to demonstrate it in the new environment.

Increasingly the non-Christian peoples will demand of Christianity evidence that it is concerned with the intolerable conditions under which they live and that it is not a religion only for races that have attained high economic levels and standards of life.

New Emphasis upon the Urban Church. The strong emphasis put upon the rural field of missions in the last decade has, to some extent, shifted attention from the urban church. A vital and steadily growing city church will continue to be basic to the future of the Christian movement. The city church has several advantages not enjoyed by the rural church:

a) Contact with Christian institutions,
b) Contact with other churches, pastors, and leaders,
c) A comparatively strong pastoral leadership,
d) A considerable middle-class constituency,
e) Help of the missionary body,
f) A comparatively strong financial basis.

Some opportunities before the city church are:
a) A program for enlisting and training its lay members in Christian service,
b) A program for attracting and enlisting in service the many students and graduates of higher institutions who are employed in the city,
c) A message and a program for winning men of affairs in the life of the city,
d) A message and a program for the industrial workers and the depressed classes of the city,
e) Extension to and contact with the rural church field,
f) The comprehensive parish program,
g) Emphasis upon home and family life,
h) Organization of church finance and business management, including techniques and methods of self-support,
i) The use of research and survey techniques.

The missionary and the native pastor will be required to deal effectively with these problems and to use these techniques.

The Approach to Intellectuals. There is danger in many mission fields that the cultured and influential leaders of the community will be ignored, avoided or repelled by the Christian movement. Among the reasons for this are:

The identification of leading families with the religious and traditional institutions of their lands;

The nationalism and pride of these people and the social and civic ties which hold them to the old order;

The frequently humble status of the Christian group, its foreign and unattractive church equipment, and the frequent lack in social and cultural standards and intellectual power of its pastor;

The halting use of language and lack of preparation of some missionaries for meeting and influencing people of the upper classes;

The absorption of the missionary and pastor in the nurture and problems of the church constituency;

The identification of the Christian movement in the minds of upper-class people with foreign economic and cultural penetration.

The desire of some high-caste Hindus to know missionaries was expressed in 1938 by an influential member of the Legislative Council of the Punjab:

We upper-class Hindus are sometimes wistful at the way the missionaries ignore us and devote themselves entirely to the low-caste people. We almost never meet a missionary. I have known only two and one of them, C. F. Andrews, seemed to me to be the personification of Christ Himself. I wish you would tell your missionary friends that we want to know them better and wish to learn for ourselves what they have come to give to India.

Another type of intellectual is the modern, highly educated man who has no religious faith or connection and prides himself upon his "emancipation from all superstition." This type is exceedingly numerous in Latin American lands, and is a growing class in Asia.

Yet another aspect of the problem is the man who has been educated in a mission institution in which he identified himself with the Church, but on reaching prominence in government or secular affairs has severed his connection with the Christian movement. There are thousands of such men in all the larger mission fields.

Youth and the Church. The devotion of youth to heroic, venturesome, and self-sacrificing causes is an unmeasured resource of the Christian movement that has not yet been effectively drawn upon by many of the Younger Churches. The source of the problem is deeper than the frequently negative policy of the Church toward the social and recreational life of youth and the failure to provide adequate substitutes for banned activities. If the Christian Church does not take a stand in nations which are struggling with colossal issues such as national freedom, illiteracy, poverty, undernourishment and land serfdom, and does not provide programs of action, as well as of preaching and teaching, which will challenge youth, youth will follow other ideological movements which enlist it in definite lines of service.

Literature Production. Paralleling the world-wide demand for literacy service which the post-war age will offer, there will be the call for books and reading material suited to conserve the results of literacy campaigns. Here is a comparatively new line of service awaiting the missionary. A situation typical of many fields exists in Jamaica where thousands of young boys and girls who have learned to read in classes of the first standard, on leaving school, have lapsed into illiteracy.[1] They received no encouragement from their illiterate parents, they had no money to buy books or papers, and even if they had had the money, reading matter suited to their needs did not exist in Jamaica.

The notable results of the work of the International Committee on Christian Literature for Africa, under Margaret Wrong's leadership, is a guide to the possibilities and methods of creating literature in other fields.[2]

Visual Adult Education. The post-war missionary will find the still or motion picture a powerful means for portraying to the adults of non-Christian communities the meaning and values of the world to which their children are being introduced in mission schools. The relation to native tribal life of the mission program in school, church, hospital, agriculture, child care and diet can all be vividly shown in pictures. The life history of a child educated by the mission from the time he leaves the parental hut until, ten or fifteen years later, he returns to his village as teacher, pastor, or doctor can be presented in a motion picture story of intense interest. However, such pictures to be effective must be laid in native surroundings with native actors and must deal with native interests. It is useless to show pictures of a Western mother caring for her babies, or scenes of harvesting or dairying on a modern farm. The practical experience of the Bantu Educational Cinema Experiment as recorded in the book, *The African and the Cinema,*[3] would be most helpful in this connection.

A picture program of this nature can help to bridge the chasm which is created between the mission-educated child and his home community.

Research and the Missionary. The post-war decades will be not only an era of reconstruction and of resumption of old activities; they will also be an era of exploration and of blazing new trails. The missionary and the national pastor will need the ability to

[1] J. M. Davis, *The Church in the New Jamaica,* pp. 38, 91.
[2] International Committee on Christian Literature for Africa, Edinburgh House, 2 Eaton Gate, London, S. W. 1.
[3] Notcutt and Latham, Edinburgh House Press, London, 1937.

assess the principal social factors in the rapidly changing scene about them, and to relate these to the many-sided aspects of the Christian movement and to experiment in new fields of Christian service. For this, they will need a knowledge of simple survey techniques and the measurement and evaluation of economic and social data and phenomena.

Facility in social measurement and evaluation would widen and deepen the missionary's understanding of his task. The mission boards have among their personnel many potential discoverers and trail-blazers, and those who, upon their own initiative, have gathered accurate data related to their fields. Such returned missionaries, as well as new candidates for service, should be encouraged, given facilities for preparation before going abroad, and an opportunity after reaching the field to carry on surveys and research as a part of the total task of the mission. A central bureau in the mission field would be invaluable to coordinate, counsel, and make widely available the results of such studies.

The Gospel of Christian Stewardship. The principle of Christian stewardship is placed among the patterns for the post-war age because, while not new, it has yet to be discovered and taught by a majority of missionaries and Younger Church workers. The power of the stewardship principle to revolutionize the inner life of the Church, when intelligently and persistently taught, is not generally realized. This is true not only of securing self-support but, what is yet more basic, of the spiritual vitality and outreach of the members. However, to secure these results, the missionary will need to understand thoroughly the Gospel of stewardship so that he may communicate its principles and practices to the church leaders with whom he will be associated.[4]

Church Financial Organization and Management. If the chief work of the missionary is to extend the Church of Christ in non-Christian lands, he will need to be versed in its business management and financial organization. In this regard, there is almost a blind spot in the preparation of the training schools for the national pastors and not infrequently in the training of the missionary as well. The church—large or small—thrives or languishes to the de-

---

[4] a) See publications of the United Stewardship Council, Hillsdale, Michigan.
b) "Practical Stewardship Suggestions for the Pastor," The Committee on United Promotion, The Presbyterian Church in the U. S. A., 156 Fifth Avenue, New York.

gree that it uses business methods and practical procedures for the conduct of its affairs. If missionary or pastor is ignorant or lax as to this side of the church's life, the members will rarely of their own initiative supply the lack.[5]

An inescapable task of the missionary will be to help the National Church, its leaders, and its institutions to accept *the principle of self-support* and to be prepared to demonstrate the ways and means of attaining it. Difficult under any circumstances, this discipline will be made doubly hard by the economic dislocations caused by the war and the necessity of extending large financial aid during the initial period of special crisis. The war, however, has prepared the way for a new era of church independence in at least two respects: it has proved to congregations long accustomed to foreign subsidies the possibility of self-help. It has also formed a base line from which new standards of economy in church construction and management and new concepts of member responsibility can be demonstrated. Before going to the field, the missionary will need preparation in church finance and business management, in the principles of stewardship, and in the proved techniques and methods which have been used by some of the Younger Churches in various lands to reach a self-supporting position.

The Christian Church and Practical Affairs. In the post-war strategy of missions, the stabilizing of the Christian movement through the development of its own leadership in practical affairs needs to take a far more prominent place. If the indigenous church bodies in many non-Christian lands are to be more than foster children of the Western Church, the missionary societies with the National Churches must "raise their sights" and look beyond gathering the depressed and poverty stricken classes into congregations to the development of a progressive, independent movement, eventually capable of creating and financing its own institutions. This cannot be done by raising professional leaders alone, i.e., ministers, teachers, and doctors. Business and commercial men, and men who can lead in practical affairs are required by the Younger Church no less than by the Church of the West.[6]

In addition to the cabinet makers, bricklayers, blacksmiths, machinists and typesetters who are being trained by mission industrial

[5] See Appendix, "The Organization of Church Finance," by John Ritchie.
[6] Madras Series, Vol. V, pp. 81, 82.

schools, there will also be required master carpenters and masons, contractors and builders, architects and draughtsmen. The mission will be called upon to provide technical training for its students in figuring costs and in the taking of contracts. Reserve funds also will be needed for advancing the initial capital to start such enterprises.[7]

There are commercial markets peculiar to India which, if organized with adequate leadership and capital, would serve to rehabilitate the great low-caste group of leather workers who collect and tan the cattle hides. However, the marketing of leather is largely in the hands of Mohammedan middlemen and brokers. The bones of India's cattle have been exported to Europe by German and Scotch firms, processed into fertilizer, and shipped back to India for sale to the peasant farmer.

Rarely does the missionary or native pastor have the instinct or training to organize these unused commercial opportunities about him. Moreover, such business ventures usually have been outside the scope of the missions. Here is a line of mission strategy in which the leadership of Christian business men in the West might be splendidly utilized for strengthening the Younger Churches.

Rehabilitation of War Devastated Areas. The missionary who goes to war devastated areas should be conversant with the problems and methods of the military, official, and private organizations for public welfare and reconstruction in order that, as opportunity arises, he may be able intelligently to counsel with and assist the short-term administrator, and correlate the mission's longer-term rehabilitation activities with the official programs.

Questions related to the health and sanitation of communities, diet, food supply, rehabilitation of farming and small industries, schools, the training of welfare workers, nurses and home visitors are matters on which experienced mission members could offer their counsel. Such collaboration in emergency situations might lead to useful long-term cooperation of the mission with local or provincial authorities.

The Leadership of the Younger Churches. The mantle of leadership will increasingly fall upon the Younger Churches in the

---

[7] E. C. Bhatty, "The Economic Background of the Church in the United Provinces," pp. 22-26. Ewing Christian College, Allahabad, 1938.

post-war era. In the next fifty years the sources of the spiritual regeneration of the world and the leadership of its Christian destiny will more and more be found in the youthful vitality and powers of consecration of the Younger Churches. The concept and planning of the Ecumenical Church, including its world mission and the rôle of the missionary and his preparation for service, must hold this great objective constantly in view. A central task of the missionary, as never before, will be discovering powers of initiative and leadership in his national associates and encouraging and training them to carry responsibility.

II

MISSIONARY TRAINING IN NORTH AMERICA

The theological seminaries of North America and Europe are determining the shape of the Church on the mission field, for the training of the candidates of the mission boards is very largely in their hands. The missionary, therefore, tends to reproduce on the field the type of Church and pastoral training with which he, himself, is acquainted. In this sense, the Western theological seminary is the key to the future development of the Church on the mission field.

The Church, with its principles of organization, management, and finance is foreign to the experience of the members of the Younger Churches. If the missionary does not have a clear grasp of these principles and does not promote them in the churches with which he is associated, it can hardly be expected that the national pastor or members will take initiative or show enthusiasm for these subjects. Thus, the path to the development of well organized and locally supported Younger Churches leads directly from the mission field to the training of missionaries in the "sending lands."

The Theological Seminary. From a recent examination made by the Department of the curricula of forty-six of the theological seminaries that train American candidates for missionary service, it is clear that they are predominantly concerned with the sources, history, and content of the message of Christianity, and with the method of presentation as contrasted with the adaptation of the message to the environmental conditions under which it is received, appropriated, and rooted. There is also a marked absence of courses which prepare the candidate to deal with these special conditions.

Five years ago, Professor Ralph A. Felton made an analysis of the courses of study offered by forty-three leading theological seminaries in the United States. His analysis shows that, out of the total of 246.09 course hours per week offered by the average seminary, only 2.51 hours were given to the highly specialized problems of the field of the rural church—a field which includes one-half of the churches. The average seminary devoted three times as many hours to the teaching of Aramaic and Syriac as to the study of the family; as much time was given to Egyptian Hieroglyphics and Ethiopic as to the health factor in church work; a knowledge of sacred archaeology, when measured in course hours, was considered to be as vital to the young pastor as training in the business management, organization, and financing of his church.[8]

What can be done to induce the seminaries to broaden the scope of their training to include subjects that will better prepare prospective missionaries, as well as future American pastors, to deal with the environmental conditions of their fields? This question was put to several men who are well informed upon theological education in North America. One man replied that this was not the job of the theological seminary. Another that the chairs of the seminaries are endowed in perpetuity and that the system was "crystallized." Another man passed the responsibility back to the mission boards. Yet another relegated it to supplementary training in other institutions. The last man questioned said, "I have tried for twenty years with very little success to get new courses into our seminary. We may have to 'by-pass' the seminaries as Admiral Nimitz by-passed a fortified island in the southwest Pacific and set up our own type of institution which will do the job as it ought to be done." He added that this course would be particularly useful in dealing with the "replica" seminaries on the mission field.

[8] Ralph A. Felton, "The Training of Rural Ministers," Drew Theological Seminary, Madison, New Jersey, 1940.

The School of Missions. The school of missions has appeared as a practical and timely effort to supply the need for specialized missionary training. The Kennedy School of Missions of the Hartford Seminary Foundation at Hartford, Connecticut, offers courses in the rural church, ethnology, anthropology, linguistics, phonetics, and the philosophies and cultures of China, India, the Moslem lands and Africa. Sixteen foreign languages are taught in the Department of Linguistics.

The Canadian School of Missions at Toronto provides courses in missionary theory and practice, history of missions, primitive religion, culture contacts, the non-Christian faiths and phonetics. The relations that have been developed with the University of Toronto are such that virtually every supplementary subject for equipping a missionary may be studied under first-class academic leadership. The school is a cooperative undertaking of the mission boards of the Canadian churches.

Scarritt College for Christian Workers at Nashville, Tennessee, offers yet a different pattern of high-grade missionary preparation with a group of wide and practical courses which are worthy of careful consideration. It is in close contact with the needs and realities of the rural church and offers to its students useful facilities for field work.

The Bible Institutes. This type of institution is widely used by the candidates of the independent missionary societies and is responsible for the training of a very large number of missionaries. Many of these schools are highly organized and well manned, and, while offering a wide selection of courses, concentrate their training upon the Bible as the foundation of the work of the missionary.

SUPPLEMENTARY TRAINING FOR SPECIALIZED PREPARATION

Agricultural Colleges. The introductory courses in rural life, agriculture, and home economics which have been developed by Mr. John Reisner[9] at Cornell Agricultural College, Ithaca, New York, and the State Agricultural Colleges of Iowa and Oregon, represent a notable forward step in the supplementary preparation of the missionary. Fifty or more missionaries are annually enrolled in the special rural courses offered at Cornell.

[9] Director of Agricultural Missions, Inc., 156 Fifth Avenue, New York.

The Merrill-Palmer School at Detroit, Michigan, is probably the best equipped center in North America for training in the wide range of problems related to home and family life.

The Summer Institute of Linguistics, Bacone College, Muskogee, Oklahoma, is sponsored by the Wycliffe Bible Translators, Inc., and specializes in phonetics and the techniques for reducing primitive languages to writing, and for translating the Bible into these languages.

A Course in the Rudiments of Medicine for Non-Medical Missionaries, under the auspices of the Christian Medical Council for Overseas Work,[10] provides training in hygiene, household and community health measures, first aid and the rudiments of preventive and curative medicine and minor surgery. Its aim is to enable missionaries to conserve their own health, prevent the spread of disease in the communities where they work, and to render intelligent service to those who are sick.

Training for Post-War Rehabilitation Service. The Pacific School of Religion at Berkeley, California, through its Department of Overseas Service, provides a short-term training to graduate students for work in the devastated areas in China which can be credited toward advanced degrees given by this school. Among the courses available are: the language, geography, history and culture of China, Chinese Christian institutions and the work of the Christian mission, community reconstruction, public health, sanitation and mass relief. Courses in Christian education, theology, ethics and Church history are also available.

The University of California and neighboring Berkeley seminaries offer the student a wide variety of supplementary studies.

Only one of the schools briefly described offers courses in the business management of the local church or in methods for attaining self-support. It is obviously impossible for the prospective missionary to spend the time needed for thorough training in many of these supplementary subjects. At best, in an additional year at his disposal, he must choose between concentrating on two or three subjects or spreading his energies in a superficial introduction to a wider selection.

Anthropology, agriculture, psychology, rural sociology and economics, the home and family, health and sanitation are not offered

10 156 Fifth Avenue, New York.

in the Western seminary since these subjects have not been considered essential for the American pastor and, if desired, they may be studied in the liberal arts colleges and universities.

The missionary candidate who applies to a board for appointment has usually completed his university and theological training, and is faced with a new group of subjects which are intimately related to his future career, but with which he is probably unfamiliar. The reluctance or inability of the candidate to spend further time in study is often matched by the eagerness of the mission board to send him at once to the field, and frequently he sails without further preparation. A practical difficulty is finding, in a minimum period of study, suitable introductory courses in these supplementary subjects which are adapted to meet the missionary's needs.

This problem was reflected in the replies to a questionnaire that was sent to one hundred mission boards in North America upon the subject of anthropological study for their missionaries.[11] A majority of them considered that special preparation in the customs and institutions of the people to whom they are to be sent is most desirable for their candidates, but less than one-half of them made any provision for such preparation. Less than twenty per cent of the sixty-eight boards that replied to the questionnaire provide their furloughed missionaries with opportunities for study while at home. A difficulty frequently expressed was in finding institutions which offer suitable courses for meeting the needs of the candidate or furloughed missionary.

THE MISSION BOARDS AND POST-WAR PREPARATION

During the last two or three years, there has been an imposing amount of conference and study on the problems of post-war missions. In the nature of the case there has, as yet, been little action in implementing the many proposals which have emerged.

There are three or four immediate steps that boards can take—individually and unitedly—to transfer the problem of training workers for the post-war program from the realm of discussion to that of action:

[11] Ralph Dodge, "Missions and Anthropology," Hartford Seminary Foundation thesis, 1944.

1. Center attention upon those conditions which, with certainty, the missionary enterprise will have to deal in the decades immediately before us.
2. Upon these conditions as a base, determine the type of ability and training the missionary, who must deal with them, will require.
3. Measure the present training facilities of our institutions by the yardstick of the preparation required for the specific field conditions to be dealt with.
4. If existing facilities are inadequate, create supplementary instruments of missionary training to meet the new demand.

This procedure is used by the large secular projects which are dealing with the international scene, i.e., orientation courses for civil service candidates of the British Colonial Office, language schools for diplomatic and commercial attachés, and the training courses for their overseas employees provided by the Standard Oil Company and North American banks. Should not similar practical and adequate methods be used by world missions?

A theological training for missionaries cannot be discounted; on the contrary, such training is basic for the future builders of the Church. Rather, attention is called to the importance of devising a supplementary plan for the specific preparation of the worker since the conditions to be met on the post-war mission field will be so varied and specialized that they cannot be dealt with by a theological training alone.

Why should not the mission boards, which annually send hundreds of representatives to their fields, unite upon a suitable course of supplementary missionary training for the post-war age which would provide for the specialized studies required? Would this not obviate the candidate's expenditure of time in "shopping about" and the often inadequate preparation the missionary carries to his field?

In North America, such a plan for supplementary studies could provide for several centers accessible to different parts of the continent, viz., central Canada, the northeastern seaboard states, the South, the Middle West, and the Far West. There would be obvious advantages in centering upon institutions already engaged in the special training of missionaries provided such institutions were able to reconstruct their curricula in the measure required. Several of the institutions in question have already begun to supplement their courses with this purpose in view.

THE TRAINING OF THE NATIONAL PASTOR

The general outline for the training of the native pastor will continue to be patterned upon the Western seminary but there will be definite divergence at certain important points,—points that are related to the stabilizing and adjusting of the Church to its environment.

It is not only the Western institution which is reflected upon foreign mission fields. Similarly the native pastor and worker tend to reflect the stature of the missionary with whom they are associated and by whom they are trained. The vision of the native leader often is bounded by the horizons of the missionary. The missionary's interests and his estimate of the task of the Church are reflected in those of his native associate. The weight of influence on some fields of older missionaries who have long been out of touch with the widening vision and practice of the home Church makes it difficult for the young recruit to follow the new emphases and programs to which he is devoted. There is also the tendency for the national pastor to be content to work on traditional lines and to be reluctant to change the accustomed pattern. Here is a vicious circle which missions in the post-war age should find the means to break. The preparation of the new or the returning missionary can contribute greatly to this end, particularly if he has been trained in the methods of demonstrating the activities that he proposes to his associates.

The Western seminary is responsible in large measure for the type of native pastor and for the kind of church he develops, for the native pastor is usually the product of a "replica" of the Western seminary. If there is a lag between the needs of pastoral training in the sending lands and the courses of study offered in their seminaries, a similar lag is reflected, often in an aggravated form, in the mission institution abroad. In not a few mission fields a tragic result is that both the missionaries and the pastors are unprepared to cope with the environmental and practical aspects of the life of their churches. In sixteen of the theological seminaries of twelve mission fields which we have visited in the last five years, two seminaries only were providing courses related to the training of their students to meet the overwhelming social and economic problems of the churches. Most of the schools were faithfully duplicating the principal courses offered by the seminaries of their denomination in the homeland but, because of limitations in leadership, funds, and vision, had not provided the special courses which, in recent years, many of the home seminaries had begun to add to the conventional theological curricula.

Typical of the problem was a West Indian country in which eighty per cent of the people live in rural areas and where the bulk of the population, including a majority of Evangelical Church members, exist under almost incredible conditions of ill-health, undernourishment, poverty, debt and illiteracy. The Union Theological Seminary did not offer a single hour of instruction on the social and economic conditions of either the rural or urban peoples or suggest ways in which the pastor or church might improve them. Since the vitality and growth of the Church rest in great measure with its leadership, it follows that the replanning of pastoral training upon the mission field is a first requirement for a thoroughgoing and permanent stabilization of the Younger Churches in their environment in the post-war age.

THE SHUNHWACHEN TRAINING CENTER FOR RURAL PASTORS

The Shunhwachen Training Center of Nanking Theological Seminary has set a high-water mark on the mission field in its pastoral training for the vast rural areas of China. The following description is given since the project is capable of being reproduced upon other fields of the Younger Churches.[12]

In 1929, Nanking Theological Seminary opened a Department of the Rural Church in order to give students going into the rural ministry a more specialized training for their work.

Shunhwachen, the market town of a natural group of villages near Nanking, was selected as a community where teachers and students might live near the village people, study rural needs and problems, and practice ways of Christian service and methods of building up a rural church.

The University of Nanking had conducted surveys and extension work in Shunhwachen for many years. The people were friendly, a small Presbyterian church already existed, and the rural community was representative and not too far from Nanking. The first theo-

[12] Frank W. Price, "Shunhwachen Rural Training Center of Nanking Theological Seminary," May, 1936.

logical students went out for field training in 1931, a new church program was begun in 1932, and on January 1, 1933, the farm and buildings of the Nanking Seminary Rural Training Center were dedicated. The center provided accommodations for the staff of the Rural Church Department of the Seminary and for students in training, facilities for directing experiments in Christian rural service, conferences, religious education and demonstrations in improved farming. It also served as a practice field for the theological students.

The work of the Shunhwachen Training Center consisted of:

1. Research into various problems of rural life and of the rural church, experimentation in Christian service and reconstruction in a rural community, and in the ways of building up the rural church;
2. Training of professional and voluntary workers for service in the church and the training of village leaders;
3. Extension service to the fifty other rural communities of the Shunhwachen district;
4. Production of literary and visual materials for use in Christian rural work.

The methods that were tested in the local groups and organizations to which the Seminary staff was adviser could be used by rural churches and adapted to many other communities. Among these groups were the church, the village agricultural improvement association and cooperative society, the evening schools, the community welfare and health organizations and children's clubs. All these groups made use of local leadership and the simple resources that were available in the average rural community. From the beginning, the Seminary aimed to develop self-help in all church and community effort. The training center and the Shunhwachen church cultivated the friendliest possible relations with the people and local organizations and worked with them for community betterment. The confidence and willing cooperation of a large number of people in the surrounding villages were also won in the six years of active life of the center.

The local program at Shunhwachen included the following:

1. *Agricultural Extension and Economic Improvement.* Many demonstrations were conducted with improved varieties of seed,

wheat, rice, soy beans, cotton, corn, buckwheat, peanuts, potatoes, and kaoliang. Improved peaches, grapes, pears, figs, and persimmons were planted. A nursery with ten varieties of trees and 10,000 seedlings was developed and vegetables and flowers were cultivated.

Experiments were made in the breeding of imported poultry and hogs and in crossing them with domestic strains.

Agricultural improvement societies to introduce better seeds and stock were organized in ten villages. Seven credit and producer's cooperative societies were trained and organized in as many villages.

2. *Drought Relief and Improvement of Irrigation*. Branches of the Shunhwachen Social Welfare Association were organized in thirty-seven villages. Two reservoirs were repaired, 214 ponds deepened, and 50 irrigation ditches were dug or deepened, benefitting 1046 farms.

3. *Public Health and Medical Service*. Shunhwachen Center maintained a health station, with two nurses in attendance, which was incorporated in the government health service of the *hsien*. Its program provided daily clinic treatments, preventive medicine, public and school health, baby welfare and service to mothers. The annual budget was met by government grants, clinic fees, and local contributions.

A research project in rural health and nutrition was carried out in cooperation with Nanking University.

4. *Social Work and Recreation*. The Christian group at Shunhwachen influenced the social life of the community through friendship with and influence upon individuals in local social organizations, through its own social programs which it promoted, and through opposition to social evils, influence upon public opinion, lifting of social standards and modification or change in wrong systems.

The rural training center in 1934 became one of the cooperating units in the Shunhwachen branch of the New Life Movement.

Through the Social Welfare Association organized by the rural center and with the financial help of Shunhwachen, four main roads were widened and branch roads were improved.

The rural center and the church became members of a new association of town organizations with the purpose of civic betterment.

Representatives of eight local organizations met once a month for supper and discussion. A Young Men's Club was formed, social and recreational activities were started, a building was rented and a good membership was built up. With the help of the seminary students in training at the Center, an experiment in industrial education and in cottage industries was undertaken.

5. *The Church.* Active religious work in the community was carried on by the Shunhwachen church. While the seminary rural center and the church were separate in organization, there was a very close relationship between the two. The Shunhwachen church was the laboratory church of the Center and its large parish was the Center's experimental parish and through it the rural church in the parish was being built up. When the rural center was started in 1931, the Shunhwachen church was a typical rural church of thirty members with a limited evangelistic program and an evening literacy class. By 1935, it enrolled ninety-three members, of whom more than one-half lived in seventeen of the surrounding villages. There were fifty-two people who were enrolled in enquirer's classes. Every member was asked to serve in some way in the wide church program. The church was well on the way to become self-supporting, self-governing, and self-propagating. The members' contributions to the church had increased from $36.10 in 1930 to $194.27 in 1935. All but $50.00 of its annual budget was being met locally. Branch chapels had been built by the people in two outlying villages and the aim was to extend the Church to each village of the district in which Christians lived.

A LAY LEADER TRAINING PROJECT

One of the most practical and efficient projects in any mission field for training lay leadership for village church and community service is described by Miss Alice E. Murphy of the North China Mission of the American Board.[13]

The mission work in the Tehchow and Lintsing fields, Shantung, had been conducted along the traditional lines of medical, educational, and evangelistic work with hospitals in Tehchow and Lintsing, numerous primary schools, one high school and a number of relatively weak churches scattered in the county seat, towns, and

[13] "Training and Guiding Lay Leadership in the Village Church," Agricultural Missions, Inc., Mimeograph Series, No. 157, 156 Fifth Avenue, New York.

larger market centers. The Christians were mostly men, only a few living in the same village, and about one-half of them being the only Christians in their respective families. Church work consisted almost entirely of preaching by evangelists who were paid with mission funds. The duty of the Christian was to attend church, to abstain from certain sins, such as idol worship, and to send his children to the mission school. Station classes for instructing new converts were held once or twice a year but there was little systematic instruction of church members. The area of the two fields was about equal to that of the state of Massachusetts. Before the war, it was densely populated, with 2,129 persons to the square mile. The average family had 5.94 persons and consumed annually goods valued at $46.08 (U. S. currency).[14]

There was plainly need of a more intelligent and active church membership and a program of church life in which the improvement of the social environment and the spiritual life should go hand in hand. This need was expressed by Liang Shu Ming, head of the experimental district of the Shantung Institute of Rural Reconstruction:

The history of China during the last hundred years may properly be thought of as a record of rural decadence. . . . Rural life has been brought close to the point of complete ruin. . . . China is not only bankrupt in an economic sense, but also in a moral sense. By this we refer to the shaking and collapse of the old ideas, beliefs, folklore and customs, without anything new to take their place. . . . Consequently, the rural folk have been thrown into a state of baffled confusion and depression. Until there is some transformation and enlightenment, this state of mind renders futile any effort to better their condition.

Madame Chiang Kai-shek stressed the need of spiritual uplift in rural reconstruction, as follows: ". . . We cannot create the social life of the people, but it is within our power to regenerate it, and wholly transform it by breathing into it a new soul."[15]

The laymen's training program evolved from keeping in mind the question, "What sort of a church do we want?" together with the motto, "The redemption of the whole of life through a church deeply rooted in a village." The plan adopted aimed to organize

[14] J. Lossing Buck, *Chinese Farm Economy*, p. 389, University of Chicago Press, 1930.
[15] Address before the National Christian Council of China, May 7, 1939.

the village churches into parishes for strength and mutual help. In each parish, at least two well-trained workers—a man and a woman —and, if possible, a public health nurse cooperated with the mission station for specialized help. The village church was the heart of the program. It consisted of the Christians of one village together with those who lived within a radius of two miles. These people were organized under their own voluntary workers, with a regular program including worship services in their own place of meeting. The pastoral district was made up of a group of from five to twenty such churches, each church with three representatives on the parish council which had a unified program and budget and employed the paid workers.

The first duty of this village church group was to recruit, train, and supervise volunteer lay workers. The mission training staff consisted of a missionary, a Chinese leader, and two women district supervisors together with the lay training teams which served both areas. These teams helped with materials, literature, with training programs, moral support and guidance and made contacts with hospitals, schools, and government agencies.

Between 1939 and 1941, under war conditions, ten new churches were built or purchased without mission help, the labor, materials, and funds being given entirely by the people.

The lay workers training teams consisted of an adult education and church worker, a women's and children's specialist, a public health nurse and an agricultural expert. At the invitation of the parish council these teams spent an entire year in a parish, giving the intensive training for laymen and women that the pastor did not have time to give. A year allowed time to visit all the churches, to study local conditions, get projects started and give training to the lay workers who were to lead them. This was on the principle that the help was temporary, the church was theirs, and that the project was the responsibility of the villagers.

The team carried a lending library, textbooks, a phonograph and records, pictures to sell, dress patterns and handcraft materials, posters, hymn charts, etc. The teams did their own housekeeping in rooms provided by the Christian farmers, and a part of their work was a demonstration of sanitary and hygienic living, cooking, and eating. The local pastor and woman worker spent as much time as possible with the team so they might take part in the developing program after the visitors had gone.

Believing that self-help with intimate, expert counsel is the only permanent way to self-improvement, the team went to the country people, lived with them until it knew them and their problems, and until they knew and trusted the team members.

The following principles were used:

1. Begin with felt needs and enlarge the plans as the people grow in vision and ability.
2. Do not do things for people that they can do for themselves. Let them find a way out of difficulties as these arise.
3. Start with a few simple projects that the villagers may gain confidence through success. Let the laymen and women decide what they will undertake.
4. Help the people to feel that it is God's work and to count heavily on prayer and spiritual resources.
5. Study the parish with the laymen. Help them to feel a responsibility for the whole parish and not for the church members alone.
6. Hold special celebration or "Achievement Days" to fix definite objectives and to mark progress.
7. Place special emphasis upon youth and upon reaching all the members of families.
8. Develop the Lay Workers' Training Camp or Institute.

The purpose of the Lay Workers' Institute is to give a short period of intensive training to persons who have been chosen for certain tasks by their group. These representatives associate with people from other villages who are trying to do the same sort of thing, and they have a chance to make new friends and gain a sense of belonging to a larger, more far-reaching organization. Each camp has from twenty-five to fifty members, and meets for from fifteen to twenty days. Camp programs are divided into special subjects—literacy class leadership, training of deacons, leaders of worship services, Christian homes workers, Sunday School teachers, and agricultural demonstrators. The members bring their own food supplies and live in simple quarters provided by local Christians. The camps are held mostly in the winter months when the farmers have free time.

The Japanese occupation of Shantung has created difficulties in securing adequate staff for the parishes and teams, and has interrupted the normal growth of the whole program. However, during this confused period, there has been a steady gain in church membership, an unprecedented sale of Bibles, many new church buildings and a number of newly organized groups which have reached full churchhood. There has also been a large increase in financial support by the local Christians with a much stronger feeling that the Church and the work is theirs and a greater understanding of Christianity and the Church's task. The years of lay training undoubtedly account for the remarkable record of this group of churches under war conditions.

THE PROGRAM OF THE RURAL CHURCH

The program of the local parish should be voted and voluntarily assumed by the local Christians and not superimposed by the mission or supervisors.

The following goals were undertaken by one or more of the rural parishes of the Tehchow-Lintsing area:

1. *Worship.* A worship service each week within easy walking distance of any part of the parish. Nightly prayer meetings at the church.

2. *Literacy.* Every Christian up to forty-five years able to read the New Testament. Literacy classes open to non-Christians. A New Testament in every Christian home. A loan library of books and magazines.

3. *Homes.* Every member of the family a Christian. Every member literate. Simpler weddings and funerals; grace at meals and family prayers in the home; making children's toys and play equipment; flowers, fruit trees, and vegetable gardens for each home; women's weaving cooperatives; mother's and grandmother's clubs for handwork, worship, good times and discussion of problems.

4. *Health.* First aid box in each community with someone trained in its use. A bottle of iodine in each home; vaccination campaigns each spring; sanitary toilets in homes, schools, and churches; windows that can be opened; education regarding flies, mosquitoes, trachoma; whitewashing walls, tetanus control, better diet; milk for babies; midwife training.

5. *Agriculture.* Distribute and use better wheat and millet seed provided by Cheeloo University; introduce tomatoes, spinach, beets, alfalfa; distribution of pure-bred White Leghorn chickens; control of destructive insects and plant diseases; education in and organiza-

tion of cooperatives; representatives sent to agricultural short courses; well-digging for truck gardens and fields.

6. *Home Industries*. Industrial school to teach shoemaking, carpentry, basketry, tinsmithing and stocking knitting with itinerant stocking knitters; making and selling straw hats; hooked rug project for poor women; carding, spinning, and knitting of wool; bee culture; cotton-marketing cooperative.

7. *Gospel Extension*. Parish-wide four-day revival meeting each year; laymen responsible for all church services, prayer meetings, and parish visitation; "Win your relatives and friends" campaign.

8. *Religious Education*. Enquirers won by personal witness; station classes led by pastor, assisted by laymen; Bible study classes; Sunday Schools; singing of Bible verses; advanced classes for baptized Christians; classes for learning new songs and hymns; lay leaders attendance at Lay Training Institutes.

9. *Church Building and Equipment*. Adequate auditorium with sufficient light and air; worshipful altar with pulpit; blackboard, hymn charts, pictures, scrolls, church bell, guest bedrooms and kitchen.

10. *Education*. Primary schools for villages without a government school.

11. *Recreation*. Social evenings, plays, exhibits on health, home, and agriculture; Harvest Home Festival, Easter, Christmas and New Year's celebrations; church dedications; literacy class socials and literacy games; Chinese checkers, tournaments, playgrounds, kite-flying, deck-tennis; daily vacation Bible schools, Sunday School game hour; women's meetings, toy making, etc.

In conclusion, the author wishes to emphasize that the purpose of this book is to further the progress and the stability of the Younger Churches of the world. Attention has been called to the varied and rich resources—economic, social, cultural and spiritual— of the Church, and to the interdependence and interrelation of these resources.

There can be no true or lasting vitality in a church apart from the experience of God's saving grace through His Son, Jesus Christ.

Where this is absent, no amount of exhortation to give, expedients for economic strengthening or devices for saving funds can inspire a church or a Christian to sacrificial giving of self or substance. Where this experience is present, the weakest church or member is impelled from within to do the utmost to extend His Kingdom and the key to church support is at hand.

The Word of God is a source of inner life, available to every church, for which no results of economic or social research, or stimulus of money or method from without, can be substituted.

The task of the missionary and national pastor is to kindle this inner fire and this aim must be central in their preparation. All else is subsidiary to this, for without themselves possessing that fire, how can they kindle it in others?

Yet under God's plan of human redemption, He has provided a store of immutable laws and of rich resources whose recognition and use by His workers will undergird and extend the spiritual edifice of His Church in the post-war age.

APPENDIX

THE ORGANIZATION OF CHURCH FINANCE

BIBLIOGRAPHY

INDEX

APPENDIX

THE ORGANIZATION OF CHURCH FINANCE

THE following plan has evolved from the forty years of missionary experience of the Reverend John Ritchie of Lima, Peru, with several score groups of Indian Evangelical Christians scattered through the lofty central Andean Corridor. The program which follows was carried out with gratifying results in certain selected churches and was then modified and adapted to the needs, limitations, and capacities of the more primitive mountain congregations.

With Mr. Ritchie's permission, we present a digest of the sixth section of the forthcoming book which he has written on *Indigenous Church Principles in Theory and Practice*.[1] It is a clear and detailed analysis of the steps by which the problem of financing the Church should be approached and developed.

A Christian church may be successfully started in a private home without the services of a salaried pastor and with little or no expense. But as it grows and moves out into a more public life and activity, expenses increase. When and if a salaried pastor serves the church, the budget is very materially augmented.

If the church is part of a larger and expanding movement contributions also will be required from the associated congregations to meet the expenses of the organization.

If the support is to grow correspondingly with the progress of development and expansion without foreign funds, a definite process of education is necessary.

EDUCATION FOR SELF-SUPPORT

The members of the church require to be taught whatever pertains to the proper conduct and success of its financing. This process of education, though a basic factor in self-support, is frequently lacking in mission churches.

[1] Published by Fleming H. Revell Co., New York, 1945.

Many sincere Christians attend church services and contribute to the collection without having any idea of what should be their share in the support of their church. They give a coin and feel that they have made their contribution. They have never been taught that God has a claim on their money or been shown how much is required to maintain the church and its services, or how much would be required from each one to cover the expenses. Most of those who attend church would make an honest effort and many would make considerable sacrifices to do their part, if they were properly informed and consulted.

INSTRUCTION THROUGH BIBLE STUDY

The first step in the educative process may well be a course of Bible studies to find what is the will of God concerning the support of His Church. Such a course may be given in a series of talks by the missionary or pastor. But believers are impressed by what they find in their Bible, and what we discover for ourselves stays with us longer than anything told by another. The simple study outlines given below were sent to a number of churches, mostly rural, accompanied by the following instructions:

We recommend that you do not appoint a speaker to deliver discourses on the themes, but that the members attend bringing their Bibles, and all take part in the study and express their views.

Copies of the notes for the next study should be made available to the members in advance by writing them on a blackboard for each to make his own copy. Then the person in charge should arrange who is to read and comment on each passage, so that they may prepare to read it well and to state briefly what it teaches concerning the will of God.

When you gather for these studies, whoever presides should conduct the opening exercises and then call on the person appointed to read the first Scripture passage. When he has read and commented on it, the others should be encouraged to express their views of the significance of the passage. Then the next will read the following portion and comment on it, and so on till the end. At the close, the chairman may give a brief review of what has been learned concerning God's will for His people in the matter of offerings.

FOUR BIBLE STUDIES ON THE OFFERING TO GOD

I. *The Offering in the Pentateuch*

1. *The Tithe*

Abram gives tithes to Melchizedek, priest of God. Gen. 14:20
Jacob promises to give God a tenth of all. Gen. 28:22

2. *The Law of the Tithe*

A tenth of all is the Lord's. Lev. 27:30, 34
A tithe the offering for the Levites. Num. 18:19, 21, 24
The Levites gave a tenth of the tithes to Aaron. Num. 18:26, 28
Tithes for the needy. Deut. 14:28, 29

3. *Other Offerings* (in brief review)

The offering of expiation. Lev. 6:1, 7
Burnt offerings, sacrifices, tithes and other offerings. Num.
28:3, 4

II. *The Offering in the Historical Books and the Prophets*

1. The Tithe in Hezekiah's revival. 2 Chron. 31:1, 6, 12
2. The Tithe in the Restoration after the Captivity. Neh. 10:37,
   38; 12:44; 13:10, 12
3. The Prophet Amos denounces the women who oppress the poor
   and make a show of piety by giving the tithe. Amos 4:4
4. The Prophet Malachi denounces robbing God. Mal. 3:7, 10
5. How to honor God. 1 Chron. 16:28, 30
6. The offering which dishonors God. Mal. 1:7, 14. Compare 1
   Chron. 21: 22, 24
7. The joyful giver. 1 Chron. 29:6, 16 (note verse 9)

III. *The Offering in the Gospels*

1. The tithes of the Pharisees. Luke 11:42, 44; 18:12
2. To bring an offering is not enough. Matthew 5:23, 24
3. The poor widow's offering. Mark 12:41, 44
4. The Christian measure for giving. Luke 6:38
5. How the converts of Jesus gave. Luke 5:27, 29; 19:8
6. Gifts should be given with discretion. Matthew 7:6
7. God entrusts His gifts to those who are faithful. Luke 16:10, 12

IV. *The Offering in the other Apostolic Writings*

1. A voluntary communism. Acts 4:34, 37
2. A saying of Jesus recalled. Acts 20:35

3. The Apostle Paul lays down a Principle. 1 Cor. 9:11, 14.
   Gal. 6:6
4. Paul teaches Method and Measure. 1 Cor. 16:1, 2
5. Paul cites an Example. 2 Cor. 8:1, 4
6. A purely Christian Motive. Eph. 4:28
7. God loves a cheerful giver. 2 Cor. 9:6, 10

INSTRUCTION THROUGH THE BUDGET

The next step is to teach the congregation how much is required to meet the needs of their church. The natural method is the preparation and approval of the church budget. The conditions of the mission churches which should deal with this problem are very varied. Many village churches exist with a minimum of financial involvement, paying neither rental nor pastor though contributing to the support of itinerant preachers. They were becoming accustomed to a cheap but insufficient church life.

On an appointed mid-week evening each year, the congregation gathers in special session to deal with the budget, preparation being made beforehand and interest built up among both members and adherents. It is an advantage to have someone present with experience in the budget system who can present it clearly and simply. The following circular, sent out to over eighty village churches, may be suggestive:

WHAT IS THE CHURCH BUDGET

At the beginning of each year it is necessary that each congregation know exactly how much money they will require to spend during the year, and also how the funds are to be collected. This is done by means of the budget, which is a statement and calculation of the amount to be spent during the year.

The budget should include, in addition to the local expenses of the congregation, funds for the presbytery with which to support the preachers and pay their travel expenses. Also it should provide funds for the synod with which to sustain the Church periodical and the general secretary. Further, if the delegates to the presbytery do not pay their own expenses, the budget should include such amounts. All these expenses are necessary for the life and progress of the church.

HOW IS A BUDGET PREPARED?

The church budget should be prepared and approved in a full meeting of the congregation, in which each one should have complete liberty to express his views and to vote on each item. Before this meeting the treasurer should draw up a provisional estimate, in view of the expenses of past years and the plans for the coming year. After approval by the elders, this provisional budget should be presented to the meeting, preferably written up on a blackboard, beginning with the expenses. These should be written up one by one, each one being discussed and approved before adding the next. If any item is not approved it should be modified according to the wishes of the church. The following is the expenses side of an imaginary church budget:

BUDGET OF THE EVANGELICAL CHURCH IN ———

Expenses

Rental of meeting place	S. 600.00	per year
Rates and Taxes	30.00	
Light	60.00	
Secretarial expenses	30.00	
Expenses of delegates	60.00	
Contribution to presbytery	200.00	
Contribution to synod	50.00	
Tracts and Sunday School literature	120.00	
Benevolence	100.00	
	S. 1250.00	per year

HOW ARE THE FUNDS TO BE PROVIDED?

Supposing that the congregation has approved expenses amounting to S.1250.00 per year, this sum is divided by 52, the number of weeks in a year. The amount required each week is found to be S.24.04. A calculation should be made of the number of contributors, members, and adherents who may be expected to contribute their share of the funds. If there are twenty, the weekly sum of S.24.04 is now divided by 20, which shows that each one should give S.1.20 each week.

By this simple process, everyone may see what is his proper share in the expenses. But not all can give the same amount, and no one should be obliged to give any stated quota. The calculation is made to establish the basis and to let everyone see how much is required from him. If some give less, others will have to give more.

God has given us a simple plan for gathering the necessary money: The method of the tithe. The Bible teaches that a tenth part of all our income or of the produce of our fields, belongs to God. Let us take as our guide the Bible rule of the tithe. Let each one conscientiously valuate his income before God. The money should be put apart each time we receive our wages, or sell our crops, and placed in a small box or bag specially kept for this purpose. This money should be used exclusively in the service of God. The first call on it is for the support of the church and those who serve it. We should also support the Sunday School, Christian Endeavour, Women's League, students in the Bible School, etc. The elders may not be able to carry this through successfully in the first year. It may take several years to attain the goal.

None of the churches to which this circular was sent was supporting a pastor. Most were contributing to the support of itinerant preachers appointed and maintained through the presbyteries. But this support was inadequate and not always available when due. Many of the congregations were composed very largely of poor, though not unintelligent, Indians who had a very limited understanding of financial affairs. It was therefore deemed prudent not to go further at first than the Bible studies and the budget. The introduction of the complete system of the double budget and every-member-pledge at the beginning, would have been overwhelming to many of these rustic groups. But as soon as each congregation has instituted the budget method, they can be shown how to organize the quota payments by adopting the every-member-pledge and thus keep their finances in order and their accounts clear.

When dealing with an urban congregation, however, it is possible to institute the double budget and every-member-pledge at once.

Church officers commonly impose the budget on the church without the members having any opportunity jointly to discuss its details. To impose the budget without discussion forfeits the most valuable opportunity for educating the members in the conviction that the quota asked from them truly represents their share in carrying on their church as they desire. It will be found altogether advantageous to have the budget presented in a church meeting and discussed line by line. Even though the discussion should bring out acute differences of opinion, it is healthy for the church to have these stated and understood.

If the church has a paid pastor, his salary will be the largest single item in the budget. If he is being paid entirely or partly from mission funds, the members are probably not aware of the total amount. He will therefore tend to oppose a budget discussion which would disclose how much he receives and perhaps lead to expressions of disapproval. He may also be unwilling to have the amount of his salary depend on the vote of the congregation. His resistance in these circumstances is quite understandable, and his opposition should be treated with sympathy. Whoever has the matter in hand for the mission might assure the congregation that the mission recognizes that the services, ability, and devotion of their pastor should be paid more highly, that only the excessive demands on the treasury have kept the amount so small, and that the mission in urging self-support desires that justice may be done in this matter by the congregation which enjoys his ministry. An appeal to the nationalistic sentiment of the congregation to do better by their pastor than the foreigner did, is likely to arouse a sympathetic response.

Should the discussion lead to a decision to do without a paid pastor, let such a choice be welcomed and honestly supported. The experience of carrying on their church without a pastor, if due to a deliberate decision, will put the church officers and members on their mettle, and constrain them to exercise their own gifts. The day will probably come when that congregation will again ask for a pastor and be the more willing to support him.

INSPIRATION FOR SELF-SUPPORT

Many Christians will readily respond to the education which has been suggested, and will give their church quota faithfully. But this is not enough to sustain all the members in its practice. To the knowledge of what is right there has to be added an inspiring motive. Such inspiration is greatly to be desired, but the ministry of some mission churches does not promote it. There are two elements which enter largely into this state of soul which deserve special consideration—worship and service. The soul that knows God through evangelism and Bible study also feels the need to worship Him. Now an offering is one of the expressive and natural elements of worship and a worship service is an appropriate setting for an offering to God. A worship service which helps the believers to realize the divine presence would be incomplete without an opportunity given to express the soul's love and adoration in an offering.

The other vital inspiration to sustained giving is the enthusiasm of Christan service which is accomplishing something for the welfare of others. The writer has the privilege of visiting from time to time a mission field congregation which is a veritable beehive of gracious and wise Christian service, affecting the lives of members, adherents, and the community. The income, received in boxes placed at the door, from a numerous but poor congregation, is a source of encouragement to go on to larger things. They pay all the expenses of the church, support two pastors, and some eight or nine other workers besides.

THE ORGANIZATION OF SELF-SUPPORT

In the earlier stages of the growth of a mission church, support may be adequately taken care of by the annual budget discussion and the calculation of the amount due from each member of the group. But with growth, a stage is soon reached at which the collection of the offerings should be organized if income and expenditure are to be balanced, and the education of the church properly carried forward. This may be done by adapting to local conditions the methods of the every-member-pledge.

In the rural churches, it may be wiser to adopt the budget discussion and quota calculation, and have this put into practice before saying anything about the every-member-pledge and weekly envelopes. In a town congregation the whole system may be presented and carried into effect at once. The church officers will recognize the need for a method to convert the calculated quotas into calculable income. Whoever presents the method should be fully informed as to its details, and be ready to show its adaptability to local conditions, otherwise it can be made by any critic to appear too cumbrous.

Beyond the annual budget for church support, another budget for missions and benevolence should also be prepared. This should include an amount for the care of the poor, and all other funds required for purposes other than the support of the church, such as contributions to missions, the Bible Society and Tract Society, and help for seminary students. This should be discussed, approved, and divided to find the weekly quota in the same way as the other budget.

Every member and adherent should then be approached for his pledge. He is asked to state on a card provided for the purpose, how much he will give each week for the church, and how much for benevolences. He may, of course, give only for the support of the church. The signed cards are given to the treasurer, who arranges them in alphabetic order of names and numbers them consecutively. He then prepares for each person a series of thirteen envelopes, dated for the Sundays of the quarter, numbered with each contributor's number and annotated with the amounts pledged. These thirteen envelopes are then given to the person whose number they bear. On opening the envelopes each week, the amount in each is checked with that noted on it. Should these not agree, the amount received is clearly marked. The envelopes are then arranged in their numerical order, and the amounts received on both accounts noted on the account sheet for the quarter.

A sheet measuring 16 x 13 inches can be ruled to keep a clear account of the contributions of fifty-five contributors for three months. Used on both sides, it carries either 110 names for the quarter, or 55 names for the half year. Each column gives the total offerings for the week, each line the total contributions of the member for the quarter. The account-keeping is therefore perfectly simple. The weeks' used envelopes should be tied together and kept till the year-end audit of the accounts. At the end of each quarter a note of thanks sent to each contributor shows the amount of his pledge and the amount received. This serves as a reminder to any who have been absent some Sundays and failed to bring their offering, and gives every member a check on the amount entered to his name in the account.

The conditions of the mission church should dictate the scope of items in its budget. A few years of practice will teach the church officers what items to include if they will keep clear the distinction between the two budgets.

Where the parents and family are hostile to the new faith of the convert, he should be approached by the every-member canvasser at the church. But wherever possible the visit should be made in the home as it yields returns in the spiritual welfare of the church.

It should be carefully planned with this in view and be made, if possible, by a member of the budget committee with an elder or deacon who should be supplied with copies of the budget and pledge cards. It should be made perfectly clear that the church is not asking for a pledge of the quota amounts but that as some may give less, others will have to give more, as their tithe permits. The member should understand that the amount pledged is voluntary and that it can be suspended in case of unemployment or sickness. A signed card should be obtained for every pledge·

The visitors should enquire whether the children are attending Sunday School, and the adolescents are sharing in the youth activities of the church. Members are more likely to express their criticisms on such an occasion than on a pastoral visit. In most cases they can be dealt with and misunderstandings cleared up. When the pledges are in on the following Sunday, an announcement by the treasurer of the total amount pledged and of any uncovered balance, gives the members to feel that they are partners in the enterprise and are expected to take an interest in its success.

The use of the envelope involves expense and work, but it more than compensates for both. One of the great surprises in the writer's missionary experience was the remarkable stabilizing effect on church attendance which resulted from its introduction. Members who formerly had been very inconstant in attendance, when asked for the explanation of their new regularity, replied that they had to come to bring their envelope. Further, the contributor who does not have envelopes does not give his offering when he is absent. The envelope user brings the back envelopes when he returns after an absence.

The treasurer's record serves not only to keep account of the fulfilment of pledges but at the end of each month he can see at a glance if anyone has ceased to give without having notified him. The member may be out of work, or there may be sickness in the home, or his spiritual life may have been chilled. In any case, a pastoral visit will do him good and may prove both helpful and timely. Nothing need be said about the offerings: He knows about these. If the visit fulfils its spiritual purpose, both the member and the offering will be restored.

The confidence of the members in the scrupulous handling of the funds is indispensable in any method of church finance which de-

pends on their contributions. This is the heart of some acute problems in self-support on certain mission fields. Confidence can be
fostered by the annual audit of all church accounts. This audit
should check the existence of the cash balance, if any, and where or
how this is held. It is further helped by the circulation of the annual statement to the members. It may be that few can understand
it but the fact that it is given out inspires confidence. Any de-
falcation affecting church funds will shake the confidence not only
of contributors in the congregation, but in all others to whom the
news spreads.

The Central Synod of the Evangelical Church of Peru has found
it desirable to adopt the following instructions to the elders:

Church money may not be used for any purpose other than that
for which it was given.

Church money may not be loaned.

A detailed and audited account of the church funds should be
presented to the congregation each year, either written or printed,
so that all may know whereon the funds have been spent. A copy
of this account should be sent to the committee appointed by
the Synod.

Church funds should be deposited in the bank in the name of
the church, two persons being authorized to sign, and they should
not be deposited in the name of any individual.

Wherever this method of church finance is adopted by rural
churches, arrangements should be made to have the necessary materials available for purchase in small lots at some central depot.

Among the most frequent objections to this system of church
finance will be that it involves too much work. It is true that it
requires more work than the usual hit-and-miss methods, but the
labor is amply repaid. The larger the number of members having a
specific part in the life and work of the church, the richer will be
their fellowship and the greater their interest. This method of dealing with the financial affairs provides a field of activity for some
whose gifts are administrative rather than oratorical or didactic.

The Central Synod of the Evangelical Church of Peru has appointed a Committee on Financial Development which devotes its
attention to propagating and developing this system throughout the
Synod. On this committee also devolves the duty of fostering the

support of the presbyteries, and therefore of encouraging each congregation to assume its proper obligation in support of the general bodies of the Church.

BIBLIOGRAPHY

Addison, J. T., *The Medieval Missionary*. International Missionary Council, New York and London, 1936.

Ako Adjei, "Imperialism and Spiritual Freedom: An African View." *The American Journal of Sociology*, Vol. L, No. 3, November, 1944. The University of Chicago Press.

Allen, H. B., *Come Over Into Macedonia*. Rutgers University Press, New Brunswick, (N. J.), 1943.

Azariah, V. S., *Christain Giving*. Christian Literature Society for India, Madras, 1940.

Barclay, W. C., "Christian Education of the Methodist Church in Brazil." The Methodist Church, New York, 1943.

Bates, M. S., "Missions in Far Eastern Cultural Relations." Eighth Conference of the Institute of Pacific Relations, December, 1942. Institute of Pacific Relations, New York.

Bhatty, E. C., "The Economic Background of the Church in the United Provinces." *The Madras Series*, International Missionary Council, New York and London, 1938.

Blair, H. E., "Christian Stewardship in Korea." *The Madras Series*, International Missionary Council, New York and London, 1938.

Bogardus, E. S., *Introduction to Social Research*. Suttonhouse, Ltd., Los Angeles, (California), 1936.

Braga, Erasmo, and Grubb, K. G., *The Republic of Brazil*. World Dominion Press, London, 1932.

Browning, W. E., *The River Plate Republics*. World Dominion Press, London, 1928.

Brunner, E. deS., *Rural Korea*. Vol. VI, Report of the Jerusalem Meeting of the International Missionary Council, New York and London, 1928.

Buck, J. L., *Land Utilization in China*. (3 Vols.), Institute of Pacific Relations, New York, 1938.

Buck, Pearl, *Tell the People*. John Day, New York, 1945.

Buell, R. L., (a) *Problems of the New Cuba*. Report of the Commission on Cuban Affairs, Foreign Policy Association, Inc., New York, 1935. (b) *The Native Problem in Africa*. (2 Vols.), Macmillan, New York, 1928.

Burton, J. W., (a) *Missionary Survey of the Pacific Islands.* World Dominion Press, London, 1930.
(b) "The Methodist Church in Fiji." *The Madras Series,* Vol. II, International Missionary Council, New York and London, 1939.

Butterfield, K. L., See Report of Jerusalem Meeting of the International Missionary Council, (8 Vols.), Vol. VI, New York and London, 1928.

Camargo, G. B., and Grubb, K. G., *Religion in the Republic of Mexico.* World Dominion Press, London, 1935.

Chao, T. C., *The Christian Movement in China in a Period of National Transition.* International Missionary Council, New York and London, 1937.

Clark, C. A., *The Nevius Plan for Mission Work in Korea.* Christian Literature Society, Seoul, 1937.

Clark, E. M., *The Other Half of Japan.* The Evangelical Press, Harrisburg, (Pa.), 1934.

Clark, S. J. W., "The Indigenous Church." (Second Impression), World Dominion Press, London, 1928.

Clarke, Dumont, Pamphlets—"The Country Church and The Lord's Acre Plan." The Farm Federation, Asheville, North Carolina, 1943.

Condliffe, J. B., *China Today: Economic.* World Peace Foundation, Boston, 1932.

Dale, J. T., See *The Indians of the High Andes.* Committee on Cooperation in Latin America, New York, 1945.

Darling, M. L., *The Punjab Peasant in Prosperity and Debt.* Oxford University Press, London, 1932.

Davis, Kingsley, "Demographic Fact and Policy in India," from *Demographic Studies of Selected Areas of Rapid Growth.* The Milbank Memorial Fund, New York, 1944.

Davis, J. M., *Modern Industry and the African.* Macmillan, London, 1933.
Economic and Social Environment of the Younger Churches. International Missionary Council, New York and London, 1938.
Finance Policies of the Missionary Societies. International Missionary Council, New York and London, 1938.
"The Batak Church." International Missionary Council, New York and London, 1938.
The Economic Basis of the Church. Vol. V, *The Madras Series,* International Missionary Council, New York and London, 1939.
The Economic Basis of the Evangelical Church in Mexico. International Missionary Council, New York and London, 1940.

The Cuban Church in a Sugar Economy. International Missionary Council, New York and London, 1942.

The Church in the New Jamaica. International Missionary Council, New York and London, 1942.

The Church in Puerto Rico's Dilemma. International Missionary Council, New York and London, 1942.

The Evangelical Church in the River Plate Republics. International Missionary Council, New York and London, 1943.

How the Church Grows in Brazil. International Missionary Council, New York and London, 1943.

Dening, Walter, *A New Life of Toyotomi Hideyoshi.* The Kyobun Kwan, Tokyo, 1904.

Dennis, J. S., *Christian Missions and Social Progress.* (3 Vols.), Revell, New York, 1897-1906.

Elkin, A. P., "Missionary Policy for Primitive Peoples." *The Morpeth Review,* No. 27, University of Sydney.

Elmer, M. C., *Technique of Social Surveys.* Jesse Ray Miller, Los Angeles, (Cal.), 1927.

Enser, H. J., "A Brief History and Critical Analysis of the Rheinish Mission Among the Bataks of Sumatra." Hartford Seminary Foundation, 1945.

Evans-Pritchard, E. E., "Witchcraft." *Africa,* Vol. VIII, No. 4, October, 1935, Oxford University Press, London.

Felton, R. E., *The Rural Church in the Far East.* International Missionary Council, New York and London, 1938.

Fishman, A. T., *Culture Change and the Underprivileged.* Christian Literature Society for India, Madras, 1941.

Fleming, D. J., (a) *Ventures in Simpler Living.* International Missionary Council, New York, 1933.
(b) *Heritage of Beauty.* Friendship Press, New York, 1937.
(c) *Each With His Own Brush.* Friendship Press, New York, 1938.

Franklin, A. B., *Ecuador—Portrait of a People.* Doubleday, Doran, Garden City, N. Y., 1943.

Gibbons, C. W., "Project for an Experimental Mission Centre in Africa." London, 1933.

Global Epidemiology: A Geography of Disease and Sanitation. Vol. I, Lippincott, Philadelphia, 1944.

Graham, J. M., and Piddington, Ralph, "Anthropology and the Future of Missions." The University Press, Aberdeen, (Scotland), 1940.

Gulick, S. L., *Toward Understanding Japan.* Macmillan, New York, 1935.

Lord Hailey, *An African Survey*—A Study of Problems Arising in Africa South of the Sahara. Chapter XI, "The Problems of Labour," Oxford University Press, London, 1938.

Hall, R. O., *The Christian Movement in China in a Period of National Transition*. International Missionary Council, New York and London, 1938.

Hallowell, A. I., "Sociopsychological Aspects of Acculturation," in *The Science of Man in the World Crisis* by Ralph Linton. Columbia University Press, New York, 1945.

Hatch, D. S., (a) *Up from Poverty in Rural India*. Oxford University Press, London, 1936.
(b) *Further Upward in Rural India*. Oxford University Press, London, 1938.
(c) "My Job Is Village Reconstruction." Christian Rural Fellowship Bulletin, No. 98, December, 1944, New York.

Heinrich, J. C., *The Psychology of a Suppressed People*. Allen and Unwin, London, 1937.

Helser, A. D., *Education of Primitive People*. Revell, New York, 1934.

Hill, A. V., "Health, Food, and Population in India," in *International Affairs*. Vol. XXI, No. 1, January, 1945, London, Toronto, and New York.

Hocking, W. E., *Rethinking Missions*—A Laymen's Inquiry After One Hundred Years. Harper's, New York, 1932.

Hooton, E. A., "Tribute to Missionaries," in *Christian World Facts*. No. 22, Autumn, 1941, Foreign Missions Conference of North America, New York.

Howland, C. P., *American Relations in the Caribbean*. Yale University Press, New Haven, 1929.

Hubbard, J. W., "The Cause and Cure of African 'Immorality.'" *International Review of Missions,* Vol. XXI, No. 78, April, 1931, London.

Hypes, J. L., See *Laymen's Foreign Missions Inquiry*—Fact Finders Reports—Vol. IV.

Ishii, R., *Population Pressure and Economic Life in Japan*. King, London, 1937.

Jerusalem Meeting of the International Missionary Council. New York and London, 1928.

Jones, T. J., *Education in East Africa*. A Study by the Second African Education Commission, Phelps Stokes Fund, New York, 1924.

Joseph, P. C., "The Economic and Social Environment of the Church in North Travancore and Cochin." *The Madras Series,* International Missionary Council, New York and London, 1938.

Junod, H. A., *The Life of a South African Tribe*. (2 Vols.), Second Edition, Macmillan, London, 1927.

Junod, H. P., "Anthropology and Missionary Education." *International Review of Missions,* Vol. XXIV, No. 94, April, 1935, London.

Keesing, F. M., *The South Seas in the Modern World*. John Day Co., New York, 1941.

Klein, C. L., "An Historical Study of Self-Support in Some Karen Missions in Burma." (Thesis), Berkeley Baptist Divinity School, Berkeley, California, 1936.

Kraemer, H., *The Christian Message in a Non-Christian World*. Harper's, New York, 1938.

Latham, G. C., and Notcutt, L. A., *The African and the Cinema*. Edinburgh House Press, London, 1937.

Latourette, K. S., *A History of the Expansion of Christianity*. (7 Vols.), Vol. I, "The First Five Centuries," Vol. II, "The Thousand Years of Uncertainty," Harper's, New York, 1938.

Laubach, F. C., *Toward a Literate World*. Columbia University Press, New York, 1938.

Laymen's Foreign Missions Inquiry. (7 Vols.), Harper's, New York, 1933.

Lee, E. M., and Wasson, A. W., *The Latin American Circuit*. Board of Missions and Church Extension, The Methodist Church, New York, 1942.

Levo, John, *The Romantic Isles*. Society for the Propagation of the Gospel, London, 1936.

Lindsay, A. D., Report of the Commission on *Christian Higher Education in India*. Oxford University Press, London, 1931.

Linton, Ralph, (a) *The Study of Man*. Appleton-Century, New York, 1936.
(b) *The Science of Man in the World Crisis*. (Edited by Ralph Linton), Columbia University Press, New York, 1945.

Lorimer, Frank, "Population Trends in the Orient." *Foreign Affairs,* (Council on Foreign Relations, Inc.), Vol. XXIII, No. 4, July, 1945, New York.

Lowie, R. H., *An Introduction to Cultural Anthropology*. Farrar and Rinehart, New York, 1940.

Lucas, E. D., and Das, F. T., "The Rural Church in the Punjab." *The Madras Series,* International Missionary Council, New York and London, 1938.

Lord Lugard, *The Dual Mandate in British Tropical Africa*. Blackwood and Sons, Edinburgh and London, 1923.

Mabillon, *Acta Sanctorum, Vita Wilfridi.*

The Madras Series, (a) Meeting of the International Missionary Council at Madras, December, 1938. (7 Vols.), New York and London, 1939. (b) *The World Mission of the Church.* Findings and Recommendations of the International Missionary Council, Madras, December, 1938, New York and London, 1939.

Malinowski, Bronislaw, *The Dynamics of Culture Change.* Yale University Press, New Haven, (Conn.), 1945.

Manikam, R. B., *The Christian College and the Christian Community.* A report based on Research Studies by Eighteen Christian Colleges in India, International Missionary Council, New York and London, 1938.

Marquard, Leo, See, *Modern Industry and the African.* Chapter XIV, "Indirect Rule," Macmillan, London, 1933.

Matheson, M. C., *Indian Industry—Yesterday, Today, and Tomorrow.* Oxford University Press, London, 1930.

Mathews, Basil, *Unfolding Drama in Southeast Asia.* Friendship Press, New York, 1944.

Mayhew, Arthur, *Education in the Colonial Empire.* Longmans, Green, London, 1938.

Melland, Frank, (a) *In Witch-Bound Africa.* Seeley, Service and Co., London, 1923. (b) "Ethical and Political Aspects of African Witchcraft." *Africa,* Vol. VIII, No. 4, October, 1935, Oxford University Press, London.

McDowell, H. C., "Adjusting the Missionary Enterprise to the Supporting Capacity of the People." Report of the Galangue Station, American Board, Angola, 1933.

Montalambert, *Monks of the West.* Vols. 2 and 6.

Mosher, A. T., (a) *The Christian Mission Among Rural People.* Foreign Missions Conference of North America, New York, 1945. (b) "God in the Countryside." Christian Rural Fellowship News Letter, January 18, 1944.

Mott, John R., (a) *Cooperation and the World Mission.* International Missionary Council, New York and London, 1935. (b) *The Larger Evangelism.* Abingdon-Cokesbury Press, New York and Nashville, (Tenn.), 1944.

Moule, A. C., "The Primitive Failure of Christianity in China." *International Review of Missions,* Vol. XX, No. 79, July, 1931, London.

Murphy, Alice E., "Training and Guiding Lay Leadership in the Village Church." (Mimeograph Series No. 157), Agricultural Missions Inc., New York.

Nitobe, Inazo, *Bushido—The Soul of Japan.* Putnam's, New York and London, 1905.

Notestein, F. W., "Problems of Policy in Relation to Areas of Heavy Population Pressure," in *Demographic Studies of Selected Areas of Rapid Growth*. The Milbank Memorial Fund, New York, 1944.

Odum, H. W., and Jocher, Katharine, *An Introduction to Social Research*. Henry Holt, New York, 1929.

Oldham, J. H., *Christianity and the Race Problem*. Association Press, New York, 1926.

Lord Oliver, *White Capital and Coloured Labour*. The Hogarth Press, London, 1929.

Orde Browne, G. St. J., *The African Labourer*. Oxford University Press, London, 1933.

Osias, Camilo, *The Filipino Way of Life*. Ginn, Boston, 1940.

Oxford Conference on Church, Community, and State. Allen and Unwin, London, 1937.

Park, R. E., "Missions and the Modern World." *The American Journal of Sociology*, Vol. L, No. 3, November, 1944, The University of Chicago Press, Chicago.

Paton, William, *Christianity in the Eastern Conflicts*. Edinburgh House Press, London, 1937.

Pertz, *Monumenta Germania Historica*. (84 Vols.), Vita St. Sturmi.

Phillips, R. E., (a) *The Bantu Are Coming*. Student Christian Movement Press, London, 1930.
(b) *The Bantu in the City*. Lovedale Press, Lovedale, C.P., (South Africa), 1938.

Pickett, J. W., *Christian Mass Movements in India*. The Abingdon Press, New York, 1933.

Ponniah, J. S., "The Christian Community of Madura, Ramnad, and Tinnevelly." *The Madras Series,* International Missionary Council, New York and London, 1938.

Price, F. W., (a) "The Rural Church in China." Nanking Theological Seminary, 1937.
(b) "The Shunhwachen Rural Training Center of Nanking Theological Seminary." 1936.

Quintanilla, Luis, *A Latin American Speaks*. Macmillan, New York, 1943.

Ranson, C. W., (a) *A City in Transition*. Christian Literature Society for India, Madras, 1938.
(b) *Theological Education in India*. A Survey under the auspices of the National Christian Council of India, Nagpur, 1944.
(c) "The Gossner Evangelical Lutheran Church in Chota Nagpur and Assam." Nagpur, 1944.

Rauws, J., (with H. Kraemer, F. J. F. Van Hasselt, N. A. C. Slotemaker de Bruine), *The Netherlands Indies*. World Dominion Press, London, 1935.

Rawlinson, Frank, "Western Money and the Chinese Church." *Chinese Recorder*, Vol. LIX, No. 11 to Vol. LX, No. 7, November, 1928 to August, 1929, Shanghai.

Redfield, Robert, *Tepoztlan,* A Mexican Village. University of Chicago Press, Chicago, 1930.

Rhea, J. S., "Rural Program, Central Training School, Kambini." (Mimeograph Series No. 18), Agricultural Mission Inc., New York.

Richards, A. I., (a) *Hunger and Work in a Savage Tribe.* Routledge, London, 1932.
(b) *Land, Labour, and Diet in Northern Rhodesia.* Oxford University Press, London.

Ritchie, John, *Indigenous Church Principles in Theory and Practice.* Revell, New York, 1945.

Roy, S. K., "The Church in Chota Nagpur." *The Madras Series,* International Missionary Council, New York and London, 1938.

Rycroft, W. S., (a) *On This Foundation*—The Evangelical Witness in Latin America. Friendship Press, New York, 1942.
(b) *Indians of the High Andes.* (Editor), Committee on Cooperation in Latin America, New York, 1945.

Sáenz, Moisés, "The Peruvian Indian." The Strategic Index of the Americas, Coordinator of Inter-American Affairs, Washington, D. C., 1944.

Sailer, T. H. P., *Christian Adult Education in Rural Asia and Africa.* Friendship Press, New York, 1943.

Schrieke, B., *The Effect of Western Influence on Native Civilizations in the Malay Archipelago.* G. Kolff and Co., Batavia, 1929.

Scott, Roderick, "The Christian Movement in China in a Period of National Transition." International Missionary Council, New York and London, 1938.

Schebesta, Paul, "Recent Literature on Bantu Tribes." Some Ethnological and Linguistic Publications, *Africa,* Vol. I, No. 1, January, 1928, Oxford University Press, London.

Shaw, Mabel, *God's Candlelights.* An Educational Venture in Northern Rhodesia. The Friendship Press, New York, 1933.

Shropshire, D. W. T., *The Church and Primitive Peoples.* Society for Promoting Christian Knowledge, London, 1938.

Simpson, E. N., *The Ejido*—Mexico's Way Out. University of North Carolina Press, Chapel Hill, 1937.

Smith, E. W., (a) *The Golden Stool.* Edinburgh House Press, London, 1930.

(b) "The Sublimation of Bantu Life and Thought." *International Review of Missions,* Vol. XI, No. 41, January, 1922.
(c) Presidential Address. *Journal of Royal Anthropological Institute,* Vol. LXIV, 1934, London.

Smith, G. H., *The Missionary and Anthropology.* Moody Press, Chicago, 1945.

Stuart, J. L., "Conflict of Cultures in China." *Chinese Recorder,* Vol. LX, No. 7, August, 1929.

Swope, Gerard, "The High Cost of Living in South America." *Atlantic Monthly,* June, 1940.

Timothy, N., "Economic Environment of the Church in the United Provinces." *The Madras Series,* International Missionary Council, New York and London, 1938.

Tschopik, Harry, "The Aymara," in *The Handbook of South American Indians.* Vol. II, "The Andean Civilizations," Bureau of American Ethnology, Smithsonian Institution, Washington, D. C., 1945-46.

Uchimura, Kanzo, *Diary of a Japanese Convert.* Chapter X, "Net Impressions of Christendom," Revell, New York, 1895.

Wasson, A. W., (a) *Church Growth in Korea.* International Missionary Council, New York, 1934.
(b) "The Methodist Church of Brazil," (1930-1943). The Methodist Church, New York, 1943.

Westerman, Diedrich, (a) *The African Today and Tomorrow.* Oxford University Press, London, 1939.
(b) "The Place and Function of the Vernacular in African Education." *International Review of Missions,* Vol. XIV, No. 53, January, 1925.

Williams, J. J., *Psychic Phenomena of Jamaica.* The Dial Press, New York, 1934.

Wiser, C. V., and W. H., *Behind Mud Walls.* Richard R. Smith, Inc., New York, 1930.

Wiser, W. H., (a) "Building the Social and Economic Foundations for an Indigenous Church in the United Provinces." Lucknow Publishing House, Lucknow, 1940.
(b) "Financial Foundations for the Church in Rural Areas." Lucknow Publishing House, Lucknow, 1941.
(c) *The Jajmani System.* Lucknow Publishing Co., 1936.

Yen, James Y. C., "The Thousand Character System," in *The Talking Leaf.* Foreign Missions Conference of North America, New York, 1944.

Ziegler, E. K., (a) *A Book of Worship for Village Churches.* Agricultural Missions Inc., New York, 1939.
(b) *Rural People at Worship.* Agricultural Missions Inc., New York, 1943.

SUPPLEMENTARY LIST—REPORTS AND PAMPHLETS

Mass Education in African Society. Colonial Office, Advisory Committee on Education in the Colonies, Colonial No. 186, British Information Services, New York.

United Missions in the Copper Belt. Annual Reports, 1936-1944. Edinburgh House Press, London.

Report of the Royal Commission on Agriculture in India, June, 1928. Chapter VIII, "Irrigation," Chapter IX, "Communications and Marketing," H. M. C. Stationery Office, London.

Report of the Central Advisory Board of Education on Post-War Educational Development in India. ("The Sargent Plan"), New Delhi, 1944.

Report of the Royal Commission on Labour in India, June, 1931. H. M. Stationery Office, London.

Eighteen Research Studies Made by Christian Colleges in India in Preparation for the Meeting of the International Missionary Council at Madras, December, 1938. New York and London.

Report of the Fiftieth Anniversary of the Chosen (Korea) Mission of the Presbyterian Church, USA. 156 Fifth Avenue, New York.

Reports, Jamaica Welfare, Ltd., 1938-1944. Kingston, Jamaica, B.W.I., and British Information Services, New York.

Agricultural Missions Inc., Bulletins, Mimeograph Series, and News Letters. 156 Fifth Avenue, New York.

Annual Reports, Government Soil Conservation Service. U. S. Department of Agriculture, Washington, D. C.

Reports of Puerto Rico Reconstruction Administration. U. S. Department of Agriculture and Commerce, Washington, D. C.

Report of the Imperial Reconstruction and Social Welfare Commission for the Colonies. Colonial Office, London.

Report of the Commission to the Indians of the High Andes. Committee on Cooperation in Latin America, New York, 1945.

Statement of Policy on Colonial Development and Welfare, C.M.D. 6176, 1940. Colonial Office, London.

INDEX

Adams, Santiago, 240, 241
Addison, James Thayer, 65
Agricultural Colleges: 192, 275
Agricultural Missions, Inc., 235, 242, 254, 275, 283
Ako Adjei, 18, 41
All-India Congress Party, 32
All-India Lutheran Federation, 165
American Baptist Mission, Burma, 159, 234
American Board, 48, 150, 167, 204-06
American College, Madura, 96
Ancestor Worship, modification of, 53-4
Andrews, C. F., 268
Angola, Portuguese West Africa, 77, 85, 166-70, 204-06
Anthropological approach, 47-61, 265-66, 277
Anthropology:
 definition of, 47
 and missionary preparation, 265-66, 277
 and missions, 26, 34, 38, 47-8, 69, 265-66
 and the mission board, 277
 and presenting the Gospel, 50
 rôle and functions of, 47-8
Argentina, 123, 186, 203-04
Arianists, 71
Assemblies of God, (Pentecostals), 181-82, 197
Assumptions:
 of incapacity, 8, 9, 78, 110, 123, 134
 of poverty, 8, 119, 123, 219
 of superiority, 17, 18, 39, 48, 79, 82, 93-4, 110
Azariah, V. S., (Bishop), 111

Balloch, E. C., (Bishop), 218-19
Bantu, 14, 35-6, 48, 54, 100
 Educational Cinema Experiment, 269
 Miners, 12-3, 35-6, 67
 tribal life, 12, 60, 67
Baptist:
 Canadian—mission, Bolivia, 66-7
 church, 194, 197, 210-11

missions in Latin America, 139-40, 215
Barmen Mission of Germany, 150
Basutoland, South Africa, 14
Batak, Sumatra:
 Adat and use of, 43, 153
 Church, 43, 67, 77, 85, 121, 124, 149-54, 186, 191
 financial policies, 151-52
 missionary spirit, 151-52
 presbyter, 151
 teacher-preacher, 150-51, 153
Bates, M. Searle, 27
Belgian Congo, 8, 14, 19, 39, 56, 102, 136
Bhatty, E. C., 99
Bible:
 and Church growth, 135, 156, 212, 292-93
 institutes, 120, 136, 156, 275
 study, 135-36, 155, 292-93
Biradari, 41, 122
Blair, Herbert E., 216
Bo Hie Dong, China, 133
Bolivia, 57, 66-7, 101, 103, 147
Borneo, 61, 67
Braga, Erasmo, 180
Brazil:
 churches of, 116, 124, 134-35, 177-82, 190-91, 202, 211, 215
 Congregational Union of, 178-80
 Independent Presbyteries of, 180-81, 215
 South—Union of Seventh Day Adventists, 182
 Southern Baptist Convention of, 139-40
Bridgman, Mrs. F. B., 67
British Colonial:
 Development Board, 263
 Development and Welfare Act, 19
 policy, 12, 19
Budget:
 discussion of, 187, 296-97
 double, the, 298
 formation of, 296-97
Buell, Raymond Leslie, 13, 19